Advance praise for *Born with a Tail*

"Entrancing and fascinating—an absolute must-read."

  —Gillian Flynn, *New York Times* bestselling author of *Gone Girl*

"What an entertaining, bizarre, sometimes delightful, sometimes disturbing story. Thank you, Doug Brod, for this great book about an overlooked character in America's gloriously weird history."

  —A.J. Jacobs, author of *My Year of Living Constitutionally*

"What happens when Satan meets show business? Please allow Anton LaVey to introduce himself. A quizzical cultural icon, this Zelig-like huckster with horns and cape became entwined with a veritable nightmare alley of celebrities, among them Jayne Mansfield, Kenneth Anger, Marilyn Manson, and Sammy Davis Jr. Doug Brod strikes just the right tone as he takes a magnifying glass to this tiny world, and the results are highly amusing. The Church of Satan high priest preferred to chow down at the Olive Garden—who knew? This and many other blasphemous secrets are revealed in *Born with a Tail*. I command thee to read it, and, like Sammy, raise one red fingernail in tribute."

  —Jimmy McDonough, author of *Shakey: Neil Young's Biography*
  and *Soul Survivor: A Biography of Al Green*

"You don't have to sell your soul to enjoy Doug Brod's wickedly entertaining take on the incredible true-life tale of master showman and devil's advocate Anton LaVey. If it didn't actually happen, you wouldn't believe a word!"

  —Larry Karaszewski, co-screenwriter of *Ed Wood* and
  The People vs. Larry Flynt

"Doug Brod is a wonderfully gifted writer. Come for the devil, but stay for the writing! This is a delightful and strange portrait of an unusual man, made glorious by Brod's insight and witty prose. You'll laugh all the way to the underworld!"

—**Jonathan Ames,** author of *A Man Named Doll*

"San Francisco, 1967. As seekers and stoners flood into Haight Ashbury to kick off the Summer of Love, another less-publicized movement is in its infancy across town—a dark and demonic flipside to the Age of Aquarius's peace and patchouli. It's called the Church of Satan, and its leader is a goateed figure in a black cape named Anton LaVey. Part evangelist of evil, part P.T. Barnum showman, LaVey would attract a bizarre galaxy of eccentrics into his orbit: sorcerers and sexual deviants, hip pagans and high priests, even a handful of danger-loving celebrities drawn to the occult. In *Born with a Tail*, Doug Brod takes us on a stranger-than-fiction tour of the dark side. More than just a fascinating biography, *Born with a Tail* is a high-resolution X-ray of America's weird psyche in the second half of the twentieth century."

—**Chris Nashawaty,** author of *The Future Was Now: Madmen, Mavericks, and the Epic Sci-Fi Summer of 1982* and *Caddyshack: The Making of a Hollywood Cinderella Story*

"The devil is in the details—and Doug Brod brings them all together in this deeply researched, fiendishly entertaining account of the life of celebrity Satanist Anton LaVey, one of the twentieth century's most fascinating pop-culture provocateurs."

—**Brian Raftery,** author of *Best. Movie. Year. Ever.: How 1999 Blew Up the Big Screen*

"Anton LaVey's breathless, lifelong hustle through seemingly every social circle in postwar California sewed an unlikely thread from Jayne

Mansfield to army PSYOP officers, from the Age of Aquarius to the Satanic Panic and beyond. With devilish wit and even tenderness, Doug Brod shows how LaVey's committed cosplaying held a mirror up to the darker parts of America—not just the obvious hypocrites, but the murderers, mobsters, and fascist-flirting trash-culture vultures who swirled around and glommed onto the Mephistophelian mascot."

—**Sean Howe,** *New York Times* bestselling author of *Agents of Chaos: Thomas King Forçade, High Times, and the Paranoid End of the 1970s* and *Marvel Comics: The Untold Story*

"Hail Satan? Perhaps not. Hail Doug Brod? Definitely. He's written one hell of a book, a witty, cogent chronicle of one of the most noteworthy grifts American culture ever conjured up."

—**Glenn Kenny,** author of *The World Is Yours: The Story of Scarface* and *Made Men: The Story of Goodfellas*

BORN

WITH A

TAIL

Also by Doug Brod

They Just Seem a Little Weird: How KISS, Cheap Trick,
Aerosmith, and Starz Remade Rock and Roll

For Rachel and Sasha
And for Shari, one helluva sister

"He wears a mask, and his face grows to fit it."

—George Orwell

"Give him a mask, and he will tell you the truth."

—Oscar Wilde

"Do we really want to give these people the truth, because if they had the truth, what would they do with it?"

—Anton Szandor LaVey

Contents

Invocation

"PLEASE dim the lights."

So commands the black-caped high priest, six feet tall and solidly built, an ebony Van Dyke customized to expose the philtrum just below his nose. Improbably peaked eyebrows cap inky, squinting orbs that are bookended by vaguely pointy ears. Around his neck hangs a large round pendant. His sinister appearance evokes that of Ming the Merciless, the enemy of intergalactic comic-strip hero Flash Gordon, or really any number of villains from the golden age of pulp magazines. That malevolent countenance is belied, however, by a somewhat comical headpiece, which features four-inch horns protruding from both sides and an exaggerated widow's peak, the material's frayed edges suggesting the wear and tear from a decade's worth of aggressive trick-or-treating.

He stands before a stone fireplace on whose purple velvet–covered mantel a red-tressed woman lies face-up, barely covering her nakedness with a leopard-print blanket. Candles stuck into human skulls limn the contours of her pulchritude. Over the mantel hangs a large round sign, a rendering of a goat's head inside an inverted pentagram whose five points hit on the Hebraic letters *lamed, vav, yod, tav,* and *nun,* spelling out "Leviathan": a sea monster, the Devil. It's the sigil of Baphomet, the same image that's on the priest's medallion, whose two upward points

1

symbolize the duality that sustains natural processes—negative/positive, masculine/feminine, push/pull—and three downward points represent the rejection of Christendom's Holy Trinity.

In this makeshift chapel tucked inside a black Victorian house on an otherwise ordinary residential street in San Francisco, California, taxidermized owls, ravens, and rats bear witness to the infernal rite from their perches high upon shelves, while a real, live five-hundred-pound lion named Togare lets out the occasional roar and slaps a paw against his backyard cage.

The minister bangs a gong. A pretty blonde woman, his domestic partner, holds a brass chalice. With a large open book in one hand and a bell in the other, he rings to "the four cardinal points of the compass: Satan meaning fire, Belial meaning earth, Lucifer meaning air, and Leviathan meaning sea and water."

He then replaces the bell with a sword, pointing again. "*Nomine Satani Lucifer excelsis*," he chants in an accent of discordant origin, more Fargo twang than Hades bellow. "In the name of our great god Satan Lucifer, I command thee to come forth and bestow your blessing upon thee." He twirls the sword overhead.

The latter "thee" of his incantation are otherwise known as John Raymond, a thirty-five-year-old journalist, and twenty-six-year-old Judith Case, a former New York socialite who works for a pension consultancy. Raymond, graying and handsome, with a dark curl drooping over his forehead, wears a dark turtleneck sweater and herringbone blazer. The brunette Case, sporting a modish short haircut with bangs, is draped in a smart black wool dress. That same round pendant rests on their chests.

Raymond places on her finger a ring in the shape of an ankh, the Egyptian hieroglyphic symbol of life.

"Your vows being made by intent," the minister intones, "by the power of Satan, I now confer the possession of each other upon you." He tells Raymond to "take this woman." And he takes her all right, stretching out his left arm to pull her toward him, grabbing her neck and locking her into a theatrically extended kiss.

"*Rege Satanis!*" exclaims Lucifer's apprentice, Latinizing the phrase "Reign, Satan!"

The clergyman reads to all assembled the poem "Resurrection" by morbid pulp-fiction writer and poet Clark Ashton Smith. Then "Hymn to Pan," by occultist Aleister Crowley: "Thrill with lissome lust of the light! O man! My man! Come careening out of the night."

Next, he chants in Enochian, an esoteric language that originated in sixteenth-century England. At one point the minister blesses his guests with a phallus (not real) before letting out a sigh of relief at the conclusion of the service.

"Well, that's it," he utters. Mission accomplished.

Anton Szandor LaVey, the high priest of the Church of Satan, performed this fifteen-minute ceremony no fewer than five consecutive times that night, under oppressively hot lights, for the benefit of television cameras and international news agencies.

In addition to church members, those assembled at this devilish wedding, held on the evening of Tuesday, January 31, 1967, in LaVey's residence at 6114 California Street in the Richmond District, included a few notable personalities. Among them: Fritzi Armstrong, owner of the Metaphysical Town-Hall bookshop and a leading San Francisco astrologer since the early 1940s; writer Lenore Kandel, whose collection *The Love Book* had recently been found in violation of state obscenity codes for containing the poem "To Fuck with Love"; and singer-actress Barbara McNair, hobbling on crutches, her broken foot in a cast, a pink ribbon around a toe. Where was Allen Ginsberg? Alas, the eminent Beat poet was a last-minute no-show.

More than fifty journalists and photographers—including Joe Rosenthal, who shot the iconic picture of the US Marines raising the flag on Iwo Jima at the end of World War II—crowded into the small living room of this black-painted townhouse for a ceremony that left the rickety place a shambles. "Reporters clustered in knots around each authentic guest they could find," an observer noted, "and sometimes interviewed one another by mistake."

At one point during the evening, a wailing fire truck stopped in front of the house, and out leaped firemen brandishing axes. False alarm.

After the service, Lois Murgenstrumm, the twenty-one-year-old woman atop the fireplace, asked for a glass of water. "It was awfully hot up there on the altar," she said. LaVey later clarified that she wasn't lying on the altar: "She *is* the altar." The altar, he explained, shouldn't be a "cold, unyielding slab of sterile stone or wood. It should be a symbol of enthusiastic lust and indulgence."

Through a gap-toothed grin, he described the wedding as being "conceived not in heaven but in hell, which is the mold from which heaven was cast, and which has kept religion alive from the beginning." But was this service, billed as the first Satanic wedding, even a wedding? The couple, after all, hadn't bothered to get a marriage license.

"I am an ordained clergyman in the Satanic Church, which I founded and which the law may not recognize," LaVey said.

"I did it just as a favor," LaVey told one reporter. "They're still going to have to go down to City Hall and dish out two dollars to make it official."

Raymond admitted to reporters he had been married twice before. "They were both Christian weddings. The lions demolished the Christians years ago. We get along fine without them," he explained, before adding, "I look forward to a nice life now, indulging vigorously in the seven deadly sins."

In interviews with the assembled press, Raymond—who had worked for the left-leaning *Sunday Ramparts*, the *Honolulu Advertiser*, and the

Christian Science Monitor—replied to a bunch of other questions with cynically evasive answers, such as "Do you mean what religion I was raised in or what religion did I raise?" Radically minded, he responded to one query by launching into a political tirade: "This marriage is as valid as the war in Vietnam or the treaties we have with other countries. The state doesn't recognize the Satanic Church and until it does, I don't recognize the state."

For the reception, guests repaired to a subterranean bar, carefully descending via ladder through a trapdoor. "As you step off the last rung of the ladder and turn around in the semi-darkness, you are confronted by a strange sight," went one report, "a full-size effigy of a man in a sailor suit. Extended from its open fly is an enormous erect penis." After entering this room, which LaVey called "the Den of Iniquity," guests toasted the newlyweds with glasses of vodka punch containing mandrake root—an aphrodisiac—and scented with eucalyptus oil.

The *San Francisco Examiner* reported that astrologer and sexologist Gavin Arthur, grandson of twenty-first US president Chester Alan Arthur and a presumed LaVey pal, had presented the couple with a black cat named Pisces. (An indignant Arthur soon wrote to the paper, "I had nothing to do with these people, let alone giving them a gift.")

One journalist noted that LaVey's sense of humor was in evidence by a sign on the bathroom door, which from one angle read "Men," and from another, "Women." "Inside, above the toilet, is a placard taken from an old theater: 'Ladies remain seated during the entire performance.'" Before the ceremony, reporters interviewed Raymond and Case as they stood in front of one of the parlor's more whimsical accoutrements: a display case containing what appeared to be a human skeleton with the top of its skull separated as if it were tipping its cap.

Considering the turnout, it's no surprise the wedding made the news all over the world, appearing on front pages from Stockton, California, to Huddersfield, England, and from Bismarck, North Dakota, to

Burlington, North Carolina—in stories distributed by United Press International, the Associated Press, and Reuters. "Sorcerer Conducts Satanic Wedding," "'Satanic Wedding' Alarms from Beginning to End," "Nude Dresses Up Wedding Held in Den of Satan," the headlines screamed—or, in most cases, tittered.

On July 28, the couple decided to make things legal, having the recorder of San Francisco issue a marriage certificate, signed by LaVey and listing Diane LaVey and artist David Trufant as witnesses. "I consider it to be official recognition," LaVey said, before adding, "but I would not go so far as to say that the state sanctions or condones it." The state would not go so far as to say that either, its Department of Justice refusing to offer an opinion on the union's legality. "We're not saying this is good or bad because we just don't know," a spokesperson said. But since the California civil code recognized marriages officiated by any minister over the age of twenty-one—licensed or not—yes, the nuptials were deemed legitimate.

LaVey parlayed all this attention into a trip to Los Angeles for an appearance on *The Tonight Show* starring Johnny Carson, who at the time was America's most popular late-night TV host. While typically a forum for showbizzy creatures like Desi Arnaz, Bill Dana, and Phil Harris—other guests on that October 3, 1967, episode—*The Tonight Show* sometimes highlighted more serious newsmakers, such as one of LaVey's inspirations, the philosopher Ayn Rand, who appeared on the show three times that same year.

A few months earlier, LaVey occupied the hot seat on the nationally syndicated *Joe Pyne Show*, whose brash host has been credited with inventing the modern style of the combative media interview. Bedecked in a black, crimson-lined cape, his egg-shaped pate Vaselined to a blinding sheen, the high priest—cool, articulate, seductively appealing—remained unflappable and in good humor as his interlocutor took every opportunity to not only label him "shifty" and a "bit of a ding-a-ling" but also to point out his dirty fingernails and call the Baphomet medallion around his neck a "little red yo-yo."

"To marry two people without a license in front of a naked babe lying up on an altar," Pyne sputtered. "I don't know what *that* is!"

What that is was a story that even made its way into another kind of pulp magazine, one that trafficked in hearts that were broken, not ripped out of chests. A magazine called *True Confessions*.

More than thirty years after the event, John Raymond decided it was time to make a true confession of his own. That Satanic wedding? It was a sham, a put-on, a stunt. In response to a story that appeared in the alternative newspaper *SF Weekly* about the feeble state of the Church of Satan, he wrote in a letter to the editor, published in July 1998, that he first met LaVey one month prior to the nuptials, when he profiled him for the *Berkeley Citizen*, a community newspaper he was editing. He found the Satanist to be "hip, cynical, and funny. . . . He was a man with a dream. But instead of looking to heaven, he focused in the other direction." LaVey liked how the article turned out and called Raymond to see if the writer would want to help generate some publicity for the nascent church.

Raymond considered the offer for a few days, until, he said, "the neon bulb over my head started flashing like a ten-dollar hooker with a heavy habit." His epiphany: they'd stage the world's first Satanic wedding, joining Raymond and his live-in girlfriend, Case, in unholy matrimony.

He phoned the *Berkeley Daily Gazette*'s Fred Gardner, a friend and former colleague, to help put together some press releases. "Later that day," Raymond recalled, "I even asked Judy to marry me. 'Why not,' she replied, stirring the Kraft macaroni and cheese. Her passion had always been the glue that held us together. That and her cooking."

Case told *True Confessions* that the couple had been introduced to LaVey the previous fall. "As soon as we attended some of Anton's lecture classes and his Inner Circle, the Friday-night ritual meetings," she said, "we realized that the ideas of this church expressed our own beliefs better than any other organized credo."

Reached by a reporter before the ceremony, Case's father, Edward, an attorney and former trustee of the New York State Power Authority, offered no comment on the marriage but did say he "certainly will not attend."

He needn't have worried. By October 9, *San Francisco Chronicle* columnist Herb Caen, who had breathlessly covered the run-up to the wedding, wrote that the couple had separated and were headed for divorce. Still, the outlandish, hastily arranged ceremony managed to thrust LaVey and his year-old church headlong into the cultural conversation. Over the next three decades, he would become not only a subversive celebrity and a best-selling author, but also the often misunderstood and frequently vilified face of blasphemy and evil in America.

"After the last guest and the press had left, Fred, Anton, Judy, and I burst into laughter," Raymond recalled.

"We really pulled it off," LaVey told him. "And you can bet the rubes are gonna come back for more."

I.

A Dark Star Is Born

A caudal appendage, or a true human tail, can take many forms. It sometimes appears as a tumor, an elongation of vertebrae, or muscle tissue, blood vessels, and nerves all wrapped up in skin. It is an extremity so rare that before 2017 only 195 cases had been identified in medical literature. But that's exactly what Anton Szandor LaVey claimed to have had growing out of the top of his tuchus when, on April 11, 1930, in Chicago's Franklin Boulevard Hospital, he was expelled from the womb of Gertrude Levey.

"It really was profoundly disruptive to everything I did," he would later say. When he was around twelve, he had to have it lanced and drained a few times and started sitting sideways. Once while camping, he said, "I rolled around and must have banged it. Next day it started itching. Two days later it really flared up." The intense pain sent him to the ER. He said that because of a room shortage, he underwent surgery on a gurney in a hallway to have an extra vertebra removed near the bottom of his spine. The doctors didn't want to knock him out completely, but the local they gave him didn't help. He dealt with the pain by biting through a rubber pillow cover and bending a metal bar at the edge of his cot.

Anton Szandor LaVey gave himself that florid, abracadabran name (sometimes styled as La Vey) when he was a teenager. His birth certificate belonged to one Howard Stanton Levey, and before it was amended, mistakenly listed his date of issuance as March 11, his mother's birthday.

Gertrude, twenty-seven, and her twenty-six-year-old husband, Michael Joseph Levey, Howard's father, had recently lived with her parents and sister Gloria at 3826 Maypole Avenue in Chicago's West Garfield Park, a neighborhood where many Jews settled among Irish, German, and Italian immigrants. Michael, a Chicago native, was one of eight kids born to Meyer Levey, a fruit merchant, and his wife, Anna, both Russian Jewish immigrants.

Born in Cleveland, Ohio, to Baris and Luba (Libby) Coulton, Gertrude had seven siblings as well. Her folks, also Jews from Russia and Ukraine, emigrated to the United States around 1892. Baris worked assembling stoves in Hamilton, Ohio, in the early years of the new century, then moved his family to Chicago, where he would run a newsstand.

By the time Howard was three years old, his parents journeyed westward to Modesto, in Northern California, where his dad was a manager for the Rainier Beverage Company, a brewery. Within three years, the Leveys would head one hundred miles even farther west to Corte Madera, a leafy hamlet (population: around one thousand) in Marin County, whose redwood trees supplied some of the lumber used to build the city of San Francisco just fifteen miles to the south. By 1940, they had moved crosstown to 18 Redwood Avenue, and Michael worked selling auto accessories at S. Levin's Auto Supply on Van Ness Avenue in San Francisco while Gertrude, who as a teenager was a typist at an advertising agency, remained at home.

As a child, Howard had little use for sports and was a bookish sort, drawn to Jack London's and Mark Twain's tales of adventure as well as to entertainment of the fantastical and macabre. Enraptured by radio plays featuring the heroic likes of the Green Hornet, the Lone Ranger, and the Shadow—a noirish vigilante who knew what evil lurked in the hearts of men—he also devoured classic novels. He'd read *Franken-stein* and *Dracula* at six years old and became a fan of William Hope Hodgson's supernatural detective Thomas Carnacki and the pulpy monstrosities of *Weird Tales* magazine, which published the work of H.P. Lovecraft, Robert E. Howard, and Clark Ashton Smith. As an adolescent, he read books on magic and hypnotism and was particularly fond of *The Command to Look*, a photography manual by William Mortensen that offered a psychology-based approach to picture-taking.

Though he had friends, with his admittedly oddball looks—big ears, narrow eyes, elongated oval head, thick wavy hair—he took pride in being something of an outcast. "I never was a 'rebel,'" he later said, "because I was never part of anything to rebel against. I was never accepted by groups in the first place."

One group that did accept him was the Cubs, the boys' adventure and good-deed organization. As a member of Cub Pack No. 3 at Larkspur School in nearby San Anselmo, Howard was awarded a Bear badge at eleven years old. Though his parents were not religious, one of the obligations of that rank required him to discuss with a caring adult "what it means to do your duty to God." The badge itself, a diamond-shaped, bright red felt emblem, featured the embroidered outline of an ursine head in gold with the letters "CUBS BSA," for Boy Scouts of America, stitched underneath.

Howard's parents, both of whom were registered Democrats, were an indecisive pair who, he would later recall, never voiced many opinions. "From a young age," he said, "they followed my advice on things like what kind of cars to buy, anything that involved an aesthetic eye." They also gave him a wide berth to do what he wished, though his mother told the budding musician to watch out for his hands. He liked brass, percussion, woodwinds, and strings, but took up the keyboard because he appreciated its range. At Tamalpais High School in Mill Valley, as an oboist with the classical ensemble, he'd play Bach and Mozart and the like during Christmas assemblies.

Fascinated by engineering and architectural wonders, he claimed to have been one of the first to walk over the Golden Gate Bridge when it first opened to pedestrians in 1937. But it was the Golden Gate International Exhibition in San Francisco in 1939–1940, on the man-made Treasure Island, that would have a more profound effect on the boy. There, among the marvels of modern technology, he managed to sneak into Sally Rand's Nude Ranch, the burlesque queen's provocative attraction, where he ogled topless cowgirls spinning lassos and pitching horseshoes. After a friend told him he saw his Sunday school teacher among the scantily clad ladies, LaVey later said that this hypocrisy led him to experience a Satanic epiphany.

Another exhibition, a government-sponsored replica of a dilapidated tenement, gave him a voyeuristic charge and inspired him to create his own miniature city at home. But if any attraction at this World's Fair could have been deemed Satanic, it was Incubator Babies, which displayed live preemies in a modern hospital setting in the Gayway, the amusement concessions located in Treasure Island's "fun zone."

He would later say that at around five years old, when he saw a playmate wet herself, he acquired a predilection for watching girls pee. It was an example of "erotic crystallization inertia," which he defined as the point at which a sexual fetish became ingrained. Men born in different eras, he theorized, would have dissimilar fixations. If LaVey, who came of age in the 1940s, had a type, he said, it was a fleshy, heavily made-up moll with pale, translucent skin. Who pissed her panties.

A defender of animals, LaVey claimed that at eleven he used a BB gun to shoot another boy who had been aiming at a bird. And as an unrepentant prankster, he was gobsmacked when he first encountered the Johnson Smith & Company catalog. With its ads for joy buzzers, whoopee cushions, and sneezing powder, the compendium of novelty items and toys provided him with more benign weapons to cause embarrassment and not injury. "It had all the most horrid examples of man's inhumanity to man," he would later say, "all of course presented in the form of good fun and entertainment."

When World War II began in 1939, his thoughts, like those of many boys of that era, turned from BB guns to military weapons, uniforms, and strategy. He saved up to buy a catalog of naval munitions. For school, he'd dress like a French legionnaire or don a flight jacket and white scarf. He claimed that an uncle who went on submarine patrol during the war helped develop in him a love of the ocean and said that after the war, in spring 1945, he accompanied an uncle to Germany to rebuild US Army airstrips. There, he said, he was introduced to Nazi occult films and German Expressionism, which would later help shape his philosophy and aesthetic.

In the '30s and '40s, there was no shortage of heroic figures for a young man to idolize. LaVey, instead, reveled in the exploits of real-life outlaws. Demagogic politician Huey Long, Chicago gangster Al Capone, Russian mystic Grigori Rasputin, eighteenth-century Sicilian occultist Alessandro Cagliostro, arms dealer Basil Zaharoff—men who forged their own paths in their own way—as well as writers like John Milton and Friedrich Nietzsche, who explored the virtues of self-interest.

A natural autodidact, LaVey left high school in his junior year, preferring to hang around with disreputable types: gamblers, pimps, and prostitutes. He claimed to have learned secrets of the criminal trade and living outside the straight world through his father's brother Bill "LaVey," who was tight with mobster Bugsy Siegel's crew until he was sentenced for tax evasion to McNeil Island, a federal penitentiary in Washington state. (A salesman named William Levey/LaVey did do time at McNeil, but it was for mail fraud. He served from March 1938 to November 1941, years before he would have been taking his nephew on a tour of the criminal underworld.)

LaVey claimed that in spring 1947, after finding himself in a legal jam, he took off with the Clyde Beatty Circus, where he worked first as a roustabout, caring for the lions and tigers, then as a trainer. He became so adept at handling the big cats, he said, that during feeding time he would lay his own food next to theirs and imitate their snarling as he chowed down. The mutual trust was so great, he claimed he'd sometimes sleep in their cages.

It was on the road with Beatty that LaVey said he began playing the calliope professionally, grabbing the opportunity one day when the regular musician, Fred Mullen, got too drunk. The instrument, an organ that uses gas or steam or compressed air to produce buoyant carousel sounds through a set of large whistles, was to become a favorite of his. Not only would he accompany animal acts, he said, but also such circus stars as Hugo Zacchini ("the Human Cannonball"), aerialists the Flying Wallendas, horse-riders the Hannefords, and trapeze artists the Concellos.

For all his supposed contributions, LaVey's name is nowhere to be found in Beatty's 1947 *Season Route Book & Souvenir Program*, which appears to list every person associated with that tour, down to the last butcher, electrician, and musician, including Fred Mullen. It wouldn't be the last time LaVey went uncredited for work he said he did.

After the circus season ended, the West Coast carnival circuit beckoned. If the Beatty habitués represented the tippy top of the big top, the carnies growled in its dark underbelly. LaVey claimed to have spent some time playing the midways at Crafts 20 Big Shows, the Foley & Burk carnival, and the Pike, an oceanfront amusement park in Long Beach, California. During these carnival days, LaVey said, he met such sideshow performers as Francesco Lentini, who was born with three legs; Bill Durks, who was born with two faces; and the Human Ostrich, who had the ability to regurgitate objects at will. He became particularly fascinated with the goings-on in the "mitt camp," where fortune tellers read palms and mentalists worked suckers. That's where LaVey got to watch and learn.

Around this time, LaVey claimed to have had another Satanic epiphany, one that would echo his experience on Treasure Island. While working the midways, he'd also freelance on the organ for evangelists doing tent-revival shows nearby. The same guys he'd see in Sunday's congregation, he had just witnessed gawking at the carnival strippers doing their bump and grind. "I knew that the Christian Church thrives on hypocrisy," he later said, "and that man's carnal nature will out no matter how much is purged or scourged by any white-light religion."

He developed his own peacocky style, modeled after noirish gangster chic, with wide-lapeled, big-shouldered suits, pocket squares, crisp Panama hats, and delicately landscaped facial hair. And in the fall of 1948, he said, he moved his trade indoors to burlesque houses. In one of them, downtown Los Angeles's Mayan Theatre, he claimed to have accompanied a young dancer-actress named Marilyn Monroe, who was then between gigs. Later, he told one interviewer that she'd been billed as "Marion Marlow," which seems unlikely as a onetime roommate of Marilyn Monroe's was a singer named Marion Marlowe. He said Monroe had been stripping there after Columbia Pictures declined to renew the twenty-two-year-old ingenue's contract.

The pair, naturally, fell into a torrid two-week affair and lived together
in a fleabag motel on Washington Boulevard, he told a reporter and a
biographer decades later. He'd tell another journalist that he shacked
up with her for a month at Hollywood's Oban Hotel, on Yucca Street,
because not only did she own a car and earn twelve dollars a day—
two more than he did—she also enjoyed "a good fuck." He would also
elaborate on her erotic proclivities: "She approached sex like a little
girl, adjusting shyly to the demands of her mate. . . . She moaned and
groaned and sweated like so many of us do, but when she came, she
would begin gnashing her teeth.

"And she sometimes farted when she lost all control."

After that dalliance, Los Angeles lost for him whatever grimy allure
it may have had. By 1949, he was living in San Francisco with his peri-
patetic parents and eighty-one-year-old grandmother, Libby—who had
been widowed when he was six—at 790 Thirty-Second Avenue, a block
north of Golden Gate Park on the city's west end. Anton, listed in the
census as unemployed at the time, claimed to have picked up the odd
gig playing the organ for local strip shows at lodges and stag parties
and worked at an agency where he took photos of naked women. To
avoid having to serve in the Korean War, he said he bluffed his way into
criminology classes at the City College of San Francisco, despite having never finished high school. (According to a 1991 magazine profile
of LaVey, the college had no evidence of his enrollment.)

As he pursued music in the evenings, he said he also fell in with Zion-
ist organizations that were running guns to Israel, which had just recently
declared its independence. "I would be hired to play for a fashion show
or variety show," he said, "and then I'd get through and go right down to
the docks where crates of guns were being loaded onto ships to Israel."
Some of the smugglers, whom he called "ideological mercenaries,"
were ambivalent about the cause they were contributing to, which he
also said had been an element of his arms-dealing hero Basil Zaharoff's

philosophy and appeal. "Many seemed more concerned about refining and perfecting innovative weapons technology they were experimenting with than who their new relay or explosive was blowing up, though."

One night at Playland at the Beach, a seaside amusement park on the western rim of the city, he met a pretty blonde girl named Carole Lansing, the San Francisco–born daughter of a banker and a deputy registrar at city hall. She was petite, glamorous, and all of fifteen years old when they married in 1951. The following year she gave birth to their daughter, whom they named Karla Maritza. The LaVeys initially lived in a flat on Forty-Seventh Avenue, right near Playland. "I'd be in the crib and I'd hear the screams of the children on the rollercoaster," Karla would later recall.

LaVey claimed to have parlayed his talent for picture-taking and interest in crime into a job as a photographer for the San Francisco Police Department. But the blood-drenched murder victims and mangled bodies removed from car wrecks quickly took their toll on the young father, who decided, "There is no God. . . . There is nobody up there who gives a shit. Man must be taught to answer to himself and other men for his actions." (After the SFPD later said no one with his name ever worked for the department, LaVey reckoned that documentation of his employment was likely expunged.) Soon, he said, he was picking up work as a sort of professional ghostbuster, investigating cases the police deemed frivolous—strange sounds coming from the attic, flying-saucer sightings—using a tape recorder, a camera with infrared film, and a theremin to detect any paranormal presence. It was, for him, an ideal gig, one that allowed him to indulge his skepticism along with his taste for the bizarre. In the process, it revealed to him why people craved religion: they needed to believe in a force beyond themselves to explain away the things they couldn't. Clients began paying him to exorcise supposed malevolent spirits and work out their personal issues through hypnosis.

On the first of November 1955, LaVey became a member of San Francisco's musician's union. Though he played many instruments, the only one listed in the rolls was "electronic organ." Soon, he'd be performing at watering holes all over town. While jazz trumpeter Chet Baker and Borscht Belt comic Shecky Greene entertained the swells at the Blackhawk and Bimbo's 365, Anton Szandor LaVey (often billed as "S.F.'s Unique Organist") played for lounge lizards and barflies at Ethel's and the Wilshire.

In 1956, his parents bought an old Victorian house at 6114 California Street for $9,500. Soon, LaVey moved his young family in. He later said he had discovered the property himself while on a house hunt, claiming it was a former bordello and speakeasy that had belonged to a madam named "Mammy" Pleasant. (Mary Ellen Pleasant, an abolitionist, entrepreneur, and philanthropist, is said to have been one of America's first self-made Black millionaires.)

To reflect the image LaVey was building for himself, the house's slate-gray exterior would not do. He had to paint it black.

II.

Dandy in the Underworld

THE local media started taking notice of this strange character in their midst. Herb Caen wrote in his September 30, 1957, column about "a tall, thin cat wearing a beard and a trenchcoat" whom he met as LaVey peddled paintings of a skeleton and a vulture at a local arts festival. "Nobody'll buy my pictures," said LaVey, who insisted that these were examples of his more pleasant work. "I've done some really grim ones since." Sensing an in, LaVey invited Caen over to his home to meet his pet tarantula, Bruno. "He sits on the mantelpiece and I scratch his back and he lifts one of his hind legs and waves it around to show he's enjoying it."

On Sunday afternoons and evenings in late 1959, LaVey played the organ at Mori's Point Inn, a restaurant and bar next to a golf course in Pacifica, California, a half-hour's drive from the city. At some point his schedule changed and the place advertised "Dancing Friday Night to Anton La Vey's Orchestra." With a versatile keyboard, he could indeed approximate the sound of a band.

One night, Diane Von Joo, a seventeen-year-old usher at a nearby movie theater, stopped by the bar while on a date with her manager. "Anton was playing a Hammond organ and there was an unlit candle sitting on top of it," his grandson Stanton later wrote. "Diane took the opportunity to meet the man she would later not-marry by striking a match to the candle on her way to the ladies room." It wasn't long before the two fell into an affair.

In December, LaVey made an appearance in the *San Francisco Chronicle's* Question Man column, a person-on-the-street interview that asked eight people stopped at the intersection of Twenty-First Avenue and Geary Boulevard the burning question: "What is the best way to get along with people?"

"Everyone likes to be thought of as an individual and not be put into a group with everyone else," began LaVey's reply, which led into a succinct encapsulation of his philosophy. "If you treat them so that they sincerely feel that you don't recognize them as just another person, then they respect you."

With a wife and young daughter at home, LaVey kept busy freelancing. On May 10, 1960, as part of the Peninsula Organ Society, he played the Burlingame Women's Club at an event called "Circus Daze," which promised clowns and acrobats. Later that October, at a performance sponsored by the Capuchino High School Parent-Teacher Association in San Bruno, he presented an evening of pipe-organ music, including jazz, blues, pop ballads, and the sound of the circus.

Steve Leialoha first met LaVey around 1960, when the organist started dating Diane. Leialoha, then eight, lived with his family across the street from hers in Pacifica, near Mori's Point Inn. It was LaVey's unusual car parked on the street that caught the neighbors' attention: a

1937 Cord with retractable headlights, which the owner was more than happy to show off to the kids. "He was dressed to match," recalls Leialoha, who grew up to become a popular comic-book artist, "in a white turtlenecked sweater under his black sports coat and his equally black hair and goatee. Beat fashion at its most cool."

LaVey eventually landed a fairly solid gig at the Lost Weekend, at 1940 Taraval Street, four miles south of his home. Long a staple of the Sunset District, the Lost Weekend was a cocktail lounge with a difference. And it wasn't because in 1961 George Salinger, brother of President John F. Kennedy's press secretary Pierre Salinger, was the manager. The Art Deco–style listening room was a rectangle, maybe fifty feet deep. At the back, on the right, was a fake brick fireplace, and against the chimney hung a painting of actor Ray Milland, the star of the joint's namesake, a 1945 film about an alcoholic on a binge. The space also happened to house a mighty Wurlitzer pipe organ.

Unlike the more ubiquitous two-keyboard Hammond organs, a Wurlitzer, with its elaborate construction and electro-pneumatic piping, could mimic a symphony orchestra. "It was a neighborhood bar, except that organ nuts knew about it," says Edward Millington Stout III, perhaps the world's foremost Wurlitzer restorer. He was in his early twenties when he began maintaining the Lost Weekend's centerpiece at the request of Larry Vannucci, the resident organist. Another of the bar's organists was Dewey Cagle, whose son, decades later, would become close with LaVey's family.

As Stout describes it, the housing for the Wurlitzer, one of only 2,200 or so produced by the company, was quite complex: "In the center of the club was an aisle that went to the two bathrooms, which were on the left side. On the right side was the office. When you went back further, you went up around six steps, and you're at a different level." That's where the Wurlitzer relay, which acts as the organ's brain, was secured. Above a cigarette machine at the end of the bar, up on four legs, was the chrysoglott, a percussion instrument that sounds like a vibraharp, which connected to the relay. The two ten-by-ten chambers housing the organ's pipes were located above the bathrooms, protruding into the building's attic, side by side with the shutters. The sound that blasted through them often woke the neighbors, occasionally even shaking them from their beds.

LaVey was there subbing for Vannucci, who had the night off, when he met Stout. The men became fast friends.

For guys like LaVey and Vannucci, "it was a decent living," Stout says, though tips were often hard to come by since the organist would be mostly inaccessible to the crowd. Since the console, where the musician would sit, was on a platform above the bar, he ended up looking down on the audience. A huge mirror on the wall behind him hung at a forty-five-degree angle so patrons could see his hands move along the keys.

Vannucci, who in 1960 put out a record of Wurlitzer favorites, peppered his sets with ballads and jazz standards like "Mood Indigo" and "Sophisticated Lady." LaVey, in contrast, would proffer a kitschy mix of stuff like the bullfight staple "España Cañí," Ravel's "Boléro," and "Yankee Rose," a jaunty dance-band number from 1927. LaVey, Stout admits, had a distinctive approach, describing it as "merry-go-round, circus-type music." And he didn't think much of it at the time. "LaVey was limited," Stout says. "His repertory was limited."

"My sister gave me a bunch of family scrapbooks, and one of them was of the San Francisco Theater Organ Society," says Dewey Cagle's son, John Aes-Nihil (short for Aesthetic-Nihilism), a filmmaker and archivist of fringe subcultures. "And so I thought maybe Larry Vannucci was in it, and he is. Then I thought maybe Anton was in it. And there's one page on Anton: 'The Golden Gate Organ Club invites you to join in cocktails for two at the Lost Weekend, June 12, 1960. Professor Anton LaVey at the pipe organ. Anton has traveled the world over with major circuses, making people happy by playing the calliope.'"

Stout, the younger of the two by a few years, remembers LaVey's playful side, rating him a prankster par excellence. Together, they specialized in making a scene. Their targets were often restaurant workers and patrons.

"Let's go down and have some fun," LaVey would say.

"I've got to go in there with a character of some sort," Stout would respond. "Do you have any old suits that are in real bad shape?"

"Well, there's one down in the basement that's moldy."

"Perfect."

Stout, a small guy, would put on the larger man's old suit, add the safety goggles he carried around for his repair jobs, then smudge the lenses with a mix of cigarette ash and spit. "They were all clouded up and looked like they hadn't been cleaned in a hundred years," he says. "Then I assumed a character, which was easy to do, of a halfwit named Edgar."

With LaVey playing the straight man, they'd enter a restaurant and cause a commotion. "We had a lot of fun upsetting people and getting stares," Stout says.

A woman named Virginia Cullen often accompanied the men on their excursions. She was a veteran San Francisco cop who at twenty-six was one of the first on the force to earn the official designation "policewoman." Adopting the pseudonym Sister Marie Koven, she became an early member of LaVey's Magic Circle, a kind of occult salon he came to host at his home.

Cullen, a former marine who, early on, went undercover as a junkie prostitute for the vice squad, continued to have a colorful career. One late August night in 1963, an off-duty Cullen enjoyed a few drinks while watching her friend Anton entertain at the Lost Weekend. After getting in her car and driving away, she claimed a vehicle following hers forced her to the curb near her home. A man, who she said appeared menacing, came over to her window and made an indecent remark, so she drew her service revolver, shot him in the thigh, and arrested him for assault. When he was put on trial the following February, the man, a carpenter named Carl Dee, said she fired at him for no reason. LaVey testified on Cullen's behalf, saying he witnessed her being followed, though it's hard to imagine how he could have. Dee was acquitted, while Cullen's reputation received a shiner.

A few months later she found herself in trouble again when she was charged with "unofficerlike conduct" and suspended ninety days for both excessive drinking and allowing children to handle her unloaded gun. Still, she managed to get promoted to assistant inspector in 1972. Twelve years later, Cullen, then sixty, was returning home from a bar on her motorized tricycle when it was struck by a pickup truck. She escaped uninjured.

Anton and Carole split by 1960. Karla stayed to live at 6114 with her father and Diane, who took his last name though they never married. In Carole's divorce papers, she claimed her husband's only income came from his Lost Weekend residency and various other music bookings, which amounted to $29.91 per week ($314 in 2024, adjusted for inflation).

It was at the Lost Weekend, LaVey said, where another San Francisco police inspector buddy, Jack Webb (who shared a name with the star of the popular TV series *Dragnet*), gave him the idea to codify his obsession with magic and the occult and create a new religion.

Sandwiched between, and seemingly dwarfed by, two otherwise unremarkable rectangular buildings, the two-story, peaked-roof house at 6114 California Street—with three windows aligned on the second floor and three others forming a large bay window on the main level— appeared homuncular, out of step. And recessed a few yards in from the curb, it seemed even more alien, as if it were willfully withdrawing from the surrounding community. In the same spirit, LaVey saw the interior as a canvas on which he could project his wicked, feverish art— creating a total environment out of his grisliest dreams. And in Diane he had found a willing accomplice, one whose encouragement charged his creativity.

A dozen red brick stairs ascended to the front door. Inside, a staircase at right led to the second-floor bedrooms, while to the left, checker-board tiles marked the path down the long dark hallway. Over time, he painted his and Diane's main-floor bedroom a glossy red, the living room and kitchen a shiny black. On a huge mural in the kitchen, a cartoonish bat-winged demon, based on the one from the "Night on Bald Mountain" segment in Disney's *Fantasia*, rose from red and yel-low flames. Underneath it, LaVey would eventually configure banks of keyboards. Other, more whimsical creatures adorned the wall around the door leading to the backyard.

His and Diane's bedroom contained a loft bed, with a small office below. Maces, swords, and other weapons hung nearby. Off to the right was a bathroom with a large octopus painted on a wall.

He decided on purple for the sitting room, where a trick bookcase opened up to the red bedroom and a trapdoor in a fake fireplace gave access to the basement. Sunlight was not welcome in this house filled with memento mori, reminders of the inevitability of death. Skulls. A full-size human skeleton. Stuffed (real) animals. His own paintings of cadaverous ghouls and haunted mansions.

Over the years, he filled the purple room with such conversation pieces as a combination barber/dentist chair, an examination table (complete with stirrups), and a tombstone belonging to one Lucas Machado that the LaVeys used as a coffee table.

And then there were books. Dozens upon dozens of books. Floor-to-ceiling shelves heaved and sighed with the weight of multitudinous volumes from a vast assortment of genres, including macabre short fiction, fantastic adventure, true crime, magic, the occult, pop psychology, and show-business nonfiction. Grim anthologies like Fritz Leiber's *Night's Black Agents*, Ray Bradbury's *Dark Carnival*, and A.E. Coppard's *Fearful Pleasures* fought for space alongside Donald John Smith's *Amateur Acting and Stage Encyclopedia*, Erving Goffman's *Behavior in Public Places*, and Herbert Asbury's *The Great Illusion: An Informal History of Prohibition*. A number of the spookier titles belonged to Arkham House, an imprint cofounded by pulp writer August Derleth, which initially published H.P. Lovecraft story collections. For LaVey, books were the keys to life's secrets, doorways into worlds unknown and unimaginable. He was so serious about his stash that he affixed a sign onto one of the bookcases, which served as a warning to potential biblioklepts: ANYONE CAUGHT REMOVING BOOKS FROM SHELVES WILL HAVE THEIR HANDS AMPUTATED.

The black living room would eventually become a key space in the house, a chamber where LaVey would enact rituals using the stone fireplace's mantel as the focus under a red ceiling, illuminated by electric-candle sconces, and among a Yamaha organ, an upright coffin, a gong the size of a garbage can lid, and a wooden sleigh chair he claimed once belonged to Rasputin. A replica of King Tut's sarcophagus served as another trick door into the red bedroom.

The bar in the low-ceilinged cellar, the Den of Iniquity, would become the setting for his wanton menagerie of artificial human companions, mannequins whose faces he altered, posed in a room that resembled a species-behind-glass diorama at a natural history museum seemingly curated by Diane Arbus and Weegee.

The Black House, as 6114 came to be known, stood as a monument to one man's obsessive aesthetic, leavened with his peculiar gallows humor.

The only things missing were actual gallows.

Ed Stout would become a frequent guest at the house, where he'd gather with LaVey's social circle for screenings of silent movies nearly every other week. "He was very gracious," Stout says. "I was one of several friends who enjoyed the fact that he enjoyed being a character. His whole life was a performance."

However entertaining that character could be, Stout had zero interest in LaVey's occult endeavors. "I thought it was a load of horseshit," he says, adding that he was deeply suspicious of any institution that called itself a church. "I wanted to be anchored in a reality that I could comprehend. I figured I'd better be responsible for my own actions and not blame it on some supernatural creature. I mean, when a baby's born, it hasn't even bounced on the floor twice before it's given a gift by this loving and benevolent institution. And this gift is a pox called original sin, based on some story about a snake and an apple in a garden. And this church, this organization that invented this deadly pox on this innocent child, who hasn't passed wind once—this child is given this pox.

"And for the rest of its miserable fucking life, it has to go to the authorized dealer once a week and have its spiritual oil changed," he continues.

"That's a fucking good business."

III.

6114: House Number of the Beast

NO TRESPASSERS. SURVIVORS WILL BE PROSECUTED.

The sign, no bigger than a license plate, hung in the kitchen of the Black House beneath a window through which one could see a toothy lion named Togare pacing in his metal cage on the back porch. Visitors would do well to heed its warning.

In 1965, the neighborhood weirdo, his brood, and their house made a splash on *The Wonderful World of Brother Buzz*, a local children's TV program that encouraged the humane treatment of animals. Three marionettes—two bees and one rodent—introduced the segment narrated first by a Bela Lugosi impersonator, then by an aggressively wacky lion who sounded straight off the streets of Manhattan's Lower East Side, circa 1952. After highlighting the occupants and their home's décor—Diane emerging from the trick fireplace, Anton playing the organ, Karla checking her doll's heartbeat while standing in front of a hypno wheel—the show presented the "psychic investigator" wrestling with his pet lion and later taking him on a leash to the supermarket, where the excited animal pawed at the meat cooler. Togare was nine weeks old when, LaVey claimed, a former trainer at the Clyde Beatty Circus gave him as a gift. Both *The Munsters* and *The Addams Family*, outrageous sitcoms centered on spooky clans living in macabre mansions, had debuted on TV just a year earlier. But here was the real thing, in living, breathing color.

The big cat was named for Austrian lion tamer Georg Kulovits, who performed as "Togare." And he brought LaVey a lot of attention, whether it was while mingling with the elegant likes of *Citizen Kane* star Joseph Cotten at the Sonoma ranch of eccentric architect David Pleydell-Bouverie, teaching kindergarteners from Hamlin Elementary School about the responsibilities of pet ownership, or becoming the main attraction at the Golden West Cat Club's annual all-breed championship show on October 16 and 17, where Anton judged the Household Pets Division. Togare wasn't even his first big cat. He, Carole, and Karla lived for a time with a black leopard named Zoltan.

Obviously, having a pet lion, though legal at the time, came with risks. A friend of the LaVeys recalls once seeing a row of four bloody claw marks on Diane's upper right arm. "I must have gasped," says Raechel Donahue, "because she assured me that everything was okay and it was just that Togare doesn't know his own strength."

Togare, "A Quarter Ton of Loving Lion," made the front page of the *Chronicle* on April 22, 1966, in a story that detailed his life as a domestic tabby. The piece was accompanied by two photos, one of Togare roaring and another of LaVey playfully wrestling the now two-year-old cat. When he wasn't joining LaVey on trips to the local supermarket, Togare was playing with old tires in his screened-in porch and sleeping in his owner's bedroom, chained to a ring bolt in the floor. "We just don't want him chewing up the furniture, which he likes to do," LaVey said. (Diane, who admitted it was difficult to lion-proof a house, would later say she brushed Tabasco sauce on stuff she didn't him want to bite.)

This promotional gambit began to backfire, however, when three days later the paper reported that a local attorney and political aspirant wrote in a letter to Mayor John F. Shelley that the constantly roaring Togare was a menace to the neighborhood. "You know how it is, though," LaVey later said with a sigh. "Everybody says he likes lions, but not everyone wants to live next door to one."

By then Anton had established his Magic Circle, which, in addition to policewoman Virginia Cullen, was said to have included a squad of other local eccentrics. Kenneth Anger, whom LaVey met as the young avant-garde filmmaker worked on *Inauguration of the Pleasure Dome*, a short inspired by the writings of Aleister Crowley. Novelist Stephen Schneck, whose first book, *The Nightclerk*, earned him the international Formentor Prize. Taxidermist Roy Heist. Carin de Plessen, a member of the Danish aristocracy. Anthropologist Michael Harner. Dr. Cecil Nixon, a dentist and inventor whose home contained a full-size pipe organ, an automaton named Isis who could pluck three thousand songs from a zither, and another called Galatea, who reclined on a leopard skin and played the violin. LaVey claimed another doctor in the Magic Circle, Hugo Moeller from the neurosurgery department at the

University of California Medical Center, supplied him with patients—
suffering from insomnia, nervousness, impotence, and the like—for
whom Anton could offer hypnotherapy sessions at ten bucks a pop. This
would have been quite an achievement, considering Moeller was actually a gastroenterologist.

April 30. On this date in 1939, the National Broadcasting Company
aired the first television transmission, an appearance by President
Franklin D. Roosevelt, from the New York World's Fair. On this date
in 1945, Adolf Hitler and his wife, Eva Braun, killed themselves in their
underground bunker. In religious tradition, the date marks Walpurgisnacht ("Witches' Sabbath"), a European pagan holiday celebrating fer-
tility and the coming of spring, when Christians pray to God to protect
them from witches, demons, and evil spirits.

And on this night in 1966—three weeks after *Time* magazine infamously asked on its cover, "Is God Dead?"—Anton LaVey was going
to officially revive His (or Her) adversary. He claimed he ritualistically
cut off his wavy dark locks and shaved his head. He wanted to resemble
not only the villains of the pulpy thrillers he so admired, but also as
his authorized biographer noted, "the medieval executioners, carnival
strongmen, and black magicians before him, to gain personal power
and enhance the forces surrounding his newly established Satanic
order." Where he had previously been an occult lecturer, occasional
ghost hunter, and organizer of a Magic Circle, LaVey would now be the
founder and leader of a church, one that rejected the Holy Trinity and
its proscriptions and instead allowed its congregants to indulge in their
lust for life. A—no, *the*—First Church of Satan. (He'd drop the "First"
soon after establishing the church.) He formally designated the occasion Anno Satanas, Year One on the Satanic calendar.

"Calling it a church," he'd later say, "enabled me to follow the magic formula of nine parts outrage and one part social responsibility that is needed for success." Thus officially began one man's elaborate, fanciful, artful, sometimes perilous dance with the Devil.

Satan—or the Devil, or any number of comparable figures, has appeared as an antagonistic, terrifying figure throughout folklore and religion ever since humans, wanting to make sense of a chaotic existence, had the capacity to feel shame and point a finger. The Mayans have Cizin, the Chinese have Mogwai, Muslims have Shaitan, Germans have Mephistopheles, Africans have Shetani, and so on. The Judeo-Christian figure of Satan is a fallen angel personifying pure evil who terrorizes the world and leads innocents astray, countering a merciful God's sublime capacity for good. LaVey's Satanism, however, wasn't the belief in a literal crimson, pitchfork-toting, pointy-eared demon who reigned over a fire-spewing hell (like the one painted on a wall in the LaVey kitchen). Rather, it was the idea of one—a metaphorical tempter wielding a more seductive and gratifying portfolio than the guilt-inducing Other Guy.

"Satan as a red devil is ingrained in the collective unconscious," LaVey said. "The association can't be broken, so we might as well use it and exploit it as a positive symbol." Still, some members, according to Randall H. Alfred—who went undercover in the church to research it—would come to regard the Devil as a deity to be worshipped.

LaVey's church forbade the use of illegal drugs, particularly hallucinogens, as they impeded the effective control over one's surroundings—a restriction that likely turned off students at the Berkeley campus of the University of California, where in 1968 the church made an unsuccessful attempt to missionize. Alcohol, however, was considered fine in moderation since it reduced inhibitions. Alfred recalled seeing at church parties a spiked punch called Satonic, or Goblin Juice, sometimes served out of a commode.

Edward James Moody, a lecturer at Queen's University of Belfast, Northern Ireland, spent two and half years as an active church member and came up with a profile of its participants. Those he encountered in San Francisco, he wrote, "desire successes denied them—money, fame, recognition, power—and with legitimate avenues apparently blocked, with no apparent means by which legitimate effort will bring reward, they turn to Satanism and witchcraft."

Many suffered traumatic childhoods: alcoholic parents, broken homes, abusive siblings. Some, he observed, were also characterized by "assorted psychological 'syndromes' ranging from transvestism to sadomasochism. A single factor seemed to typify all of them: all were deviant or abnormal in some aspect of their social behavior." But they themselves weren't deviants—their unconventional attitudes, he explained, caused anxiety in those who played by society's rules.

And the Church of Satan welcomed them.

"The new member," Moody wrote, "is likely to find himself praised and rewarded for the very thoughts and behaviors which brought him pain and scorn in the larger community."

Ceremonies in LaVey's church would often take the form of psychodramas conducted by the high priest. In one, the shibboleth ritual, congregants would come dressed as a person they hated and wished to curse. Over the course of the evening, each Satanist would be required to think, act, and talk like their nemesis, before that adversary would be symbolically killed. And if this feat of "greater magic"—a casting of spells and hexes through rituals and using props—was unable to conjure a real-world result, well, at least it would offer the Satanist some catharsis and provide tools to manipulate or influence the foe by using "lesser magic."

Alfred also observed that for the twenty to thirty participants, this wasn't playacting—they truly were getting something out of it. Members reported "the emotional intensity of greater magic was creating new confidence that they could recognize and then obtain their own desired goals, whether amorous, vengeful, financial, political, or whatever," he wrote, adding that "a sufficiently powerful ritual was deemed capable of implanting a suggestion in the mind of one on whom the magician wished to cast a spell."

With the establishment of a church came the administration of a church, and LaVey enlisted Diane to handle much of those day-to-day responsibilities. Karla would eventually help out too. There were promotional flyers to print up and applications to process—requiring a twenty-five-dollar fee, a current snapshot, and, for minors, written permission from a parent or legal guardian. There were changes of address to record and merchandise orders to fulfill. Those products would grow to include books, an LP record, a sigil of Baphomet wall plaque, and various medallions. Active members were sent red identification cards featuring a personalized membership number. Those and medallions, if visibly displayed, "will elicit sufficient response and will serve as a means of recognition for other Satanists you might unknowingly encounter," one handout suggested.

Diane would soon adopt the alias Lana Green on church paperwork and business calls, since Anton believed that masquerading as his secretary, and not speaking on behalf of her spouse, enabled her to be a far more effective communicator.

Eventually, a form letter went out to the incarcerated who wished to join, encouraging those correspondents to develop their understanding of Satanism under their current conditions and away from the Church of Satan (it was an elitist organization, after all). "At the present time," the mailing went on, "your opportunities to do this lie within the walls—certainly not outside them." It asked the recipients to keep the church informed of their progress, before adding fairly witheringly, "but do not expect answers to your letters; you have much time, but we have thousands of pieces of mail each week to sort and process."

On October 20, 1966, Hollywood's smartest dumb blonde came to town. In the run-up to the San Francisco International Film Festival, the *Chronicle* reported that Jayne Mansfield, the voluptuous Hollywood sex symbol, would be flying in for the event in a star-studded chartered plane along with comedian Jonathan Winters, actress Polly Bergen, and Peter Ustinov, opening night's master of ceremonies.

At the time, the actress was engulfed in chaos, both professionally and personally. Once a major-studio rival to Marilyn Monroe—thanks to her winningly self-aware roles in such late-'50s confections as *The Girl Can't Help It* and *Will Success Spoil Rock Hunter?*—by 1966 she was chasing paychecks, slumming in dreck like *The Fat Spy* and *Las Vegas Hillbillys* and touring the lowdown nightclub circuit with a tacky song-and-prance act that found her sitting on the laps of men in the audience. Locally, the Hub Theater on Market Street was currently unspooling her three-year-old sex farce *Promises! Promises!* in which she appears nude—in bed, in a tub, toweling herself dry—the kind of (over)exposure that made her unique among mainstream actresses at the time.

She had recently completed a cameo in her first major picture in a long while, *A Guide for the Married Man*, as well as a starring role in *Single Room Furnished*. The latter was a low-budget drama directed by her third husband, Matt Cimber, with whom she was locked in a bitter divorce battle, alleging extreme cruelty. Less than a week before landing in San Francisco, she had been awarded custody of their only son, eleven-month-old Tony, after a contentious, highly publicized tug of war. Along with her pink luggage and dainty chihuahuas, she brought with her Sam Brody, her divorce attorney, de facto manager, and latest boyfriend.

Theirs was a volatile and abusive relationship. And Brody knew from volatility: a few years earlier, he worked with Melvin Belli to defend Jack Ruby, the assassin of John F. Kennedy assassin Lee Harvey Oswald.

If Anton LaVey could have summoned from his ritual altar the ideal embodiment of his lust, the figure doubtlessly would have taken the form of Jayne Mansfield: full of bosom and bereft of inhibition, part squeaky cartoon doll, part ditzy gangster's moll. When they finally connected, it was a match made in Hades—the merging of two preternatural publicity hounds who exemplified the new freedoms that were rousing America out of its prudish postwar torpor.

The legend of their meeting and subsequent relationship goes something like this: either LaVey's press agents or Mansfield's reached out to the other to set up a confab and a tour of the Black House. Jayne showed up with Brody and her road manager and instantly bonded with the high priest, which made her boyfriend instantly jealous. As they walked through the rooms, LaVey warned Brody not to touch anything, particularly the skull candles on the mantel. When he took Jayne aside to present her with a Baphomet pendant, Brody went ahead and lit one anyway. "That candle is used only for curses," LaVey laid into him. "I don't know what's going to happen to you now."

Or maybe he shouted, as May Mann, a Mansfield confidante and biographer, claimed, "You will both be killed in a tragic car accident within a year. When it happens, it will be very sudden!" But, Mann wrote, if she ditched Sam, LaVey averred, Jayne would be all right.

According to LaVey, Jayne also told him to put a curse on Cimber so that she'd win custody of Tony (of whom, it must be noted, she already had custody).

After that visit, all sorts of things started to go wrong for the actress. For one, the SFIFF general manager disinvited her, claiming she embarrassed the festival with her provocative attire, and, besides, she'd never been invited in the first place.

In the meantime, LaVey dove into a busy social calendar: conducting a Halloween Black Mass in the Wax Museum at Fisherman's Wharf and donning a pith helmet to play the calliope at a coming-out party for a Sonoma rancher's debutante daughter, where he also accompanied a chimpanzee aerial act.

Raechel Donahue, who was to become a popular San Francisco radio personality, attended the LaVeys' 1966 Halloween party with her future husband Tom Donahue, a leading DJ and concert promoter. He came dressed as the literary figure Svengali and she as Trilby, the bohemian model who falls under the hypnotist's spell. Raechel recalls being greeted at the door by a six-foot-five man named Rudy, who was wearing a French maid's costume, fishnet stockings, and spike heels. "His expression implied he'd been dead for at least a few weeks," she says.

At the party, their host, swathed in his customary black cape, entertained guests by playing Bach's "Toccata and Fugue in D Minor," featuring the sinister organ riff popularized in such movies as LaVey's beloved *Fantasia* and *The Black Cat*. He also offered a tour of the house, pointing out the space between some of the walls where one could surreptitiously observe goings-on through peepholes. "It was said that [a] tunnel beneath the house was a mile long, big enough to drive a car through, and led all the way to the beach," Donahue recalls. "I never saw it, so I can't attest to the accuracy of the legend."

Just a few months after the fête, LaVey would be organizing another costumed affair, this one his first foray into the theater: a topless witches' revue.

Jayne took her kids Zoltan, six, Mickey Jr. (Miklos), seven, and Maria (Mariska), two, to Jungleland in Thousand Oaks on November 26. Nestled in the Santa Monica Mountains, about an hour's drive from her home in Beverly Hills, the private zoo housed and trained animals appearing in movies and TV shows. As his mom posed for publicity photos, Zoltan strayed too close to a chained lion. The big cat pounced, thrashing the boy about by the neck, slashing his cheek, fracturing his skull, and rupturing his spleen.

According to May Mann, as Zoltan lay on the operating table, LaVey offered to fly down to deliver "a magic healing potion." LaVey claimed he drove to the top of Mount Tamalpais, the San Francisco Bay Area's highest peak, and delivered an invocation beseeching Satan to heal the child.

A few days after undergoing successful emergency surgery, Zoltan developed meningitis, a serious infection targeting the brain and spinal cord. LaVey said that once again he held a ritual to bless the son of his new acquaintance, who herself had come down with viral pneumonia. Both mother and child recovered.

According to LaVey, the tragedy drew Mansfield closer to him, and she became his pupil and, inevitably, his lover. She would sneak out to San Francisco when Brody was in court, working. She would ring LaVey multiple times a day, even breaking into calls in progress to confess her love. At the very least, she phoned LaVey every midnight so he could cast a happy spell over her. LaVey claimed that in January, Mansfield called him for help during a particularly brutal fight with Brody, who snatched away the receiver and shouted that she was never going to speak with him again and that he'd make real trouble for LaVey if the two didn't cut off contact. Brody would be dead in a year, LaVey promised him—he'd see to it. The high priest performed a destruction ritual aimed at the lawyer, writing Brody's name on parchment, then burning it. He warned Mansfield that in whatever misfortune might befall Brody she could become collateral damage.

By December, LaVey was still publicly boasting of his lion's accessibility. "Togare has become a sort of status symbol for the neighborhood," he said in a *Chronicle* story about the group Jungle Cats of California, headed by the artist Dion Vigne. "Neighbors love to shock friends by telling them they have a lion on the block." (Vigne, another goateed bohemian, lived in an old downtown Victorian with his wife, Loralee, and an ocelot named Svengali. Loralee, a mystic, would eventually found the Temple of Isis, devoted to that ancient Egyptian goddess.)

And by January, LaVey was coyly promoting Mansfield's alleged involvement in his church. In a story that cited people he called his clients, he hinted at a glamorous Hollywood star, a Berkeley novelist (presumably Stephen Schneck), and a European baroness (Carin de Plessen), among others.

The Everly Brothers were opening a five-night engagement at San Francisco's short-lived outpost of the Whisky a Go Go. Carmen McRae was bringing her sassy jazz phrasing to Basin Street West. And over on North Bay's notorious Broadway strip, comic "Professor" Irwin Corey was spewing his quasi-profound claptrap at the hungry i nightclub, and accomplished ecdysiast Carol Doda was shaking a tail feather on stage at the Condor. Just a few doors down, sandwiched between both venues, the marquee hanging over the awning of the lounge called Gigi's—ANTON LA VEY PRESENTS THE WITCHES SABBETH—stood out for being both incorrectly spelled and grammatically dubious. (The *Chronicle* and *Examiner* had the show listed as "The Witch's Sabbath," a.k.a. the Witches' Sabbath, a.k.a. Walpurgisnacht.)

For this partially nude revue, which began its run on Tuesday, February 28, 1967, at 8:00 p.m., LaVey received $250 to deal with it all: script, props, sets, cast, rehearsals. Once the show was up and running, LaVey, who'd just struck public relations gold a month earlier with the Satanic nuptials, earned a fee for each performance and agreed to officiate weddings at the club for seventy-five dollars a pop. It's not known how many couples took him up on the offer.

Michael Aquino, who for a time would be a close associate of the high priest's, later claimed that LaVey publicist Ed Weber told him that he warned Anton about staging the performance. "We're in the process of getting the state charter," Weber told LaVey, "and if they find women running around with their breasts bared, they're just never going to do it." That must have been the straw that broke the beast's back, because a few days before the show's premiere, it was reported that Weber had gone to small claims court to demand that LaVey pay out $191 for his services. Weber told the judge that he helped LaVey expand his church from a dozen congregants to nearly one hundred. Anton didn't attend the hearing. Weber emerged victorious and, in a twist that would undoubtedly piss off LaVey, said he was asking a lawyer if he could attach Togare to the judgment. "I'll make the neighbors happy," Weber said, "and then donate Togare to the S.F. Zoo."

One of those women running around Gigi's with her breasts bared called herself Sharon King, an alias the pretty eighteen-year-old adopted to keep herself a few strides ahead of the law. She was dancing topless one afternoon at the club when the owner brought over LaVey, who was looking to hire a vampire for his show. The high priest liked what he saw and offered her the gig. Thinking, perhaps naively, that this might help kickstart a career in show business, Sharon took it. LaVey invited her and others to a meeting at the Black House, where he would run through what was expected of the performers and allow them to watch a ritual. She was already spooked by the show's Satanic content, but after seeing and hearing a roaring Togare in the backyard, she freaked out and decided to bail without attending the evening's ceremony.

She persevered, however, and despite her squeamishness, Sharon thought rehearsals had gone well. But come opening night, she felt she wouldn't be able to get into the onstage coffin dolled up in two-inch, blood-red fingernails, made-up cat's eyes, and a jet-black wig without a helpful hit of acid.

Apparently it worked. From her vantage point, the performance was a success, but her boyfriend wasn't happy with what the show was doing to her head. "We can live dealing dope," he told her later that first night in the apartment they shared. "You don't need this stuff." The next day he was gone. "I love you too much to sit and watch you lose yourself to LaVey," he wrote in a note.

One of the only circulated photographs from the show reveals the distaff bloodsucker leaving her casket, arms spread high, her dark, diaphanous see-through gown opened to reveal her pantied but otherwise bare torso. Behind her on Gigi's small stage hangs the Church of Satan's insignia, the sigil of Baphomet.

Sharon claimed the act was "a smash hit." The *Chronicle* claimed the opposite, sharing the news in March that the curtain had come down on LaVey's show and laying the blame squarely on the sorcerer-auteur for "having failed to conjure up an audience."

The show, the drugs, and her self-admitted promiscuity all led Sharon to a horrible case of gonorrhea and a long hospital stay for what she later described as "a complete physical breakdown." Soon, she would meet a man who'd have a huge impact on her life, a career criminal just released from federal prison named Charles Manson. And on the night of August 8, 1969, Sharon—whose real name was Susan Atkins—participated in the murders of movie star Sharon Tate, then eight and a half months pregnant, hairdresser Jay Sebring, heiress Abigail Folger, her boyfriend, Wojciech Frykowski, and bystander Steven Parent. On the front door of the Los Angeles home the actress shared with her husband, film director Roman Polanski, Atkins scrawled the word "PIG" in Tate's blood.

Atkins blamed Satan, and by extension Anton LaVey, for her rampage. She told Dr. Joel Hochman, who prepared her psychiatric report for the subsequent trial, that when she began hallucinating in her coffin on opening night, she didn't want to come out. "She stated that she felt alive and everything else in the ugly world was dead," he wrote. "Subsequently, she stayed on her 'Satanic trip' for approximately eight months . . ." After being convicted in January 1971, Atkins spent the rest of her thirty-eight years in prison.

"She was a junkie," LaVey said later. "She was strung out all the time. She'd come into work and said she had a fever of 108 degrees and things like that. So she wasn't necessarily insane, but she was certainly flaky, and by the time she met Charlie Manson she was probably just made to order."

Her motivation for writing her 1977 born-again memoir, *Child of Satan, Child of God,* LaVey surmised, was "to get her parole in motion by saying she found God and had seen the light—and blaming the Devil for everything. That was obviously not insanity, that was pragmatism on her part."

She did, however, serve her purpose. "In the end," LaVey said, "she made a fine vampire."

Dr. David Smith founded the Haight Ashbury Free Clinic in 1967 during the Summer of Love as a new counterculture was dawning in the City by the Bay. Having grown alienated by a society that valued materialism, big business, and the war machine over addressing economic, ecological, and social injustices, young people from all over the country converged on the Haight, announcing their independence by growing out their hair, speaking in a patchouli patois, and looking eastward for philosophical guidance, all while seeking alternative consciousness and experimenting with love and intimacy.

"We were the place you went to when you didn't have health insurance, and we were nonjudgmental," says the physician, who is widely credited with coining the phrase "Health care is a right, not a privilege." Smith recalls treating Church of Satan members referred to him by LaVey, as well as followers of many other groups. Those suffering from sexually transmitted diseases, drug addiction, or just experiencing a bad trip—all were welcome.

"San Francisco's always had a reputation for having a bohemian subculture, starting with the beatniks," he says, adding that with the influx of impressionable hippies, "it was just ripe for any guru to come in and pronounce his philosophy." Those ranks would come to include Robert de Grimston and Mary Anne MacLean, leaders of a Scientology-derived apocalyptic cult called the Process Church of the Final Judgement, whose devotees LaVey regarded as "kooks."

Smith, who remembers both Manson and Atkins stopping by the clinic, says he couldn't have predicted which of these groups would turn out to be evil. Manson's crew, he says, "were kind of weird, but they preached peace and love. To me, it depended on the leader's paranoia."

He saw the Church of Satan, with its headquarters three short miles away, as harmless. "San Francisco was the place if you wanted to do stuff like that," Smith says. "There wasn't really what you'd call a conservative backlash against those types of things.

"Unless [the followers] went out and shot people."

By March, LaVey's neighbors had grown weary of Togare's antics. The city's district attorney received a petition with 125 signatures, complaining that the lion "roars vociferously at all hours of the day and night, thereby disturbing the peace. It is also felt that the beast is a potential danger to ourselves and our children." LaVey and his neighbors were summoned to a hearing to determine Togare's fate. The grievance gained momentum when Supervisor William Blake proposed a ban on keeping wild-type animals "larger than a dog or cat" at home. Farm animals such as horses, cows, swine, and sheep were already prohibited in residences, per state housing law, but LaVey's neighbors had no patience to wait for an ordinance to be adopted. "San Francisco should not become a zoo," Blake said. "What with the hippies flocking in here, the city is already beginning to look like a zoo anyway."

Assistant DA Frederick J. Whisman held a hearing on March 14 in which he listened to arguments from both sides and signed a warrant alleging that LaVey and Togare were disturbing the peace, a misdemeanor. In his mug shots, LaVey wore a leopard-print vest under his blazer. At the inquiry, the high priest brought up the specter of religious persecution, saying that most of the complaints were being lodged "on ecclesiastical rather than zoological grounds." He said he'd received no objections for three years until he performed a Satanic wedding.

At municipal court, on March 16, LaVey's lawyer, Terence Hallinan, entered a not-guilty plea on behalf of his no-show client who, he said, had been up all night working on his topless revue. It was announced that Togare could be picked up imminently by the sheriff's department to be publicly auctioned off within ten days. Nearly $200 of the sale would be earmarked for Ed Weber to pay off LaVey's debt, but first, the press agent would have to put up money to board Togare until the sell-off.

LaVey was granted a slight reprieve when, on March 28, Blake's ordinance was backburnered after the board of supervisors' health committee labeled it "ambiguous" and "confusing."

Still, there were more feline frolics to come. Four days later, either out of loyalty or sheer hubris, LaVey and Diane agreed to cat-sit for a friend's pet. Russell Wolden III, son of the disgraced former city assessor Russell Wolden Jr., who was convicted in a bribery scandal a year earlier, needed someone to keep his 280-pound jaguar, Kitty, company. LaVey stacked the cats' cages in the backyard, separated by a wooden board. When Togare, sensing competition, began roaring and chewing the board floor, LaVey brought him to the bedroom, where the animal proceeded to grab one of Diane's loose boots and start gnawing. In true lion-tamer fashion, LaVey tried using a chair to subdue the cat, but gave up when Togare got his head stuck between the rungs, which inspired the animal to wreak even more havoc, destroying $800 worth of household items, including drapes, a typewriter, a leather coat, and an antique chair. LaVey had no other option but to call the police. Seven cops arrived along with two animal-control technicians and three zookeepers to tranquilize and remove Kitty—but not Togare—from the premises. A groggy Kitty still managed to attack one of the SPCA attendants on his way out the door.

LaVey at first admitted that, yes, it was probably time to send Togare off to the zoo, but then had second thoughts. After all, he could probably get $5,000 selling the animal to a circus. For her part, in the aftermath of the rampage, Diane sounded unbothered: "Togare was quite saucy."

"Sorcerer's Lion Goes Wild," shouted the front page of the April 1 *Examiner*. It was no April Fools' joke.

The following night, Anton and Diane returned home after a cocktail party to find their basement flooded. Togare had pawed through floorboards on the back porch and severed a water pipe. This time the lion had to go. LaVey hadn't even called a plumber before he was on the phone with the director of the San Francisco Zoo, who agreed to take the unruly pet. The cat received a police escort as LaVey drove him to his new home. "It's as if I threw part of my heart away," Diane said, with none of the glibness from a few days earlier. "It's like losing a child."

"The neighbors didn't understand Togare and made no effort to understand him," LaVey said, fighting back tears, though he and his family were told they would be able to drop by any time during regular zoo hours.

A little more than two weeks later, LaVey was found guilty of disturbing the peace after changing his plea from not guilty to no contest. It didn't matter that Togare was gone and no longer roaring in the backyard, the assistant DA argued, the peace had been disturbed. LaVey, wearing a maroon suit, white shirt, and striped tie, was fined fifty dollars and given a ninety-day suspended sentence and one year's probation. "I think it sort of shows that witchcraft trials are still in progress, and I'm very disgruntled about the whole thing," he said at an impromptu press conference outside a municipal courtroom. "I think the powers of the wrath of Satan shall descend upon all those that have had anything to do with this conviction." His lawyer, Hallinan, added that the zoo was reneging on their agreement by putting restrictions on the LaVeys' visitations with the "homesick" Togare. In the meantime, LaVey announced that he had added yet another exotic pet to his home, a twenty-five-pound South American capybara, the largest living rodent. "We won't say what size it grows to," Hallinan added with a laugh. LaVey named it Asmodeus, after the Hebrew king of demons. (The legal defeat didn't put much of a damper on the pugnacious Hallinan's career. In January 1996, he became the twenty-sixth district attorney of San Francisco.)

Togare lived for a few years at the zoo, where he sired four cubs around the start of 1969 before actress Tippi Hedren adopted him when he appeared in *Roar*, a movie she started shooting in 1976 with her then-husband, Noel Marshall. Hedren was aware of Togare's previous owner's involvement in the Black Arts and later wrote, "for whatever reason he arrived rough, tough, and defiant." *Roar*, about a family that lived with big cats, was a production unsurprisingly fraught with attacks and injuries. Togare (whose name Hedren spelled without the "e") himself mauled the assistant director, who required more than four hours of surgery. Hedren brought the lion to live at the Shambala Preserve, her private wildlife sanctuary in Southern California, where he sired more than thirty cubs, including Billy, named after William Peter Blatty, producer and screenwriter of *The Exorcist*, a film Marshall executive produced.

"Hail Zeena! Hail Satan!"

Anton and Diane's three-year-old little angel beamed brightly. She liked the way that sounded. After all, this was Zeena's night: May 23, 1967, when her father performed what has been dubbed history's first Satanic baptism—the second of the year's purgative sacrileges against Christianity and the second of his big publicity stunts.

Before a crowd of forty attendees, most of them reporters and photographers, a voluptuous brunette stripped naked and reclined on a leopard skin blanket covering the fireplace mantel in the ritual chamber. At her feet, perched at the edge, the blonde, barefoot toddler, clad in a bright-red hooded robe that her mom made that morning, sat quietly chewing gum and occasionally yawning. Around her neck hung a custom-designed Baphomet pendant featuring an ice cream cone and a lollipop.

Her dad, wearing a purple shirt, black cape, and horns, walked around the chamber ringing a bell and chanting an invocation. He pointed his sword to the sigil of Baphomet hanging behind the altar, roll-called the names of demons, and read from Clark Ashton Smith's psychedelically eldritch poem "The Hashish Eater" and Aleister Crowley's periodical *The Equinox*. He then dusted the child with soil, drank from a chalice, and flicked some of the liquid on her. After floating a candle over Zeena's head and under her feet, he bopped his "small sorceress" on the noggin with his sword as Diane stood by her side. He summoned blessings upon his second-born:

In the name of Satan Lucifer . . . Welcome a new mistress, Zeena, creature of ecstatic magic light. . . . Your power makes you master of the world of frightened, cowering, and guilt-ridden men. . . . With earth we place upon you Satan's mark that you might not forget the dark moisture, the pit from which you came, the jetting stream of manhood fertilizing Mother Earth . . .

"I always felt it was wrong to consider a child is born with black sin in his soul," LaVey told a reporter, criticizing the Christian Church's conception of the ritual. "This is baptism in reverse. There is nothing purer than a child, so we are baptizing her to symbolize everything good and to dramatize her lust for life." He performed the ceremony to instill earthly pleasure into her being, rather than ridding it of sin—which in his mind was the "true blasphemy."

"It took me a few years to realize that some of [the celebrants] may have been more fascinated with the naked [woman] sprawled on the altar than with me," Zeena later wrote. She recalled feeling "a great sense of warmth and respect" as her father gave his benediction. "'I have something they don't,' I thought proudly, in keeping with the indulgent philosophy of Satanism."

A three-week-old girl, Gloria Lilith Bach, purportedly a descendent of the composer, originally had been scheduled. And according to LaVey's press release—or "proclamation," as he called it—her mother, a priestess, was to serve as the nude altar. But after the infant's grandparents objected to the rite, Zeena was drafted as a substitute. For the journalists on hand, Anton naturally repeated the fifteen-minute spiel twice, so no one missed a thing. John Raymond, joined in marriage by LaVey three months earlier, sat prominently to the right of the altar, no doubt registering with pleasure the completion of another successful lark.

As LaVey tended to the baptism and dealt with his pet problems, in the first five months of 1967 Jayne Mansfield was often traveling overseas for work in Asia and Europe. The touring took her to a Tokyo nightclub called the New Latin Quarter, where the US military newspaper *Stars and Stripes* indelicately reported, "The last time so many Japanese were this badly shaken the results were registered on a seismograph and the entire city of Tokyo went up in flames." It took her on a goodwill visit to South Vietnam, where she consoled injured soldiers. It took her through England and Ireland, a dodgy trek peppered with canceled gigs and a photo op at the House of Commons. It took her to Sweden in May, where it also ended.

The following month, during one of Jayne's respites at home, celebrity photographer Walter Fischer, who had shot the Satanic wedding and baptism for LaVey as well as glamour portraits of the actress, took publicity stills of the pair at her Pink Palace at 10100 Sunset Boulevard, ostensibly for publication in Europe. There's Anton, dapper in a dark suit and tie, and there's Jayne, groovy in a print dress and go-go boots, the two of them having a heart-to-heart by her heart-shaped pool. There's Anton in his cape, cuddling one of her chihuahuas close to his chest. There's Anton grinning while pulling on resistance weights in her home gym. There's Anton holding her kids transfixed in the kitchen. And there's the money shot: Anton wearing his horned hood and Baphomet pendant, brandishing a sword, hamming it up on a googly-eyed tiger rug, as Jayne kneels before him, caressing a skull and drinking from a chalice. Off to the side, there's Sam Brody, sullenly slumped over in a chair.

The image of campy domestic bliss soon disintegrated when Jayne's eldest daughter, sixteen-year-old Jayne Marie, walked into a West Los Angeles police station on June 17 after having run away from home. She was there to file a battery charge against Brody, who she said beat her with a belt and slapped her, also implicating her mother in the assault.

In the front seat of the gray Buick Electra, Jayne and Sam sat squished next to twenty-year-old Ronnie Harrison, who was affianced to the daughter of the eponymous owner of Gus Stevens Seafood Restaurant and Buccaneer Lounge, which had just hosted an engagement by the entertainer. Brody normally would have driven, but he had been injured a week earlier in a car wreck while en route to a hearing regarding Jayne Marie's abuse claims. Three of Jayne's other kids—Marie, Mickey, and Zoltan—slept in the back seat, along with three chihuahuas, as they took the ninety-mile trip from Biloxi, Mississippi, to New Orleans, Louisiana, where Jayne was to shoot an appearance on daytime TV. In the early morning hours of June 29, as they thrummed down a narrow stretch of Highway 90, the fog of mosquito repellent sprayed by a truck ahead of them obscured Harrison's vision. Failing to see the tractor-trailer that was moving slowly directly in front of him, he rammed into its rear, sending the car underneath, ripping off both the top of the Buick and the top of Jayne's head. (She was not, as has been widely believed, decapitated.) Harrison, Brody, and one of the dogs were also killed instantly. The children and two pooches survived. Mansfield was thirty-four years old.

LaVey later shared an anecdote that suggested he had inadvertently caused her accident. He was at home cutting out a photo of himself holding flowers at Marilyn Monroe's crypt at Westwood Village cemetery in Los Angeles, taken by Walter Fischer for the sensationalist German newspaper *Bild-Zeitung*. After removing the picture, he noticed Mansfield was on the reverse side of the image. He had chopped off her head with his scissors on the night she died.

US tabloids and gossip magazines orgasmed over news of a supposed curse, with headlines ranging from the prosaic, "Witch's Curse Blamed for the Death of Jayne Mansfield," to the sublime, "Did Witchcraft Kill Jayne (44-23-37) Mansfield?"

Kenneth Anger, for one, suspected she and LaVey definitely had an affair. "[It] would be unnatural if they didn't," he said decades later.

But the curses?

"Curses shmurses," he said. "I frankly think it's a bunch of bullshit." As someone who practiced what he preached, he was likely on to something.

Perhaps the following sequence of events was closer to the truth.

Tony Kent, a colleague of Ed Weber's, who also had been hustling publicity for LaVey and his nascent church, happened upon an opportunity to invite a real-life movie star over to meet a real-life sorcerer who kept a real-life, quarter-ton lion in his home. On October 23, the same day she had her horoscope read by Gavin Arthur, Mansfield visited Togare at the Black House and then attended a festival screening of the Swedish drama *Night Games* before dining at Trader Vic's. (In April 1965, Arthur and the lion made the papers when the astrologer told columnist Herb Caen that during a dinner at LaVey's, Togare ripped his suit to shreds.)

Brody hadn't been keen on the visit, telling Mansfield's former press agent Raymond Strait, "This cat"—LaVey or Togare, it's not clear—"can only hurt Jayne. She must be stupid to think anything else." The boyfriend-manager concluded that, in this case, no publicity was better than bad.

Mansfield herself seemed stung by the negative reaction to news of her association with LaVey, insisting that she was not a member of his Magic Circle, nor did she ring him every midnight for magical advice. "I'm a Catholic and I don't believe in any kind of [occultism]," she said in January 1967. "I talked to Mr. LaVey when I was here for the festival and he's a very interesting man.

"I'm interested in religions, anything new. And whatever a person does is up to him."

The following month, LaVey planted an item with syndicated gossipeuse Marilyn Beck in which he claimed to have gifted Mansfield with a pendant and named her a member of the Church of Satan. She was only one of many Hollywood celebrities involved in Satanism. "I can't mention their names because most are afraid for their reputations," he said. "Some even belong to other churches as a means of cover in order to maintain their respectability, but have given up believing in the hypocritical things that are preached there."

Soon after, Mansfield again felt the need to go on the defensive. "Anton is a good friend of mine and we have some fascinating discussions concerning his religion," Beck quoted Mansfield as saying. "The man is a genius, and I enjoy tremendously talking with anyone who is an intellectual. But I am not on the verge of converting, and can't understand why Anton said I was."

In her 1973 biography, *Jayne Mansfield*, author May Mann proved to be a most unreliable narrator, spreading mythology and misinformation as if it were the gospel. On the very first page, Mann wrote this whopper: "This book was nearing completion when she was killed, her head severed from her body by the broken windshield of a speeding car . . ." She claimed Mansfield was working with her on the book before her death and that the actress's spirit urged Mann to complete it. In stilted, exposition-dense, *you-gotta-be-kidding-me* quotations, allegedly straight from the source, Mansfield shared such insights as "Anton LaVey . . . has this big black house on a hill with a 500-pound lion. He drives a black hearse. He is highly intelligent. He told me he had fallen in love with me and wanted to join my life with his."

LaVey later suggested that Mann's book, written by someone who had a lesbian crush, was around one-tenth factual, two-fifths half-truth, and the rest pure fantasy. But Mansfield's body wasn't even cold when the high priest began raining hellfire upon it.

The day after her death, the *Chronicle* ran the story "A Memory of Jayne: Actress and S.F. Sorcerer," which blithely called the actress "a devotee of the Black Arts—one of Sorcerer Anton LaVey's most dedicated pupils." As if to prove it, LaVey produced an oversized cartoony Devil greeting card inscribed, purportedly by Mansfield, "To my Satanic friend . . . my probing for truth may be satisfied by my high priest."

LaVey said she had called him two weeks earlier asking for help with a problem, and he showed up with his horns, cape, and staff. What was the issue? LaVey was not at liberty to say.

"You know, I'm a priest, whether you think it's a hokey thing or not," he said, sounding uncharacteristically defensive. "I'm sincere in what I do."

He gave that sincerity an odd airing years later in *The Devil's Avenger*, the first biography of LaVey, in which the high priest characterized Mansfield as "a lewd, lascivious virago," who would moisten her pants to make it appear that she wet herself.

In an interview with *Hustler* magazine in 1979, LaVey claimed Mansfield sought him out after reading about him in a newspaper and had asked him to put a curse on Cimber. "Jayne was not a flirt," he added, crudely playing to his presumably engorged audience. "She was an all-out exhibitionist. . . . She had a propensity for flashing her twat or baring her breasts."

The actress was happiest, he continued, "when she was rolling on the floor, fucking up a storm."

Still, the last word on the late sex goddess—or at least the last image—might belong not to LaVey, but to one of his friends. Mansfield—cavernous cleavage front and center, chandelier-like jewelry dangling from her earlobes, blood-red lipstick painted over her smile—appears indelibly, iconically, on the cover of the best-selling mass-market paperback edition of *Hollywood Babylon*, the overripe omnibus of showbiz scandal written by Kenneth Anger.

IV.

All the Rage

AS a direct result of the Satanic wedding, LaVey began attracting attention from major national publications. Shana Alexander wrote about
him for her Feminine Eye column in *Life* magazine in February 1967
("When the sorcerer excused himself to Norelco his head, Mrs. LaVey
took me on a tour of their revolving fireplace . . . then popped a TV dinner into the oven for their teen-age daughter"). *Pageant,* a mainstream
general-interest digest, devoted fourteen pages of its August issue to
the family, featuring photos of the LaVeys shopping, Zeena getting a
bath, and Diane adjusting Anton's horns. He let his membership in the
musicians' union lapse on June 30, 1967, just as enrollments in his own
union of like-minded Satanists surged.

LaVey took his press where he could find it, and if that place was
the gutter, so be it. He would become a frequent pictorial presence in

lurid, third-string skin mags with titles like *Modern Man, Bizarre, Jaybird Journal, Sundisk, Black Arts Today,* and *Nude Living,* posing in his ritual chamber with undraped acolytes—in many cases, strippers hired expressly for the shoots—as well as a more decorous Diane. (Manson follower Susan Atkins is said to have appeared in a few of these spreads. LaVey himself exposed his penis in another.)

These appearances, Randall Alfred wrote, "produced an image of the church as primarily sexual in nature and resulted in a pool of new members with this in mind." In those early days, congregants, mostly white, middle-class professionals in their late twenties to their forties, would indulge hedonistically at the church's quarterly costume parties, which sometimes transformed into orgies. (For all this early pandering to the free-love crowd, LaVey himself would later say that while he witnessed orgies, he failed to see the fun in them. He believed sex should be more personal and, instead, preferred epicureanism, "meaning that you're a little fussy about sex partners.")

Satanism's very public face did not go unnoticed by academics either. In July 1967, LaVey received a letter from a University of South Florida sociology professor named Marcello Truzzi. An expert in contemporary occult movements, the Tampa-based Truzzi had read about the church in newspapers and watched as the high priest took on Joe Pyne. Truzzi not only admired LaVey's showmanship, but also believed the Church of Satan's doctrines seemed less dangerous to humanity than those of the Catholic Church. He was going to be in San Francisco at the end of August for the annual meeting of the American Sociological Association and was hoping to call on the high priest for an interview. Truzzi, thirty-one, had much in common with LaVey. Fascinated with carny life, he was adept at hypnosis and similar skills. And he had the big top in his blood: his father, Massimiliano, had been a leading juggler for the Ringling Bros. and Barnum & Bailey Circus.

After the two did meet, they quickly developed a long-distance, primarily epistolary connection since the academic's pursuits would eventually take him to the University of Michigan, Florida's New College, then to Eastern Michigan University. It would become an extremely close friendship, one based on mutual respect, shared curiosities, and similar senses of humor. In letter after lively letter, the two would exchange book recommendations, tell off-color jokes, talk about collaborating on fiction anthologies, and mock other occult and paranormal superstars, like Sybil Leek, Hans Holzer, and Raymond Buckland, who LaVey felt were being disingenuous with their airs of respectability. For his part, Buckland had little use for LaVey's antics, saying that most of the church's members signed up simply for "kicks." "Although Crowley did not call himself a Satanist," he wrote, "he was actually far more of one than LaVey could ever be. Crowley lived the part, while LaVey acts it."

In September, Truzzi sent a proposal to *Playboy* editor in chief Hugh Hefner pitching LaVey as a potential interview subject. Writing that LaVey was far from the usual wacko one finds in such movements, Truzzi went on to say that even though ritual magic is a feature of the church, which by this time numbered some two hundred members in San Francisco alone, its primary philosophy preached indulgence, sexual and otherwise, not unlike Hefner's magazine. *Playboy* wasn't convinced.

Toward the end of the year, a different prominent men's magazine did feature LaVey. In its annual Dubious Achievement Awards, a special section cracking wise on newsworthy events, *Esquire* cited Zeena's baptism as "One reason why God did not descend in the form of a dove during 1967."

On Sunday, December 3, LaVey was the guest lecturer at the Sexual Freedom League, a social activist group that, unlike his church, was actually a front for free-love orgies. For a one-dollar donation, attendees at 321 Divisadero Street, a performance space in Haight-Ashbury, could hear him discuss "Sex and Satan." One of the attendees, a journalist named Burton H. Wolfe, had gone through a rough divorce, grown a beard, and sought enlightenment from alternative lifestyles. He was dazzled by LaVey's intelligence and common sense and thought his beliefs were unique among occultists in that they were logical and based, at least in part, on science. Soon, he became a fixture at 6114 and wrote about the church for the men's magazine *Knight* in 1968, the first of many pieces he'd do on LaVey.

The high priest made the front pages again when both the *Examiner* and *Chronicle* reported that on December 11, LaVey, in cape and clerical collar, had presided over the funeral of a US sailor who had been killed in a car accident the previous Friday. Edward D. Olsen, a twenty-six-year-old machinist's mate third class, had joined the church with his wife some six months earlier, having become fascinated with LaVey after seeing him on TV. The US Navy, believing that Olsen was entitled to the same consideration in his religious beliefs as any other armed forces member, provided a rifle squad along with an honor guard dressed in full uniform—chrome helmets, white gloves, rifle belts, and spats—for the ceremony at Cypress Lawn, a memorial park in Colma, California, twelve miles south of downtown San Francisco.

In the mortuary chapel, where black candles surrounded the coffin, LaVey read from *The Necronomicon* and other macabre works. His goal was to imbue the corpse with a magical energy that would reignite Olsen's "lust for life," a phrase he used in connection with his daughter's baptism some seven months earlier. "He chose the path of Satan," LaVey preached, "because he believed the living flesh that created and gave birth to him, his mother and father, were much more marvelous and real than any god he could not see."

Flanking LaVey during the service were Kenneth Anger, who two months earlier participated in a hippie-led effort to exorcize evil spirits from the Pentagon, and Lenore Cosseboom, a priestess of the Church of Satan. Cosseboom, introduced to LaVey by local astrologer and bookstore owner Fritzi Armstrong, had become a regular at the house. Raised poor in rural West Virginia, Cosseboom, the eldest of thirteen children, left home during the Depression as a teenager. After traveling through the roadhouses in the South, she ended up in San Francisco frequently stripped naked on the mantel, one of the church's living altars.

Cosseboom's young son, Peri, would take the bus with her to the Black House for lectures, even before the founding of the church. To him, LaVey was "Uncle Anton," a wonderful man who didn't condescend to him the way so many other adults did. When the boy was zoned for a high school that his mother didn't want him to attend, Uncle Anton let him list 6114 California Street as his address so he could go to George Washington, where Karla was also enrolled. The ruse lasted two and a half years before the school caught on.

Uncle Anton, he recalled, was also almost certainly his mother's lover. "Who cares?" Peri has said. "It was the '60s, man." To Peri, all this occult business seemed silly, but his mom was a true believer. In her flat she'd set up a sanctuary replete with an altar, a sigil of Baphomet, and a ten-inch plastic phallus.

At the gravesite, as a bugler played "Taps" and Olsen received a traditional rifle salute, LaVey, a red book in one hand, a sword in the other, gave his blessing over the silver-gray coffin draped in an American flag. "By all the powers of Satan and Hell," he declaimed, "you will walk this earth to which I bind you forever and ever. And may this plot of ground lie all the way to Hell." At the foot of the grave lay a floral arrangement of red chrysanthemums and black carnations in the shape of a goat's head.

Olsen's parents, devout Baptists who didn't attend the ceremony, were surprisingly sanguine about the whole affair, though his father did say, "It bothers me somewhat, but you must rely on faith." In light of this blasphemous display, they'd hoped the family's local church in Park Ridge, Illinois, would allow for a Christian service as well.

After the burial, it was off to dinner at the Playboy Club, which Hugh Hefner opened in San Francisco two years earlier. "We believe it's no fun to leave the party," LaVey told a reporter there. "It's life we're enthused about, not death."

The archbishop of San Francisco, John Shahovskoy, was neither enthused nor amused about the funeral. Appalled that members of the military took part, he brought his beef to the White House, sending a telegram to President Lyndon Johnson that began, "This is a nation under God and not a nation under satan." He went on to gripe that, as the chairman of the Orthodox Church Chaplain's Commission for the US Armed Forces, he felt that what went on in Colma "degrades both our forces and our flag."

His Excellency likely would have had a coronary if he got a load of what occurred at other LaVey rituals. One participant, Burton H. Wolfe, described what he observed at a Black Mass in 1968 during the early, wilder nights of the Church of Satan.

After leading a recitation of the Lord's Prayer backward, LaVey inserts a triangular holy wafer into the vagina of a female altar. When she removes the moist cracker, he breaks it up and places the pieces on the tongues of six congregants. One redheaded sinner lies across the lap of a naked acolyte to be whipped by another naked acolyte wielding a cat-o'-nine-tails. Next, another participant, dressed in papal finery, is thrown to the floor by black-robed men who proceed to pull down their pants and pretend to poop on him. "A preparation of brown, brackish mud is splattered on his vestments," Wolfe wrote. "When he is adequately covered with it, he is dragged out of the room to the strains of a Eucharistic chorus from Wagner's *Parsifal* and the shouts of 'Hail Satan.'"

Then, members of the crowd kick and whip a frail man wrapped in a white sheet who carries a cross on his back before this Christ manqué is led out of the ritual chamber. LaVey curses "that pallid monstrosity that hangs limpid upon the Cross still" and smashes underfoot a plastic religious figurine before chucking it into a chamber pot in the middle of the room and proclaiming, "Thus we drown him, and prove that he hath never walked on water, and never shall again."

"With that he stands over the chamber pot, zips open his fly and attempts to urinate," according to Wolfe. "He has difficulty, so he calls to the organist: 'Will you please play me some water music?' And the organist complies with 'How Dry I Am.'" At that point, the heretofore stony congregants crack up, and LaVey—well, his bladder, at least—is successfully moved by the music.

"When LaVey is finished, the nude female acolytes take their turns at the pot"—but for one woman, the pee just keeps on streaming. Out comes a nun who teasingly removes her habit while bumping and grinding first to Archibald Joyce's waltz "Vision of Salome," then to typical stripper music.

"To conclude the Mass," Wolfe wrote, "High Priest LaVey opens his cape wide in front of the naked altar, his hands forming the Sign of the Horns: two fingers representing the goat, thrust upward in defiance of Heaven, the other three turned down in a denial of the Holy Trinity." After three shouts of "Hail Satan," he extinguishes a candle on the fireplace and carries from the room the naked altar, now covered by a leopard skin blanket. Then they all repair to the kitchen for some coffee, tea, cake, and schmoozing.

By early 1968, Truzzi and LaVey had grown so close that the professor felt he could offer his new friend criticism without fear of causing

offense. Having seen LaVey on TV several times, Truzzi and some colleagues believed that the high priest's normal speaking voice didn't suit
his sinister image. Truzzi suggested that LaVey try to lower his pitch.
He also began offering LaVey tips to help him develop the church,
encouraging his friend to seek tax exemption and petition for an audience with the pope. LaVey appears to have ignored the latter suggestion. As for the former, he felt that "to preserve its complete flexibility
and freedom of action," the Church of Satan would not accept any tax
advantages from the government. Truzzi, who rejected organized religion, was nevertheless thrilled when LaVey offered to make him an
honorary Church of Satan member.

As Truzzi continued to look for a major publication willing to run
an interview with his friend, LaVey suggested that the professor himself
write a first-person article under the high priest's name. Truzzi could
keep the fee, minus a small honorarium, so long as LaVey could vet it
before submission.

In addition to the regular Friday night rituals and a Witches'
Workshop—where he taught women about casting spells and how to
dress and what to cook to attract a man—on Tuesdays, LaVey gave
irregular guest lectures at places like the University of San Francisco,
a Jesuit college. He was even being sought out by society swells. One
member of that smart set, television personality Pat Montandon, lived in
an apartment on the famously crooked Lombard Street in the Russian
Hill neighborhood and was known for throwing fabulous parties. As a
presenter of a movie series on KGO-TV, she received quite a bit of fan
mail. When an unmarried woman wrote in requesting a love potion,
Montandon's secretary reached out to LaVey, the only person she could
think of who would know how to brew one. He agreed to whip something up provided the women came to the house. What was he going to
do, they thought, turn them into witches? When they arrived, he served

them a pink and purple liquid in liqueur glasses, which Montandon fake-sipped and her secretary downed.

As they took in the stuffed wolf, owl, rat, and ravens on display, he offered to give them a brief tour of the house before handing Montandon a small piece of red paper. On it he had written the ingredients for "Lovey Sauce": two ounces of instant coffee, a fifth of vodka, one vanilla bean, a half-ounce of whole mandrake root, a half-cup of sugar, and a cup of water. After combining and stirring occasionally for one month, they could serve it in one-ounce portions or pour over ice cream. But not too much, he cautioned, or it will give your intended the runs.

"This is no dream! This is really happening!"

Yes, Rosemary Woodhouse, a young woman living in a baroque Manhattan apartment building with her underemployed actor-husband, is really being ravaged by Satan himself. He had been summoned by a friendly neighborhood witches' coven intent on bringing the Antichrist into the world in a scene from the 1968 thriller *Rosemary's Baby*. Written and directed by Roman Polanski and based on Ira Levin's best-selling novel from the previous year, the picture became one of 1968's highest-grossing films, cannily tapping into mainstream angst about class, careerism, and parenthood, all while sating the hunger for hip, edgy entertainment from the mavericks of the New Hollywood.

To LaVey, the movie was a miracle, presenting Satanism as something that existed among ordinary people—folks who looked just like the members of his church. "To 1966! The Year One!" declares the elderly warlock Roman Castevet, toasting the diabolical birth and the beginning of the Devil's reign. To LaVey's eyes and ears, it was all too serendipitous to be true.

Invited to an advance screening, LaVey left astonished, impressed by the casting, the acting, and the fact that the film followed the book so closely. He told Marcello Truzzi that both the novel and movie resembled paid advertisements for the Church of Satan and that he'd been enlisted to do some TV and radio promotion on behalf of the latter.

Less than a month after the movie's June opening, LaVey was already planting items in the press claiming he played the Devil who rapes the naif protagonist. LaVey and others around him—as well as journalists who parroted them—would for years boast that he served as a technical advisor on the film. "BS," says Hawk Koch, *Rosemary's Baby*'s dialogue coach, of the notion that the high priest had anything whatsoever to do with the movie. "All BS. No way LaVey was the Devil."

In a letter to Truzzi in July, LaVey made no mention of any involvement and simply praised the film again, calling it better than the book and fully deserving of its success. He singled out the performance of Sidney Blackmer, who plays Roman Castevet, a character LaVey called a dead ringer for Aleister Crowley. LaVey was also happy to report that his church had a poster on the market. On it, LaVey stands before a nude altar, scowling in a hood and cape and pointing at the viewer. Across the top are the words "SATAN WANTS YOU . . ." and at the bottom, along with the church's address and phone number, it reads, "JOIN NOW"—a parody of the US Army's famous Uncle Sam recruitment campaign. A local theater showing *Rosemary's Baby* displayed a few of them in the lobby, where they generated so much interest that the manager asked LaVey to provide some Satanic literature. LaVey also had buttons made that spoofed the official movie promo pins. Playing off of "Pray for *Rosemary's Baby*," his read, "Pray for Anton LaVey." He was proud of the double meaning, how the slogan also referred to all the religious "nuts" he encountered who hoped to save his soul.

LaVey later attributed the enduring popularity of *Rosemary's Baby* to the way the movie subverted preconceptions of Satanism. "It didn't chop up the baby in the end," he elaborated. "Rosemary took her baby to her breast exactly like Christianity's Virgin Mary. It threw all the crap down the drain and showed the public, who was expecting the sensational, the real image of the Satanist."

To capitalize on his growing infamy, toward the end of 1968 and into 1969, LaVey's lectures were advertised in the event listings of both the *Chronicle* and *Examiner* thanks to a friend who edited the entertainment section at the papers. (Beginning in 1965, and lasting thirty-five years, the papers functioned under a joint operating agreement, which saw the *Chronicle* publish in the morning and the *Examiner* in the afternoon.) The talks had become so popular that LaVey began giving the same lecture two nights a week to meet the demand.

On Wednesdays and Thursdays at 9:00 p.m., for a cover charge of two dollars and fifty cents, one could crowd into the living room at 6114 to hear LaVey expound on such topics as "E.S.P. and Telepathic Communication," "Music and Magic," "Color and Its Magical Implications," "Freaks," "The Black Mass," "Ghosts and Hauntings," "Love Potions and Monkey Glands," and "The Magical Power of Animals."

He also discussed "The Triumph of Pain" (torture methods, sadomasochistic devices), "Strange People" (hermits, flagpole sitters, string savers, sundry other crackpots and screwballs), "The Kingdom of Death" (unusual funeral practices, necrophilia, concepts of heaven, hell, limbo), "A Cup of Grue" (human sacrifice, cannibalism), "Semi-authenticated Creatures" (sea serpents, dragons, abominable snowmen), "Primitive Magic" (voodoo, head-shrinking, zombies), and "Monuments to Madness" (weird architecture, unusual inventions). In that last one, he no doubt discussed trapezoids, which held a particular fascination for LaVey. He believed that certain shapes had the ability to demand attention and could cause anxiety or pain. Though a pyramid may be pleasing to the eye, LaVey called a trapezoid—essentially a pyramid with its top removed—"the most disturbing shape of all."

"A trapezoid," he wrote, "says to the unconscious, 'I am here, solid as can be, more massive than an ordinary block, but something's missing and it bothers you.'" Mansard roofs on haunted houses, Aztec and Mayan sacrificial temples, the heads of coffins, ritual slabs—all are trapezoidal and all have the power to invoke fear. An alternate name for the Council of Nine, the church's ruling body, is the Order of the Trapezoid. LaVey's business card, as well as early Order of the Trapezoid membership cards, came in that shape—until they were deemed impractical for wallets.

One sympathetic lecture attendee, the writer and artist Jeff Berner, praised LaVey as "an educated man who displays a masterful sensitivity to conflicting and complementary energies (good and evil, life and death, etc.)," describing the high priest's mood as "wry, as if to say we are hypocrites to condemn his act while we mutilate each other every day through war, rotten marriages, plots, and the rest of 'modern life.'"

Another was Michael Aquino, a twenty-two-year-old lieutenant in the US Army. He had returned home to San Francisco to get married after nine months in Vietnam, when he saw an ad in the hippie paper the *Berkeley Barb* for a lecture on "Fortune Telling and Character Analysis." Up for some countercultural fun, he, his Mormon fiancée, and a few of their friends found themselves one night in March 1969 sitting in folding chairs in the ritual chamber–cum–lecture hall of 6114 California Street. Entering the room through the faux sarcophagus, LaVey proceeded to impress Aquino with what the admitted agnostic described as a "relaxed self-confidence." Aquino also admired the attention to detail in the shamelessly gothic environs.

After the talk, Aquino took home some church literature, which, he later wrote, struck him "as an odd mixture of common sense and 'crazy occultism.'" After filling out the requisite applications, he and his now-wife, Janet, were welcomed into the church. Following LaVey's instructions, they performed their first ritual, which Aquino described as "an affirmation of our commitment to Satan and the Powers of Darkness," in their apartment's spare bedroom. "I have made tactical parachute jumps at night with Special Forces teams that weren't half so electrifying," he later wrote, describing the sensations conjured during the black magic ritual to be more primal and profound than any physical danger he ever encountered. "Yawning pits of infinite darkness seem to open before the naked consciousness, and the magician struggles desperately for a law upon which the normal, natural functions of this mind can grasp." The experience set him on the course to become the military's first Satanic chaplain, dreams that were quickly dashed by the army's insistence on accrediting clerics only to those denominations for which there was a demand.

Aquino, who had been undergoing specialized training as a psychological operations (PSYOP) officer, would in late 1969 be exchanging letters with LaVey and a close advisor, Priest John A. Ferro, from the jungles of Vietnam.

In 1970, after Aquino returned from another tour of Southeast Asia, LaVey welcomed him into the priesthood. Aquino and his wife, now living in a tiny cottage in a small town outside Louisville, Kentucky, while he served at the Armor School at Fort Knox, organized one of the church's first regional offshoots, the Nineveh Grotto. Anton's church was leaving its dark heart in San Francisco, and its blood would soon be pumping all across America.

V.

The Cold Testament

BY the late '60s, books about the occult, the paranormal, and other arcane subjects flooded stores. In 1968, 169 paperbacks about the occult were in print. By 1969, that number had increased to 519. Hardcover titles nearly doubled from 198 in 1967 to 364 in 1969.

The choices were rich and varied. Erich von Däniken's *Chariots of the Gods* posited that alien astronauts were responsible for ancient artifacts like Stonehenge and the Egyptian pyramids. Sybil Leek, the British astrologer and occultist, told her life story in *Diary of a Witch*. In *Psychic Investigator*, Hans Holzer relayed his experiences hunting ghosts. Los Angeles–based witch Louise Huebner offered the self-explanatory *Power Through Witchcraft*. The editors of *Fate* magazine compiled *The Strange World of the Occult*.

Among LaVey's social circle in San Francisco were many authors and journalists, including Fred Goerner, a former TV news anchor and radio broadcaster and author of the best-selling *The Search for Amelia Earhart*. Goerner was the husband of Merla Zellerbach, a columnist for the *Chronicle* who frequently covered LaVey. In 1967, they attended one of his Witches' Workshops, where LaVey dropped these pearls of wisdom: "The best style of dress is modified prostitute. After all, who knows better than harlots what attracts?"; "Cream foods or anything that produces cholesterol will make a man more virile"; and "Don't hex someone unless you love or hate him very much. You can't give a little bit of a curse." (Zellerbach's son Gary also had a connection to LaVey: he was friendly with Karla who, like him, went to George Washington High School.)

One Saturday in July, Goerner and Zellerbach attended a costume party the LaVeys were throwing at the Black House. The invitation read, "Come to our 'Seamy Side of Life' Party. The costume for women is to be as sleazy as possible—harlots, strippers, madams; men will dress as panderers, gangsters, perverts, etc." (The party, Merla noted in her column, was to start at 11:00 p.m., two and a half hours after another that was being thrown by Pat Montandon. She also wondered if the two parties' hosts "coordinated plans so that mutual friends could attend both.") In line with the LaVey celebration's theme, Merla wore feathers in her hair, and Fred sported a red devil's tail attached to his black suit.

At some point, Goerner put an idea in the high priest's head. "Fred said I should write a bible," according to LaVey, "and he felt sure it would get published." When LaVey mentioned he wasn't a writer and never had any aspirations to be one, Goerner told him not to worry.

Goerner brought LaVey to the attention of Walter Bradbury, his editor at Doubleday who years earlier had been instrumental in putting together *The Martian Chronicles*, which became a breakthrough novel for Ray Bradbury (no relation).

Soon, LaVey was being courted by Goerner's agent, Mike Hamilburg. LaVey responded to his interest with an outline of the bible he'd like to write. It would contain four books. The first, "Satan," would be a fire-and-brimstone diatribe written in beatitudes form. "Lucifer," the second, would explicate the philosophy behind Satanism in clear, easy-to-digest language. "Belial" would get into the nitty-gritty of spells, charms, and hexes. The last book, "Leviathan," would offer the invocations used in actual Satanic rituals as well as the Enochian Keys. (A few years later, Hamilburg would establish his very own Charles Manson connection, representing Vincent Bugliosi and Curt Gentry on *Helter Skelter*, their 1974 book about the 1969 murders, which includes a brief mention of LaVey.)

Marcello Truzzi had been very keen to collaborate with the high priest, going so far as to offer a fifty-fifty split if LaVey would list his name as the primary author of *Cauldron Cookery*, the professor's upcoming collection of authentic witchcraft recipes, which was already written and ready to be sent to his publisher. LaVey expressed interest but wrote that he wouldn't want his name attached to a humor book before he had a chance to release his bible and a similarly serious follow-up, and he already had two ideas: *The Witch's Guide to Practical Enchantment* and *The Law of the Trapezoid*. Also, Diane was hoping to have another child once the frenetic state of affairs calmed down. Could *Cauldron Cookery* wait?

As talks with Doubleday proceeded, LaVey continued writing his holy book, not for those he deemed hyperintellectuals, but for the layman, whom he surmised would be more inclined to buy it. During his TV appearances around this time, LaVey never missed an opportunity to plug the work in progress. When Hamilburg was out tending to his ill father, the agency's Sylva Romano took over correspondence with LaVey. In June, she wrote that they were pressuring Doubleday to make an offer and would soon send what LaVey had written so far to Random House, the publisher of *Rosemary's Baby*.

When more months passed without a bite, LaVey began to grow impatient and worry that another company might rush to print an inferior Satanic bible written by someone else. He expressed to his agent his frustration at seeing his demonic influence permeate literature, film, music, and other aspects of pop culture. He started the goddamned trend. Why couldn't he get a book published?

LaVey had every reason to believe he might get left in the dust. He had signed a deal in June with a small company called Aardvark Recordings to release an LP containing a Satanic Mass and Zeena's baptism, along with readings from his proposed *Satanic Bible* on the flipside. It would appear on Murgenstrumm Records, which almost shared its name with one of his altar girls, Lois Murgenstruum. The mass would be recorded in his ritual chamber on Friday, September 13, 1968. The cover, to be designed by LaVey, would feature the high priest in ceremonial garb. He had hoped to turn the album around quickly and release it by Halloween. But Aardvark had other ideas or, more accurately, it had very few. Another year would pass before the record, with a black-and-white sigil of Baphomet on the cover instead of a LaVey portrait, would be made available.

As he toiled on the book, LaVey was presented with another literary offer that would bring in some quick, steady cash. In late August 1968, Mike Resnick, the editor of a few low-budget men's magazines and the spectacularly lurid *National Insider* tabloid—as well as an aspiring writer of genre fiction—traveled with his wife from Chicago to Berkeley, just over the Bay Bridge from San Francisco, to attend the 26th World Science Fiction Convention. To help cover their expenses, he figured he'd write a few stories while he was out there—one of them, an interview with this oddball character he'd heard about.

He and LaVey hit it off immediately, bonding over the Arkham House books in LaVey's library as well his complete run of *Weird Tales* magazine. Resnick also observed a Satanic Mass. "It was dull as dishwater," Resnick recalled, "and it's really difficult to be dull when you're chanting obscene spells over a gorgeous naked girl on a makeshift altar."

Resnick suggested that to add some thrills to the liturgy, LaVey might want to consider incorporating even more writings by such Arkham stars as Robert E. Howard, Clark Ashton Smith, and H.P. Lovecraft into his rituals. And the high priest did.

As Resnick's guest, LaVey attended the convention's costume ball, where he proceeded to be wowed by the fans who dressed up as their favorite characters. No doubt finding kindred spirits in these proto-cosplayers who wrapped themselves in taffeta and tinfoil, he declared "science-fictionism" a strange new religion. There, he also ran into his pal Forrest J Ackerman, editor of *Famous Monsters of Filmland* magazine and a foremost collector of horror-movie memorabilia, who exhausted LaVey with a seemingly endless torrent of puns.

One person not pleased to see LaVey at the convention was Karen Anderson, wife of the novelist Poul Anderson. She had refused church literature from one of his young ministers in attendance, claiming, incredibly, that the high priest had killed two of her friends. LaVey knew the men to whom she was referring; they had reached out to him before their deaths to request Satanic services without their relatives and friends knowing, and he had obliged. In a letter to Marcello Truzzi, LaVey wrote that both were great guys whose deaths touched him deeply, but he admitted that Karen Anderson's reaction didn't faze him much. LaVey had the Devil's name and played the Devil's game; if she wanted to bestow that lethal power upon him, he'd take it. A person who is feared, he reasoned, earned more respect than a clown.

Resnick, who teasingly called his new friend "Anthony Levy," thought LaVey would be an outrageous addition to the *Insider* masthead, and so he hired him to write a weekly occult advice column. In Letters from the Devil, LaVey humorously and long-windedly provided helpful tips on constructing, among other things, a voodoo doll out of a feather-filled sock, when he wasn't explaining in explicit, step-by-step detail how a virgin could masturbate to orgasm without rupturing her hymen. He was a pretty good fit for a newsprint rag whose typical headline screamed, "Exposed—American Companies That Sell ARTIFICIAL SEX ORGANS!"

In a phone call to Resnick's office a few days before Christmas 1968, LaVey asked his friend, a Jewish atheist, what he'd like as a present. "I said that it was starting to snow," Resnick recalled, "and I'd sure love for him to use his Satanic connections to get me the hell out of there in the next ten minutes, since the city figured to be in gridlock by quitting time."

After a brief incantation, LaVey told him it was done and Resnick would be able to leave in ten minutes. "And thirty seconds later the power went off," Resnick wrote, "and when it didn't come on again in five minutes, the publisher sent everyone home and closed up shop for the day."

Resnick doubted LaVey had anything to do with the outage from three thousand miles away. "Did he take full credit for it for the next ten years?" he later wrote. "Of course."

LaVey continued working for the *Insider* for another year and a half before his column was picked up by another tabloid, the *National News Exploiter*. In one letter from October 29, 1972, "Bill H." from Dallas asked LaVey how to make a friend, a fourteen-year-old girl who missed her period by two weeks, unpregnant. "Oh!" Bill went on to assure the columnist, "I am not the one who got Nancy pregnant." LaVey's advice to the presumably fictional correspondent: wait a couple of weeks to see if Nancy menstruates. If she doesn't, find an "ethical medical doctor" to provide an abortion. "DO NOT advise her to take any concoction she reads about in a book of witchcraft recipes or confidentially passed on to her by an 'understanding' witch friend," LaVey stressed, before adding, "and don't be conned into thinking any magical spell will make her 'unpregnant.'"

It was a column that just six years later would take on shocking relevance in LaVey's own immediate family.

By early October 1968, LaVey decided he had waited long enough. He delivered an ultimatum to Hamilburg: *either find me a publisher within a month, or I'll take my bible to a vanity press or figure out a way to put it out myself.* Anything of significance he ever achieved he'd done on his own, LaVey believed, so perhaps he'd make a good literary agent. The threat apparently worked. A week later Hamilburg had some news: Avon, a paperback house best known for genre fiction and reprints of classics, was interested. It was ambitious new editor Peter Mayer's mission to acquire high-quality original books for the mass market. Mayer, too, wanted the book out as soon as possible and gave LaVey a tight deadline to turn in a draft, telling the trepidatious neophyte, "Just say it the way it is. It'll be fine."

By mid-December an editor named Carol Sturm Smith was assigned to work with LaVey to get his manuscript into publishable shape. "It had floated around for a while, I'm sure, until I was willing to take it on," she says. "Most of the people [at Avon] were afraid of it. People were taking it seriously, so they were afraid of it." A few years before, Smith had edited David Solomon's acclaimed psychedelic inquiry *LSD: The Consciousness-Expanding Drug,* so she was no stranger to the counterculture. As for her commercial credits, earlier in 1968 Avon published her novelization of the Sidney Poitier romance *For Love of Ivy*, and she would later write the movie tie-in for the Burt Reynolds black comedy *The End*, collaborate on numerous cookbooks, and pen a few original novels of her own.

But she wasn't exactly a fan of LaVey's material. "I came in with a head that was pretty well certain that this project was crap," she says, adding that she saw the Church of Satan as just a fad and was turned off by its message. "It was so anti-human . . . that I did not think it had any staying power."

Smith also found that the novice author required a lot of work. "He was not a very good writer," she says. "His syntax was difficult. He had [a lot of] misspellings." There were sections in the manuscript where she knew what he was trying to say, but it just wasn't on the page. The toughest part for Smith was that she just didn't believe in what he was saying. Their collaboration was always respectful, she's quick to note, but she remembers LaVey being "a very difficult character."

Nonetheless, she found him extremely charismatic and could certainly see how he was able to command a devoted following. "He was quite extraordinary," she recalls. "He was tall and ridiculously good-looking, and he filled the space with his personality. I can understand why he ended up on my plate and in my presence, because I have a fairly good-sized persona also, and I was young and nubile. I was a fairly attractive young woman at the time, and I am fairly sure that he came in thinking that he would be able to sweep me off my feet and that I would become a welcome member of his church."

More than fifty years after collaborating with LaVey, Smith was surprised to learn *The Satanic Bible* had gone through more than one hundred printings. "I'm stunned," she says. "I'm really, really taken aback. I had no idea."

She doesn't even own a copy of it. "I had a fire that did in my New York apartment a number of years ago, and lost it and whatever else I may have had," she says. "I'm sure that LaVey would have considered that retribution. He had nothing to do with it.

"At least I don't think he had anything to do with it."

Just because he was unable to land a *Playboy* interview, that didn't mean LaVey couldn't appear within its pages. For all his appreciation of curvaceous pinups, he really did read it for the articles—particularly those that were relevant to his interests.

In the August 1968 issue, he wrote in to praise the magazine for running "Henne Fire," Isaac Bashevis Singer's short story about demonic possession, small-town life in Poland, Jewish holidays, and spontaneous combustion. LaVey believed that the "philosophy expressed throughout is pure and applied Satanism" and was impressed by the Talmudic wisdom of the author, who, he added, "has the makings of a first-rate sorcerer." But the letter, he told Marcello Truzzi, was hardly an impulsive emanation; he had received a note from the magazine soliciting a review of the story for the letters section. Suspecting that the editors wanted to ascertain his way of thinking before going all-in and assigning an interview with him, he complied with the request. Recently, he had been told by a potential interviewer that the magazine still considered him a borderline subject.

Playboy asked for and published another letter from LaVey in May 1969, this one commenting on an essay about religion and morality that appeared in a special section in January called The Decent Society. "Man does need religion, with its ceremonies, rituals and assorted trappings," he wrote, "but he needs a religion based on what he is, not on what he can never hope to be." As he did Singer, he also praised writer Harvey Cox, a renowned theologian: "I think if [he] were to marry Ayn Rand, they might produce some wonderfully Satanic children."

Just two months earlier, the high priest himself appeared, albeit briefly, in a *Playboy* article rounding up religious fads, titled "Cultsville U.S.A.," in which he is described as "a 38-year-old Transylvanian gypsy," lays out the essential tenets of the church, and extols the virtues of sex magic. Though he called the piece "snidely written," LaVey was grateful for the exposure and the fact that his name was spelled correctly.

Someone who was not happy the magazine spelled her name correctly was singer Barbara McNair, who LaVey, in the article, boasted was a Satanist. In a June 1969 letter to the editor, she wrote, "being labeled a Satanist is a degrading accusation, as this cult represents the opposite of my belief. . . . My bag is love, not hate." She didn't mention, however, that two years earlier her bag included a photo op at the first Satanic wedding; a picture of her grasping LaVey's hand during the basement reception ran in the October 1967 issue of *Sepia*, a Black newsmagazine.

In July 1969, right above a blurb about Frank Sinatra's *My Way* LP, *Playboy* ran an item that was certain to both please and dishearten LaVey. There it was, in a national magazine whose circulation totaled in the millions: a mostly positive capsule review of *The Satanic Mass*— an album that was not yet widely available. (It had been decided that the record would be best served if nationwide distribution was held off till the publication of *The Satanic Bible*.) The uncredited paragraph, which took note of the high priest's "ominous basso profundo," described the ceremony as "an impressively obscure bit of hocus-pocus" and noted that the readings combine "elements of Blake, De Sade and Hitler into a credo sure to gain converts in our time: 'Self-preservation is the highest law.'"

Randall Alfred, who infiltrated the church in April 1968 to study it, left in August of the following year. He was hardly a dabbler, as he participated in forty-four of the fifty-two weekly rituals he attended and was present at twelve meetings of the Council of Nine. LaVey even invited him to stay overnight a half dozen times.

When the researcher decided to own up to LaVey, who had grown fond of the young man, the high priest told him he suspected all along that the church had been under scrutiny. He wasn't bothered, though, since he took Alfred's initial interest as genuine. Alfred, who would later become a prominent gay journalist and Bay Area radio host, rationalized his deception by admitting his playacting and use of others for his own purposes "were all components of lesser magic."

"Thus my feint was typically satanic," he wrote, "so I was not feigning, and the last diabolical laugh is not mine after all."

Though LaVey had no use for rock 'n' roll, he was scheduled to appear on October 31, 1969, at the Black Arts Festival, celebrating music and the occult, at Detroit's Olympia Stadium, where he would proclaim the emergence of the New Satanic Age and offer a benediction from *The Satanic Bible*. Marcello Truzzi's wife, Pat—now living with her husband in nearby Ann Arbor—would appear onstage as one of his witches. At least that was the plan. The promoters, who included twenty-six-year-old Mike Quatro, advertised some of the hottest bands of the day—Pink Floyd, the MC5, Alice Cooper, Bob Seger, the Stooges, and the Pleasure Seekers (who featured Quatro's sister Suzi)—along with LSD guru Timothy Leary, psychic Peter Hurkos (conducting a séance to conjure Buddy Holly and Brian Jones), and various sorcerers and voodoo priests. A new band out of Chicago called Coven, which had recently released its debut album, would be performing a musical Black Mass.

More than twelve thousand people paid five dollars to attend the gathering. When it was discovered that many of the artists had never been under contract, and thus never showed up, the Halloween concert erupted into a mini riot. According to author Arthur Lyons, who had been trailing LaVey for his own book, *The Second Coming: Satanism in*

America, the Detroit Council of Churches successfully protested both the high priest's benediction and the proposed musical Black Mass, scotching those appearances. Relieved that the festival gig fell through, as he wouldn't have wanted to be associated with such a disaster, LaVey remained in Detroit for a few days to lecture at the University of Michigan and do some TV.

A few weeks later, to celebrate his own album, which church members were at least able to order by mail, LaVey scheduled a musical recital at his home. There, on November 19, he'd blend his old-timey pop favorites with waltzes, bump and grind, pasodobles, and many other genres. At least that was the plan until the day of, when he learned that the show-business newspaper *Variety* had recently run a story about new records with supernatural themes: among them were horror actor Vincent Price's *Witchcraft Magic: An Adventure in Demonology* and Coven's *Witchcraft Destroys Minds & Reaps Souls*. Not among them was *The Satanic Mass*, whose back cover promised "The first authentic recording in history of a Satanic ceremony." The Coven LP, on Mercury Records, featured a thirteen-minute track entitled "Satanic Mass," which arguably may have been less authentic than LaVey's, but it was inarguably the first.

For LaVey, who had fought hard to get copies of his *Satanic Mass* into the hands of those who could promote his work—and who felt his backers lacked a sense of urgency when it came to distribution—this was a huge disappointment. Such a disappointment that he canceled the celebration.

With this news coming a month before the release of his first book, LaVey could be forgiven for experiencing something of a Satanic panic attack. Had he pitched a fit and insisted that things be done his way, he'd have a record out and he'd be the first.

When *Variety* finally got around to running a review of his album, on the last day of 1969, LaVey likely wished it had never bothered. Calling the record newsworthy in light of the Manson murders, the review went on to describe LaVey as "reminiscent of Bela Lugosi" intoning "metaphysical nonsense." Albums from other occult figures followed, including Louise Huebner's *Seduction Through Witchcraft*; British Wiccan Alex Sanders's *A Witch Is Born*; the eponymous debut of Barbara, the Gray Witch (whose tagline, "Witchcraft has never looked better," said it all); and Nat Freedland's *The Occult Explosion* compilation, which features an eleven-and-a-half-minute lecture by LaVey called "Satanism."

Murgenstrumm's principals eventually transferred ownership of *The Satanic Mass* to LaVey in 1976. All told, the LP sold fewer than five thousand copies.

For all the trouble he'd endured with finding a publisher and writing his book, one thing LaVey didn't expect he'd have to fight for was what it would be called. But when he received an author questionnaire from Avon, in the space where the title went, he read in all its clunkiness: *The Bible of the Church of Satan*.

Throughout the process, LaVey insisted that the stark cover design feature a deep black background with a Baphomet symbol under the title and author. That same emblem adorned the cover of the *Satanic Mass* album, which he had hoped to promote with a mention in the book. It was an idea swiftly poo-pooed by Mayer, who called it "hucksterish." But at least LaVey's title stuck.

The first edition, which featured a biographical introduction by Burton H. Wolfe, had a dedication page that read, "To Diane." And over the course of various printings, not to mention spellings, LaVey would come to list some of his inspirations, a mix of philosophers and comedians, showmen and shamans, carnies and crackpots, Jews and Nazis. Among them: Bernardino Nogara, Vatican financial manager; Karl Haushofer, mentor to Adolf Hitler and Deputy Führer Rudolf

Hess; Rasputin, Russia's "mad monk"; Sir Basil Zaharoff, Greek arms dealer; Cagliostro, Italian magician; William Mortensen, photographer; Hans Brick, animal trainer and author of *The Nature of the Beast*; Nietzsche, philosopher; William Claude Dukenfield, a.k.a. comic actor W.C. Fields; Phineas Taylor Barnum, circus impresario; Reginald Marsh, painter specializing in burlesque and carnival scenes; Wilhelm Reich, psychoanalyst; Mark Twain, author; Howard Hughes, billionaire industrialist and movie producer; Marcello Truzzi, sociologist and pal; Marilyn Monroe, blonde movie star; William Lindsay Gresham, author of *Nightmare Alley*; Jayne Mansfield, blonde movie star; Frederick Goerner, broadcaster and author; Robert Ervin Howard, pulp writer and creator of Conan the Barbarian; George Orwell, author of *Animal Farm* and *1984*; Howard Phillips Lovecraft, horror author; Tuesday Weld, blonde movie star; H.G. Wells, science fiction writer; Harry Houdini, escape artist; and Togare, house cat.

As the manifesto of a new religion, *The Satanic Bible* is a startling concoction, blending the rational self-interest of Ayn Rand with the godless self-realization of Nietzsche and the rabid Social Darwinism of the more obscure Ragnar Redbeard (widely believed to be a pseudonym for the political activist and author Arthur Desmond), whose best-known work, 1896's *Might Is Right*, has become something of a fascist handbook. In fact, LaVey lifted most of his own bible's first chapter, "Fire: The Book of Satan," word for word from *Might Is Right*. "Hate your enemies with a whole heart," both men wrote, "and if a man smite you on one cheek, SMASH him on the other!"

Blatant plagiarism aside, LaVey's book is by turns wise, strange, pragmatic, hokey, juvenile, logical, offensive, titillating, funny, and deeply disturbing.

In the opening "Nine Satanic Statements," he tidily sums up his beliefs, which include: "Satan represents vital existence, instead of spiritual pipe dreams!" and "Satan represents responsibility to the responsible, instead of concern for psychic vampires!"

"Satan," LaVey later writes, "represents opposition to all religions which serve to frustrate and condemn man for his natural instincts."

And when the pious insist that people fear both God and Satan, he asks, "If God is so merciful, why do people have to fear him? . . . Without such wholesale fear religionists would have had nothing with which to wield power over their followers."

Portions of *The Satanic Bible* even echo the work of Christian minister Norman Vincent Peale—whose 1952 book, *The Power of Positive Thinking*, was a self-help blockbuster—minus Peale's God stuff, of course. "The Satanist, realizing that anything he gets is of his own doing, takes command of the situation instead of praying to God for it to happen," LaVey writes. "Positive thinking and positive action add up to results."

Questioning why humans worship a god invented by others, he posits this justification for Satanism's emphasis on self-interest: "Is it not more sensible to worship a god that he, himself, has created in accordance with his own emotional needs—one that best represents the very carnal and physical being that has the idea-power to invent a god in the first place?"

To leaven all of this melodramatic bombast, LaVey the vaudevillian can't resist letting fly the occasional hoary joke that couldn't possibly have inspired any knee-slapping in 1970: "With all the debates about whether or not God is dead, if he isn't he had better have Medicare!" Later, when writing about using odors to attract the opposite sex, he mentions "sentiment stimulants," those appealing to one's memories. This leads to the story of a guy trying to woo a girl who had been uprooted from her beloved fishing village. "Wise to the ways of lesser magic," LaVey writes, "he neatly tucked a mackerel into his trousers pocket, and reaped the rewards that great fondness may often bring." All that was missing in the telling was a spritz from a seltzer bottle and a pie in the face. *Ha-cha-cha!*

Though LaVey makes clear that "Satanism *does not* advocate rape, child molesting, sexual defilement of animals"—all actions that infringe upon sexual freedom—he further offers a few dubious claims about human urges. "It is an established fact that the nymphomaniac . . . is not sexually free," he writes, "but is actually frigid and roves from man to man because she is too inhibited to ever find complete sexual release." And when discussing an imbalanced relationship, in which the husband's sex drive doesn't match his wife's, LaVey opines, "she should either passively, but pleasantly, accept him sexually, or raise no complaint if he chooses to find his needed release elsewhere—including auto-erotic practices."

And lest any readers think his religion traffics solely in stifling self-regard, he offers, "Satanism represents a form of controlled selfishness. . . . If you do something to make someone for whom you care happy, his happiness will give you a sense of gratification."

Along with belittling Aleister Crowley, whom LaVey calls "a poseur par excellence [who] worked overtime to be wicked," LaVey can't resist wandering into you-gotta-hand-it-to-Hitler territory, praising the Nazi strongman's concept of Strength Through Joy: "Hitler was no fool when he offered the German people happiness, *on a personal level*, to insure their loyalty to him, and peak efficiency from them."

In August 1969, as LaVey began working with Avon's publicity department, the Manson Family murders, heinous acts labeled "Satanic" and "ritualistic," cast a malevolent pall over a country and culture already roiling with civil unrest in the streets and atrocities broadcast seemingly daily from Vietnam. Then, in December—the same month that saw *The Satanic Bible*'s publication—a member of the Hells Angels stabbed and killed a concertgoer at Altamont, the doomed "Woodstock West" held fifty miles east of San Francisco, not long after the Rolling Stones performed the song "Sympathy for the Devil." All of that bad mojo, however, failed to blunt *The Satanic Bible*'s success. The book struck an ominous chord with the hedonistic, the withdrawn, the fringe dwellers who were goth before there were goths.

"Before Anton, within the public mind, there was very little concept of Satanism," says the occult lecturer and author Mitch Horowitz. "Sure, you had Aleister Crowley. Crowley, strictly speaking, was not a Satanist, but he played with that aesthetic. And you had some romantic notions of Satanism. But not too many copies of Percy Bysshe Shelley were flying out bookstores.

"But along comes *The Satanic Bible*," he continues. "And I don't know if Satanism as a term would've gotten very widely used in the popular culture had it not been for Anton. It just wasn't out there that much." Coincidentally, many years after leaving Avon, editor Peter Mayer would again find success publishing another controversial book whose title contained the S-word: Salman Rushdie's *The Satanic Verses*.

LaVey didn't miss an opportunity to promote the hell out of his ninety-five-cent paperback, whose first printing was a generous 125,000 copies. (In 1971, he managed to sell *The Satanic Bible*'s hardcover rights to publisher Lyle Stuart's University Books imprint.) He appeared locally on KPIX's *Mid Morning* and in a short witchcraft documentary for ABC-TV. He ventured to Dayton, Ohio, for the nationally syndicated *Phil Donahue Show*, and to Burbank, California, for an interview on *Life with Linkletter*, and then back home for KGO radio's *Dunbar's A.M.* There was a major feature story in *McCall's* magazine in March 1970 and another in London's *Daily Telegraph Magazine* in July. Stops on his press tour also included New York City (where he met some of the Avon staff), Ontario (for a talk at McMaster University), and Los Angeles for *The Steve Allen Show* (whose host would later include a few pages on LaVey in his book *Curses! Or . . . How Never to Be Foiled Again*).

Though LaVey may have been welcomed and flattered by TV and radio hosts and print journalists, mainstream book critics didn't know what to make of his bible, if they even bothered to write about it.

Father Andrew Greeley, in a *New York Times Book Review* round-up of religious tomes headlined "Jesus Freaks and Other Devouts," wrote, "LaVey . . . serves up a brew of sex, aggression and witchcraft, well calculated to scare the living daylights out of anyone predisposed to Satanism." (Which raises the question: If someone were predisposed to Satanism, why would this book scare the daylights, living or dead, out of them?) The review would have no impact on the book's initial release; it was published on February 13, 1972, a full two years after *The Satanic Bible* arrived in stores.

Deirdre LaRouche, in the *St. Louis Post-Dispatch*, came up with a much more prescient take: "I suspect that, although its existence may be deplored by many, this book and its adherents will be around for a long time to come."

Then there was the unwanted press. A few months after *The Satanic Bible*'s publication, it was reported that a copy of the book was discovered by police among the personal effects of a Wyoming man named Stanley Dean Baker, an admitted cannibal murderer. The *Billings Gazette* wrote that the "fantastic, disgusting, devil-worshiping handbook would be fit only for the trash can if it were not for the fact that it may play a key role in this bizarre murder trial." LaVey called Baker and his partner in crime, Harry Alan Stroup, "a couple of strung-out hippies" before adding, "Everybody says he's a Satanist these days. It's the fashionable thing." Baker claimed in court that he was Jesus and ended up serving sixteen years of a life sentence in prison.

While it has gone on to sell more than one million copies and influence multiple generations, more than a half-century on, *The Satanic Bible* still fails to get the respect many of its admirers believe it deserves—even from its own publisher. On the back cover of Avon's 110th paperback printing, right below the portrait of LaVey bathed in shocking magenta, and right above the UPC code—which evangelical conspiracy theorists have long claimed is the actual mark of the beast— is the book's genre listing, designating the section of the store where the publisher expects the book to be stocked.

It's not "Religion."

It's not "New Age."

It's not "Self-Help."

It's not "Philosophy."

It's not "Occult."

It's "Fantasy."

VI.

A Good Goddamn

HAVING fed the hungry media with his prankish happenings and the recent publication of *The Satanic Bible*, LaVey finally made it onto the big screen when, on Wednesday, March 4, 1970, *Satanis: The Devil's Mass*, a documentary about the church, opened at the Times Theatre, a grimy former nickelodeon.

The movie was the work of Ray Laurent, who, for his thesis project at UCLA's film school, trained his camera on and around 6114 California Street for a week almost two years earlier, in spring 1968, as LaVey conjured his first book.

In an interview published the day before the premiere, LaVey seemed mixed on the results, admitting that since the film was made during what he called the church's second phase, it was not very representative of its current state. "The first phase was the inauguration, my declaration of the Year One of the Satanic Age," he elaborated. "Our second phase was one of publicity—sometimes a hokey, crass Madison Avenue approach. I regret some of the tactics, but I felt I had to get the attention of the public before it would be possible to convert them."

Satanis, he added, was somewhat misleading, because the church was now in its third phase: "formalization and discrimination."

While certainly flawed and—perhaps unsurprisingly—technically shaky, the film remains a fascinating time capsule that manages to explicate, celebrate, and denigrate LaVey's creation in equal measure.

It opens with a procession down the Black House's entrance hall, as figures—some cloaked in hoods, others covered in masks (horror-movie skulls, plaster-of-Paris animal heads, a cartoonish red-faced Satan)—crowd into the ritual chamber.

A zaftig young woman lies naked on the fireplace mantel, serving as an altar. A severe-looking man with a buzzcut and a Van Dyke rings a handbell. Notes from a funereal organ drone in the background. "In the name of our most exalted god, Satan Lucifer, I command thee to come forth. Come forth and bestow these blessings of Hell upon us," the congregant bellows. "Come forth by these names: Satan, Lucifer, Belial, Leviathan! Shemhamforash!"

"Shemhamforash!" the assembled respond in unison, repeating the Hebrew word for the explicit name of God, which was adopted for occult practices.

"Hail Satan!"

"Hail Satan!"

He passes a chalice to LaVey, head covered with his horned hood. A young man with curly hair and black spectacles (Isaac Bonewits, who would later famously graduate from the University of California, Berkeley, with a bachelor of arts in magic) passes a book to the high priest, who begins shouting the infernal names—*Asmodeus! Beelzebub!*

Mephistopheles! Baphomet!—as if he's taking homeroom attendance at rowdy Hades Junior High.

LaVey lifts his cape and, in an intense crescendo, drops his praying hands before saying, "That's it for that part."

In the film's many one-on-one interview segments, LaVey dutifully trots out his gravest hits: calling Satanism the gray area between psychiatry and religion, as well as a religion that's not based on fear. He recites his well-rehearsed bullet points with all the cheerily cynical condescension of a TV game show host. "We're realists," says LaVey, looking relaxed in a clerical collar, blazer, and red Baphomet pendant—a huge black, scarab-like ring clamped onto his right index finger.

"We also feel a person has to be good to themselves before they can be good to other people."

"The greatest sin of all is self-deceit."

"We believe in greed."

"If you're going to be a sinner, be the best sinner on the block."

Laurent awkwardly splices in observations from unidentified others: neighbors, clergymen, Mormon missionaries, Church of Satan members. One local woman admires LaVey's appearance, soft voice, and pleasant demeanor. One older gent complains that LaVey doesn't maintain his property, citing drainpipe issues and the shingles and tar paper that blow into his yard. One priest says he wouldn't dignify LaVey's church by calling it one, since it lacks ethical content.

At a gathering of Satanists in the living room, LaVey is resplendent in a shiny, satiny red shirt and vest combo, looking for all the netherworld like a guy who's about to be stuffed into a circus cannon and shot across three rings. Diane sits on the floor in front of him.

The high priest frets that Satanists are known for their curses but never their blessings. Aside from the guy next to him wearing dark aviators and a priest's collar, the salon's other attendees are dressed conservatively, mostly blazers and dresses, suggesting that at any moment this could develop into a suburban key party. "Sexual freedom," LaVey declares, "is something we feel is very important, as a necessary requisite of the Satanic Church." But it's not the most important part, he says, just "an elective."

An elegantly wrinkled elderly woman wielding a European accent and a cigarette is transfixing in her few brief segments. Like everyone else in the film, she's not identified on screen. But she is in fact Baroness Carin Marie Gabrielle Xenia de Plessen, a daughter of a Danish diplomat, and an original constituent of LaVey's Magic Circle. As an actress in the 1920s, she performed as Xenia de Plessen at New York's Metropolitan Opera House, appeared on the radio, and after moving to the San Francisco area, made the society columns in the '40s and '50s.

And as a dog breeder—of Great Danes, naturally—she advertised her "Plessendane" pups for sale in the *Chronicle* and *Examiner*. While she kept a relatively low profile, her brother George, a chicken rancher in nearby Palo Alto, had been a notorious rake around town, with quite the Satanic streak. He made the front page of the *Chronicle* in 1926 when he married one Louise Carroll, who had been freshly released from jail after burglary charges against her had been dismissed. (He himself had been arrested for bringing narcotics into the slammer during a visit.) Later, his wife was arrested in Nice, France, and charged with child substitution. It was alleged that when she found out she could not produce an heir, Louise conspired with a pregnant woman to take the baby as her own in order to secure the de Plessen family fortune.

"It has become an eccentricity to be honest," Baroness Carin says at one point, insisting that she's revolted by hypocrisy. "And I don't like bigotry. So, in some ways I'm bigoted, too, because I'm intolerant of intolerance in any form or shape."

Later, she goes on to affectionately recount the time she was almost mauled by LaVey's pet lion. "I was in love with Togare," she says, before adding that one night when she reached out to pet him, he wanted to play, so he grabbed her wrist. Her dogs often did the same to her, no big deal, only this time Togare dug his fangs in. "And then I just stood there and I was petrified and Diane said, 'He's biting you, isn't he?' And I said, 'Yes, he is.' But I didn't know what to do. . . . I knew if I tried to take my hand back again, I thought I wouldn't have a hand left."

The film, which was restricted to audiences over eighteen, offers a few examples of the raw Madison Avenue meat for which LaVey later semi-apologized. In the first of its sex rituals, a man in a bishop's miter lies prone on top of a closed casket. His pants are pulled down, and a woman loudly flogs him as LaVey chants portentously. After some lingering shots of his smarting, crimson posterior, the casket is opened, revealing a naked woman with "666"—the number of the beast, a symbol of the Devil—scrawled across her chest. As she reaches out to draw him in, three men lower the casket lid.

In an interview segment, LaVey helpfully submits that his rites are a mix of Knights Templar ceremonies, West Indian voodoo, and Norse rituals. Closeups suggest that despite possessing all this arcane knowledge, LaVey has not mastered the symmetrical trimming of his goatee.

Satanis is at its most revealing when focusing on the domestic interplay between Karla and Diane. In the kitchen, sitting in front of a travel poster for Italy's Lake Como, Karla, who was fifteen during the shoot, tells the filmmakers her parents will not allow her to attend the services. "It's unfit for my eyes," she says, mockingly. "It will corrupt my mind."

Diane playfully snaps that if Karla were back home from seeing rock concerts at the Carousel Ballroom or Fillmore Auditorium in time for the sessions, maybe she'd get to go.

"But whenever I am—'You get upstairs!' . . . I can imagine what goes on anyway," she says, her mouth taking the shape of a raised eyebrow.

"We lead a normal abnormal life," Diane later tells the camera. "In other words, we eat regular meals and sleep semi-regular hours. But life is much more interesting, I think, than for most people. And naturally we are involved in topics that are abnormal."

Karla appears remarkably easygoing about her and Diane's (unofficial) stepdaughter/stepmother dynamic. "It's really kind of strange because she's old enough to be my sister and yet she can boss me around and I have to do it," she says, before adding, "It's kind of nice having a mother, you know, the same age pretty much, 'cause she understands."

That's not the only revelatory Karla quote:

"I suppose I'm as happy here as I would be anyplace else. I've never been anyplace else."

"Inside the house it's normal—except my father, he isn't around very much because he's always real busy. My parents are busier than most parents, I think. And so we have to take care of ourselves more."

Next to Karla at the kitchen table, Diane—who admits to letting her kids live by the laws of the jungle—says, "I think it's easier raising a family with a moral code that is flexible. I think that virtue should not be based on this standard, hackneyed, trite moral code that we've been forced to live by. I think that virtue should be things like kindness and courtesy and understanding. And do unto others as they do unto you."

One particularly chatty and catty neighbor, who issues witticisms that are sprinkled throughout the documentary, tells the filmmakers that she has it on good authority that the lion participated in "some of the sexual activities."

In another ritual geared toward the film's intended raincoat-wearing crowd, a nude woman caresses a snake while another writhes on the mantel with a skull at her crotch, and still another is tied to a pole. The snake is handed over to the human altar, then to LaVey. Isaac Bonewits sticks a pin into a voodoo doll and LaVey teasingly thrusts the snake at the bound woman.

In an interview, the living altar, whose name we never learn but is in fact Lenore Cosseboom, says she's fifty-three but feels eighteen and talks about the thrill she gets up on that mantel: "I suppose we could call it Satanic ecstasy. . . . Sometimes I get so charged up that I don't think they can make a battery comparable."

Back at one of the salons, LaVey quips about one member, "When he joined the Satanic Church, he was masturbating just about every day. And now he's masturbating two, sometimes three times a day." A long conversation about self-love follows, with Cosseboom claiming she taught her son to jerk off to avoid getting pimples. It's all punctuated with peals of demonic laughter.

After a neighbor says she hopes Satanism is a true religion and that LaVey is not deceiving his followers, a priest offers sagely, "I'd be more inclined to think that this is just a means of personal aggrandizement and enhancement."

LaVey, of course, has an answer for critics who claim he's a money-grubber or a con man: other religions build cathedrals where people live in squalor and garnish followers' wages; in his church, money is being used for "much more worthwhile purposes."

Satanis climaxes with another sex ritual. It begins with Bonewits reading, backward, the Lord's Prayer and the Nicene Creed, the defining statement of belief in Christianity. A young man wearing a derby and bowtie comes forth with a request—and it serves to underline one of the more progressive elements of the church.

"What is your wish?" asks the high priest.

"I would like Satan to arouse insatiable desire in the heart of that lovely young bank teller who's just moved into my neighborhood who said his name was Roger."

"Insatiable desire shall follow Roger," LaVey says. "And he shall be summoned unto you. . . . And lust shall reign supreme. Roger shall hear this and come to you."

Shemhamforash! Hail Satan!

Bonewits is up next. He wishes to enhance his sexual performance. "I desire the power of Satan and the searing lust of Lucifer!" he shouts. "The erectness of Belial and the glistening moistness of Leviathan!"

The shaft of sin shall be yours!

Shemhamforash! Hail Satan!

The ritual ends with "the Devil's kiss," which entails Diane pressing her lips against the tush of a guy spread over the nude altar.

For all his striving toward balance, Laurent can't resist ending the film on a smash-cut punchline, this one directed at LaVey by the gossipy neighbor.

"I understand he was tremendously busy during Halloween."

In what was surely a coup for young Ray Laurent, *Satanis* was acquired by Sherpix, an independent distributor that had found success with arthouse fare like Andy Warhol's *Flesh* and *Lonesome Cowboys* and tawdrier grindhouse items like *The Stewardesses* in 3-D.

A graphically stark ad in the *Chronicle* on opening day featured a photo of LaVey under these bold words: "A cult in San Francisco that advocates evil: vengeance, witchcraft, lust rituals, black magic, human sacrifices, and total sexual freedom." A vivid eight-paragraph description of the church filled the balance of the ad, which, in the fine tradition of tawdrier grindhouse items, managed to spell the director's name incorrectly.

For its initial run, *Satanis* shared a bill with a simpatico short subject, Kenneth Anger's mesmerizing twelve-minute *Invocation of My Demon Brother.* An avant-garde bouillabaisse of trippy visuals and a simultaneously astonishing and excruciating electronic score by the Rolling Stones' Mick Jagger, the film features images of LaVey decked out in his

Satanic finery and, as could be expected considering its outré auteur, makes fairly explicit the fetishistic impulses that connect Satanists to gay leathermen.

Anger, who'd been living in London by then, sent his friend a print of the short to screen for church members. When LaVey finally saw the film, which he dubbed a masterpiece, he wrote to Anger offering praise and gratitude that, presented alongside Hells Angels and Nazis, he felt he was in good company. Among his few criticisms, he thought the film would have been more effective had Anger replaced Jagger's music with the filmmaker's own selections.

In a profile of *Satanis*'s subject in the *Oakland Tribune*, columnist Gerald Nachman wrote, "LaVey hedges a bit on the matter of the movie's quality—he shrugs, 'A magician can always rectify errors'—a cut-and-paste production that seems to have been filmed and financed largely in the dark."

"The film has many erroneous things in it," LaVey told him, "but whether well or badly done it shows real [Satanists] on the screen for the first time, not actors. It's provocative if one is interested in the occult or in sex and sadomasochism, as a lot of people are without admitting it."

Bonewits later wrote that the ceremonies in *Satanis* were exaggerated for the camera: "Since I was still an enthusiastic ritualist, I was drafted to play various silly parts in these." As he began transforming into a long-haired Berkeley radical, he found he had little in common with what he saw as an increasingly right-wing church. So he tendered his resignation, joined up with "tree-hugging Zen anarchists," and became a prominent figure in modern paganism.

Opening night, which found LaVey and Diane in attendance, doubled as a benefit for the Church of Satan. Free copies of *The Satanic Bible* were to be distributed to the Times Theatre's patrons. Lenore Cosseboom, whose raunchy, brassy appearances nearly steal the show, wore a silver sequined dress to the screening, as if she were attending a Hollywood premiere.

Reviews, for the most part, were not kind. In the *San Francisco Examiner*, which had supplied LaVey with Olympic-sized pools of ink in the previous four years, critic Stanley Eichelbaum called *Satanis* "flabby, talky, tiresome, disproportionately long," described the church as "some kind of friendship club for bored, middle-aged people," and said that LaVey himself came across as "essentially a businessman who's picked an odd line of work."

In his *San Francisco Chronicle* review, John L. Wasserman gleefully checked off the film's exploitative elements: "Topless dancers, horny boa constrictors, whippings and Gallo Port. Something for everybody."

Variety's write-up offered, "LaVey gives plenty of evidence of the persuasive personality and flair that put him at the head of a coven of Frisco devil worshippers," but called the film's technical aspects "an abomination."

Richard Ogar of the radical paper the *Berkeley Barb* was a bit more forgiving in this appraisal, which was headlined "Deviled Ham? Oi Vey LaVey!" He called the film "skillfully made and thoroughly entertaining" before opining, "behind all those Satanic trappings, this particular Devil seems like a hell of a nice guy."

In a piece for *Newsweek* rounding up "The Cult of the Occult," Nick Kazan, later the Oscar-nominated screenwriter of *Reversal of Fortune*, wrote about being evaluated for membership by seven black-hooded church members, likening the comical ceremony to a fraternity initiation. Disappointed that the mass he attended at the Black House featured little of *Satanis*'s theatricality or skin, he called it "a highly stylized, arcane bore." Even the guy getting spanked stuffed a copy of *Playboy* down his pants to soften the blows. Kazan noted that the only hints of fanaticism surrounding the otherwise composed LaVey were "a swastika and a Confederate flag beside his desk," which the high priest explained away as "symbols of power and aggression that may be used in later rituals." The writer also claimed that no Blacks or Jews attended the mass, failing to acknowledge the person conducting it. This kind of dismissive and potentially damaging national press irked LaVey, who had been used to much more sympathetic coverage. In a letter to *Newsweek* that he printed in the May 1970 edition of the church news-letter, *The Cloven Hoof*, LaVey called the use of the *Playboy* magazine in the flagellant's seat as "sardonic" and questioned why Kazan hadn't mentioned the torture instruments from the Inquisition that were also in the room. After all, he said, they represented Christian ideas of "justice."

Then again, bad press was still press, and so he incorporated *News-week*'s rebuke in a mailing to church applicants:

> The chances are that you have entertained at least a few reserva-tions in contacting us. You may have heard that we devour babies for breakfast, engage in wild or perverse sexual orgies, or even desecrate graves. We have been accused of fascism by *Newsweek* and of communism by *American Opinion*. . . . We represent a position taken against nonsense, whether religious, philosophical, or political in nature. . . . Satan accepts only an intellectual com-mitment, not ritualized abasement of his followers.

Although it had limited playdates in the '70s, *Satanis* is somewhat easier to see today, thanks to the efforts of Lisa Petrucci and the late Mike Vraney at Something Weird Video, which released the title on DVD. However, its provenance is now in dispute. "The only thing SWV knows is that we got a sixteen-millimeter film print from Lou Sher of Sherpix back in the 1990s," Petrucci says. "Apparently Ray Laurent—who's deceased—sold it to Sherpix probably back in the 1970s. SWV bought and licensed the Sherpix film library, which is how we were able to release *Satanis* on home video."

Laurent's son contacted American Genre Film Archive and Something Weird after the film was restored and released on Blu-ray in 2019, claiming the intellectual property copyright since he believed the film still belonged to his father. *Satanis* is technically in the public domain, Petrucci says, since its copyright was never registered. But instead of arguing with him and going to court, they discontinued the Blu-ray release. For years, *Satanis* provided the go-to footage for news shows looking to reveal the inner workings of the Church of Satan, notably in 1970's *The Weird World of Weird*—a TV documentary on the occult hosted by veteran broadcaster Ralph Story—on a widely viewed segment of the ABC newsmagazine *20/20* in 1985, and on Geraldo Rivera's notorious 1988 "exposé" on devil worship.

Although Ray Laurent apparently never directed another feature, he did edit movies for two very distinct auteurs: ski documentarian Warren Miller and gonzo exploitation director Ray Dennis Steckler, whose demented pictures, such as *Rat Pfink a Boo Boo* and *The Incredibly Strange Creatures Who Stopped Living and Became Mixed-Up Zombies*, are exactly the type that LaVey would have labeled Satanic.

VII.

Season of the Witch

THOMAS Lipscomb learned about San Francisco's Satanic high priest from mutual friends Marcello Truzzi and Arthur Lyons. As a senior editor at the prominent publishing house Prentice Hall, Lipscomb was only interested in books that would sell, and in the Church of Satan, he saw dollar signs. LaVey would be a perfect addition to their pop philosophy list. "The world had a whole occult lust," Lipscomb says. "We wanted it to be true. We wanted Area 51 to be real. And he exploited it."

To Lipscomb, LaVey was a uniquely San Franciscan figure—his "con," a uniquely San Franciscan one. "Everything in California was fruits and nuts," he says. "There were all these people running around, all looking for the latest con, and they had money. You had EST over here and you had the Church of Satan over there."

The difference between the two was that Anton LaVey pitched his church as a vehicle for self-empowerment, and Werner Erhard pitched his personal transformation training program, established in 1971, as a live-or-die doctrine. "The same with Scientology," Lipscomb says. "There were no easy believers in these organizations." That's because you needed to put up some real money—you had to go all in.

"The Church of Satan was a breeze compared to these others," he says. "The old joke about ham and eggs, where the chicken makes a contribution, but the pig makes a commitment—most of these things took a real commitment. EST and Scientology—they got onto the Columbia Record Club thing. They wanted you on an automatic renewal basis. That's not anything that LaVey did."

In Lipscomb's estimation, LaVey's business was, for all practical purposes, bait—with a very light hook. "These other things were gaff hooks," he says. "They went right in your gills. But that made it easier to entertain a LaVey." His appeal lay in his charm and, in Lipscomb's eyes, he wasn't too heavy. "He didn't make you feel like he was some kind of crazy guy," the editor says. "He made you think he was reasonable."

While LaVey was still banging out *The Satanic Bible*, Lipscomb, who at this point had not seen anything he had written—he'd only heard the *Satanic Mass* LP—invited him to submit ideas for a hardcover book, a more prestigious, and potentially more lucrative, showcase than a paperback original.

LaVey wrote back and proposed a woman's guide to witchery, based on the workshops he was giving regularly at the Black House. It would cover such topics as how to manipulate men, the colors that turn men on, what food to serve, casting magical spells, and mixing love potions. He even had a title, one that he tweaked since first summoning the idea: *Practical Witchcraft for Women, or How to Trap a Man Through Witchcraft*.

Lipscomb was high on the premise but wanted a softer sell. After all, women were his target audience, as they were purchasing more than 60 percent of books sold in the US. He suggested another title: *The Compleat Witch: or What to Do When Virtue Fails.* LaVey liked how the title appealed to both the occult and general markets. He quoted his desired advance—$5,000 ($40,000 in 2024 dollars)—and told Lipscomb the writing would resemble a toned-down version of his outlandish *National Insider* columns and read less like the overly formal *Satanic Bible.*

That worked for Lipscomb. When he finally read LaVey's first book, after someone from Avon passed along a manuscript, he complimented the author backhandedly, saying that it should do well in paperback. He didn't tell him how he really felt: "It was awful. It was too damn heavy." However, Lipscomb says, it was redeemed by some of the content. "It's *Poor Richard's Almanac.* It's good advice. If you kick Beelzebub out of it, it all makes perfectly good sense."

After seeing LaVey's new outline, Lipscomb sent along a contact and a note about working together, but was critical of his writing style, saying it resembled that of a medieval Christian theologian. Just as Avon's Peter Mayer did, Lipscomb encouraged LaVey to find an approach that better approximated his speech, at the same time offering him complete freedom and control. He also discouraged LaVey from discussing the book publicly and asked him to try to keep a low profile, the latter an impossibility since the author was soon to embark on a *Satanic Bible* promotional tour.

It wasn't long before Lipscomb became frustrated in his negotiations with LaVey's agents and copied the author on a letter he'd written to them, in which the editor said it would be a shame to lose a project he created, titled, and shaped for free. He annotated the note by calling this bit an exaggeration, but he nonetheless managed to rankle LaVey, who wrote back that he lacked sufficient altruism to credit Lipscomb for instigating and shaping the project.

For this book, Lipscomb wanted to leave the S-word, which he considered off-putting, out of it—even if it was being used metaphorically. "It wasn't *The Satanic Witch*," he says more than fifty years later. "I wasn't selling 'Satanic' nothing."

Instead, he saw in the material echoes of *Sex and the Single Girl*, a multimillion-seller from 1962. That book's author, Helen Gurley Brown, went on to become the long-running—and groundbreaking— editor in chief of *Cosmopolitan* magazine, which, much as LaVey's church did, promoted the concept of sex without shame. (*How to Pick Up Girls!*, by advertising copywriter Eric Weber, was another of the era's popular sex tutorials, this one targeting club-dragging Neanderthals; it would appear almost concurrently with *The Compleat Witch* in 1971.)

"What is [*The Compleat Witch*] really about? It's about soft power and how women can seduce," Lipscomb says. "In that day and age, everything was about, 'How do men get women in bed?' 'How do women get the men in bed they want?' I just took *Cosmo* and put a little Satanic flair to it."

In March 1970, Lipscomb was in the midst of a job switch, moving over to Dodd, Mead and Company's trade division for the editor in chief gig, working on topical, general-interest titles. He was tasked, said S. Phelps Platt—the company's president and chief executive officer at the time—with finding "books that will create headlines and make readers stop and think." Lipscomb certainly thought he had one in *The Compleat Witch*, which he brought along to his new publishing house. One of those other headline-creating hopefuls already on the list was Arthur Lyons's *The Second Coming: Satanism in America*, which devoted a chapter to LaVey and the church. LaVey's own book was put on Dodd, Mead's schedule for an absurdly optimistic October 1970 publication date, at a list price of $5.95.

But instead of capitalizing on Halloween month to release the work of this ghoulish celebrity—besides, the book was late and stores couldn't see it as a pre-Christmas sell—Lipscomb settled on another date, one that seemed more in line with LaVey's libidinous subject matter: February 14, 1971. Valentine's Day.

On May 20, 1970, the humorist-storyteller Jean Shepherd played excerpts from *The Satanic Mass* on his late-night radio show on New York's WOR, likely encouraged by Lipscomb, who also happened to be Shep's editor at Dodd, Mead. And did he ever have fun with it. "Jean," Lipscomb says, "understood a great big floating balloon when he saw one."

From a news item about an upcoming motorized outhouse race, Shepherd segued into the sounds of mysterious chanting before cutting in to boast that he was playing "a highly significant recording" and encouraged his audience to turn off their lights in order to participate. "Look directly at the radio with intense concentration," he implored.

"You can go to the john later."

With faux-spooky echo on his voice, Shepherd announced that what they were listening to was the high priest of the Church of Satan and that it was the first time, to his knowledge, that a Satanic Mass had been transmitted over the American airwaves.

Over atmospheric organ notes and background noise—and aided by the LP's liner notes—Shepherd talked listeners through the destruction ritual and described the four books of *The Satanic Bible*. "The membership files of the Church of Satan are confidential," he mock-somberly intoned. "The list of members of this church are never revealed to the public."

After insisting that it's "an ordained church by the way—it's not a hokey-fenokee bit," Shepherd said he had considered playing "The

Invocation to Satan" later in the program but was afraid of what might happen if the Devil started popping out of every Japanese transistor radio. Shepherd ended the show by reciting "The Nine Satanic Statements" over a bed of playful music and maniacal laughter, and later returned to speak about *The Satanic Mass* on his May 30 broadcast.

Earlier that year, a reprint of Anton's beloved *1929 Johnson Smith & Co. Catalogue* featured a new introduction by Shepherd that also likely summed up LaVey's feelings about it. The book, he wrote, "is a magnificent, smudgy thumbprint of a totally lusty, vibrant, alive, crude post-frontier society, a society that was, and in some ways still remains, an exotic mixture of moralistic piety and violent, primitive humor."

Shepherd no doubt saw in LaVey a kindred spirit since he himself was something of a prankster. Earlier in his radio career, in 1956, after he touted a nonexistent novel called *I, Libertine* on the air, his listeners inundated bookstores with orders for the title, which Ballantine Books then rushed into existence based on an outline by Shepherd (and written primarily by a pseudonymous Theodore Sturgeon). Shepherd later gained fame when stories from his 1966 novel *In God We Trust: All Others Pay Cash* became the basis for the beloved 1983 film comedy *A Christmas Story*, featuring the indelible image of a young boy's tongue frozen on a flagpole.

By July 1970, LaVey was hyperbolically boasting that church membership numbered between seven thousand and ten thousand, with twenty-five grottos in the US alone and the same number abroad. From thirteen-dollar membership fees, LaVey's income amounted to around $25,000 per year.

"I wanted to create a forum," LaVey said of the regional covens, "a loosely structured cabal for the productive aliens." The grotto system gave members an opportunity to become what one church missive called, "more than just 'mail order Satanists.'" The Babylon Grotto, headed by third-degree warlock Wayne West in Detroit, Michigan, and the Plutonian Grotto in Denver, Colorado, led by the pseudonymous Reverend Adrian-Claude Frazier, were the first two.

Michael Aquino drafted *Articles of Protocol*, a secret manual for grotto administration, which defined the groups' raisons d'être. Many people, it read, "find that they are best able to realize their desires for power and manipulative influence through the medium of a formal organization. A Grotto is able to pursue projects on a scale which would be prohibitive to most individuals." These include certain operations of ceremonial black magic, which involve meticulous preparation. Besides, "the active and aggressive impression of the will of Satan upon a given environment normally requires coordinated and cohesive efforts."

To lead a grotto, a member had to first qualify as a second-degree witch or warlock. A grotto would require a minimum of five active members before the Central Grotto, at 6114 California Street, would consider granting a local charter, and not before its progress had satisfied the Council of Nine—the church's governing body—after a six-month probationary period. "There is no prescribed level of activity that a Grotto is required to maintain," according to the manual. "The denizens of Hell are not so insecure as to require scheduled adoration by their human disciples. . . . Such rituals as the Grotto conducts should evidence the membership's conscious desire to commune with the Powers of Darkness."

Grottos sprang up all over the country and elsewhere. Santa Cruz, California, had the Karnack Grotto; Washington, DC, had the Asmodeus Grotto; Los Angeles had the Yuggoth Grotto; and the New York/New Jersey area had the Lilith Grotto, founded by the charismatic Lilith Sinclair and Spencer Waldron. Some grottos had their own newsletters, with names like *Satan's Spawn, The Devil's Advocate, The Blacklist, The Typhon Tusk,* and *Children of the Night.*

Waldron, whose father was Presbyterian and mother leaned witchy, discovered *The Satanic Bible* in college and agreed with its philosophy that Christian morality has little to do with being good. "These total fanatic fundamentalists, whatever the heck the religion is, [they could be] just nasty, evil people," he says. "And you can have Satanists that are really good people, who would give you the shirt off their back."

He appreciated LaVey's bold approach in bringing what was previously a subterranean movement to the surface, "the fact that he actually went public and said, 'We're Satanists—screw you!'

"We even joked about coming out of the broom closet."

Waldron was living in upstate New York and had become friendly with Sinclair, a witch based in Spotswood, New Jersey. Armed with the addresses of local church members provided by the Central Grotto, in June 1971 they organized a compassion ritual. Waldron, who had made second-degree warlock, had an uncle in nearby Rutherford, New Jersey, where he'd stay when attending scheduled grotto meetings and rituals. A typical meeting would consist of a discussion about an upcoming ritual, figuring out why it was necessary and what kind of preparation was needed. The night of the ritual would begin with socializing and end with the ceremony. Then, "Bam! It's done," Waldron says. "You're out the door and home."

He eventually left the Lilith Grotto to attend law school in Georgia, before becoming a park ranger in Virginia, where for a time he and his wife became involved with the Asmodeus Grotto. He recalls one particular ritual, or "working," really paying off.

"We needed a couple of hundred bucks to just make ends meet," Waldron says. "So we asked for a money working. They're kind of dangerous because it's like that classic ghost story: you ask for money in a working, and you get it because your favorite uncle died and left you a bunch of money. Or your house burns down, and the insurance pays off. That's not the way you want it."

This particular working seemed to go well. On their fifty-mile drive home from DC to Fredericksburg, they stopped for gas and discovered the attendant overpaid Waldron in change. "I gave him a twenty; we got change for a fifty," he says. "I thought, 'Oh, that's weird.' Then it happened again and again. . . . Every single purchase we made we got the wrong change in our favor." Moral concerns tied to the miscalculations aside, Waldron had never seen anything like it. The mistakes continued for around two weeks, then stopped as suddenly as they began.

"By then we figured we came up about three hundred bucks ahead, which is just about what we needed," he says. That showed him there were some talented people in the Asmodeus Grotto.

Grotto leaders were expected to keep in close contact with the Central Grotto, sending monthly reports concerning members as well as public lectures, local news clippings, and articles earmarked for *The Cloven Hoof*.

Those communiques with the front office would come to include complaints about disruptive, even potentially dangerous, members. Adrian-Claude Frazier, of the Plutonian Grotto, planned to discourage from attending rituals one homosexual member who wanted the group to help turn a straight friend gay and then threatened to kill himself or his friend if the request was denied. Frazier, a US Army colonel during World War II and the Korean conflict and a former POW, also expressed concern that a member was attempting to use the grotto to recruit for his own voodoo church, and shared that another had lost a job opportunity after announcing she was both a nudist and a Satanist. He assured LaVey that he warned grotto members not to make such open pronouncements unless they were certain of a positive reception.

Grotto leaders were also encouraged to publicize their groups with one caveat, according to *Articles of Protocol*: "You should avoid such questionable media as 'underground' newspapers, however. Not only do we wish to circumnavigate the faddist elements, but we have a standard of dignity to observe." If grotto officials should find themselves targeted for attack, they should assume an aggressive stance: "Instead of justifying his behavior, in other words, he should question that of his critic." Which explains why LaVey was furious when, in May 1971, the Plutonian Grotto failed to adequately defend the Church of Satan in the media after two teens in the Denver suburb of Northglenn were busted for allegedly robbing a Baptist church. The boys claimed to be members of a Satanic cult that sacrificed small animals and drank their blood. It was only a matter of time before LaVey's name and bible were dragged through the viscera.

Frazier responded to the high priest's censure by suggesting they divide the Denver grotto into two entities: one underground and consisting of more distinguished members; the other public-facing, featuring those who had nothing to lose. In Michael Aquino's eyes, this crisis, and LaVey's apparent capitulation to Frazier ("dividing . . . membership into those who were expendable and those who were not") signaled what he later called "the beginning of the end of the Church of Satan." Still, Aquino stayed on and even volunteered to edit a more robust version of *The Cloven Hoof,* whose circulation, once thought to be in the thousands, he claimed numbered just 270. (That number has always been fuzzy. According to Randall Alfred, the researcher who left the church in 1969 but remained casually connected for four more years, in 1971 when he was present for a mailing of *The Cloven Hoof,* "only four or five hundred active members were still paying the $10 annual 'active fee' and thus receiving [it].")

On December 9, 1971, Frazier declared his intent to resign as the leader of the Plutonian Grotto, bemoaning, among other things, the backstabbing, gossip, and security violations rampant within his group.

The Northglenn incident was hardly unique. With the expansion of the church came more accusations that its members were committing heinous crimes outside San Francisco. In May 1970, Patricia Hall, a self-described witch, was arrested with three men on charges of assault after a girl was whipped and raped in a New Orleans wax museum. "Her claim she was baptized by a 'Black Pope of the First Church of Satan of San Francisco' is an absolute lie," LaVey said, pointing out that his church had a different name, no pope, and that a check of the church's records found no "Patricia Hall" among its members. (By the following month, "the Black Pope" would become a ubiquitous honorific attached to LaVey in the press.)

That summer, two ritualistic murders committed in California once again put LaVey on the defensive. The incidents represented a problem that would dog his church for decades. Though LaVey conceived the Church of Satan as a hedonistic yet humanistic approach to life, incorporating the S-word to weed out the pretenders, others stuck to the name's traditional Judeo-Christian meaning as an excuse to indulge in the malignant and debased (not to mention, illegal).

In a page-one profile in the *Los Angeles Times*, LaVey stressed that his church was an elitist organization that didn't tolerate the kind of kooks who commit these offenses: "If someone waltzes up to our front door and says, 'Lucifer told me to come,' he gets the bum's rush, you'd better believe it." Folks disappointed to find no orgies or "nefarious activities" were turned away, and he had no use for the drug-addled. "Manson is just another mad-dog killer as far as I'm concerned," said the law-and-order Satanist, "and I think he should be taken out in Pershing Square and drawn and quartered." A couple of decades later, LaVey would revise his opinion on the cult leader.

One of LaVey's philosophical goals was the creation of a benign police state, one where "civility, good manners, and courtesy will return, and emphasis will be placed on achievement and worth, rather than on sanctimonious lip service." When it came to policing the grottos, these ideas would be strictly enforced.

It had always been his ambition to create a movement that encouraged artistic ambition and self-sufficiency. And in a handout distributed to potential agents (formerly "regional" agents), he announced a stratification system that he deemed crucial to the continued health of the organization: "Because yours is a semi-autonomous role, and represents an important link in operations, you will have no contact with other Agents, except when required." He felt that the church had expanded to the point where unrestrained collaboration could result in the sort of egalitarianism he wanted to prevent. Democracy, LaVey believed, could only work in a society with a population of one.

Arthur Lyons was visiting San Francisco from Palm Springs when he decided to pop by LaVey's place on Tuesday, September 29, 1970, to introduce a couple of friends: astronomer, computer scientist, and UFOlogist Jacques Vallée and occultist Don Hanlon. Vallée later said that he "went along as a lark," with LaVey immediately setting the larkish tone by materializing—*alakazam!*—out of the trick fireplace.

Vallée recalled the high priest insisting to his new acquaintances that "he sincerely believed in his religion, even if he did not trust his disciples farther than he could throw his massive Wurlitzer organ."

"How could I believe in them?" LaVey told them, before citing some correspondence he had received.

"A young woman in San Diego wants to benefit from my Satanic knowledge in the procuring of forbidden enjoyment regarding a certain person," he said, claiming that no dark arts could possibly help her since "the man she loves, a well-known movie star, is a notorious homosexual." Another letter was sent by a woman who wanted to be nailed to a cross like Jesus Christ for eleven days. "She can take a leave from her job after Easter, she says, offering me $400!"

After Hanlon asked fellow traveler LaVey why he would include what he regarded as abbreviated rituals in *The Satanic Bible*, the author responded, "What do these people expect for seventy-five cents?"

Superficially, LaVey may have had more in common with Hanlon, but he gravitated toward the tall, handsome Vallée, a polymath whose name read like an inversion of his own. Like Marcello Truzzi, here was another respected and successful intellectual showing a sincere interest in his work and obsessions. Thus began a friendship that would come to mean a great deal to the high priest.

That December, anticipating that LaVey's new book would have already come out in the fall, a curious advertisement for a perfume at Burdine's department stores appeared in newspapers, announcing in mostly lowercased copy:

> *she read 'the compleat witch'*
> *she is a spellbinder*
> *she has incense for every occasion*
> *give HYPNOTIQUE by max factor.*

Hypnotique, introduced in 1958, had previously been sold as "the perfume for the woman who was born to enchant men" and was even recommended by Helen Gurley Brown in *Sex and the Single Girl* as an inexpensive means to attract them. But the prematurely placed ad must have left those spellbinders scratching their beehived or pixie-cut heads: what is this *Compleat Witch* of which this ad speaks?

That same month also saw the church itself being referenced in newspaper ads for the X-rated *Witchcraft '70*, which was just opening in San Francisco. An Italian-made shockumentary travelogue in the *Mondo Cane* vein, the movie (released in the UK as *The Satanists*) purports to expose unspeakable cults, bizarre rituals, and erotic rites. From England to Brazil to Finland to the US and beyond, the movie revels in sensationalistic depictions of a ceremonial deflowering, blood shower, and naked exorcism, as well as voodoo, hypnotism, flagellation, cryogenics, animal sacrifice, and Hare Krishnas. One episode allegedly depicts the mystical union of real-life British occult celebrities Alex and Maxine Sanders. A few years earlier, the film's director, Luigi Scattini, made *Primitive Love,* starring Jayne Mansfield.

In a seven-minute segment filmed at 6114 California Street, LaVey shows off a scrapbook of press clippings before theatrically beckoning the camera crew into the kitchen while uttering in voiceover, "We believe in life everlasting, world without end." Then comes the show-stopper: the Satanic wedding of a young couple, only this time the chamber is absolutely packed with bosomy naked acolytes, along with Diane and a teenage Karla, who was now being allowed to participate. At one point the high priest appears to prepare to mount the intended, leading the film's veddy British narrator to sarcastically assert, "Satan"—meaning LaVey—"altruistically puts heart and soul into removing all traces of the honor of the bride."

Anton, who had heard the finished film presented his church in a very favorable light, had planned a promotional visit to Italy with Diane. But it was called off, he said, when producers didn't want the Devil himself there to rile up the pope and possibly thwart the movie's release.

In *The Compleat Witch*, LaVey's guide to the wily femme, men are "quarry" and "looks mean everything, despite delusions to the contrary." The average male, he writes, "is an animal first and a romanticist second. For this reason, he will always be tempted by the woman whom he considers to be of easy virtue." LaVey teaches that the ability to recognize different traits in men is essential if a woman wants to become a successful witch. Everyone, he posits, has three layers of personality. We reveal to the world two of them: the apparent "cover" and the "true" core. The third is personal, our inner image, the demonic minority self, often our opposite.

To illustrate his theory, he created the LaVey Personality Synthesizer, a clocklike diagram that classifies charismatic and physical traits (like "impulsive" and "domineering" and "no waist" and "marshmallow flesh"). Jayne Mansfield, for example, was a perfect blonde twelve o'clock. For a witch to land her quarry, she needs to figure out what kind she wants and be the person at the opposite side of the chart. LaVey adapted this concept from *The Circle of Sex*, a 1962 book by Gavin Arthur, the sexologist and astrologer who very publicly denied any involvement in the first Satanic wedding. To examine human sexuality, he charted twelve erotic archetypes that bewitch and repel. (LaVey credits Arthur's work in *The Compleat Witch's* extensive bibliography, itself a wondrous resource for arcane literature.)

Despite LaVey's basing his entire book on an overly complicated and seemingly arbitrary conceit, there is a lot of amusing weirdness to be found among the pseudoscientific hooey. He offers sections on "How and When to Lie," "Gesture, Mannerisms, Toilet Habits and Assorted Ploys," and even "The Folly in Trying to Charm a Self-Aware Homosexual." He also advises women not to scrub away their "natural odors of seduction" if they're only going to dab on scents derived from animals anyway.

In what may be the book's most notorious passage—one that epitomizes just how granular, fetishistic, and downright goofy LaVey could get—he writes about the sensual allure of salad dressings. The sharp aroma of Roqueforts, blue cheese, oil and vinegar, and the like "is similar to the male scrotal odor and reminiscent of a locker full of well-worn jock straps." Naturally, he adds, these appeal to "predominantly heterosexual women, passive males and men with homophile tendencies."

For his part, the book's editor doesn't think LaVey was too far off with that assessment. "The same conversation has been going on in every army camp for forty years," Thomas Lipscomb says. "This is stereotypical shit. It may have looked outrageous to fancy pants editors and media people who really don't know much about America."

LaVey knew that Lipscomb knew that LaVey was blowing smoke. "He did not require me to take him seriously," the editor says. "All I wanted out of him was consistent logic. If we're going to say that men's scrotums taste like blue cheese, let's define the other cheeses that are also available, consistently, in a way that the reader can say, 'Jesus, how obnoxious! *But I see what you mean.'*"

To Lipscomb, the shock value was the point. "Girls talk about that all over lunch, all over New York. When I was the publisher of *Ladies Home Journal,* I used to sit around the editorial board and say, 'What should we scare the girls with this week?'"

Still, LaVey realized when he was going too far. In a letter dated November 24, 1970, he asked his editor to make a last-minute tweak to the book's closing line, in which he wrote of man cherishing the demon within and moving on to "the Final Solution." Realizing that this loaded phrase could conjure images of Hitler's gas chambers, he suggested replacing it with "the final triumph." (Curiously, the change was never made.)

Though LaVey boasted that *The Compleat Witch* provoked book burnings and picket lines, his editor recalls none of that. To Lipscomb's dismay, for a book filled with paeans to panty sniffing and pubic toupees and instructions on making an amulet out of a soiled tampon, it failed to stir up much controversy at all. "Nobody took it even seriously," he says. "It didn't bother a soul. I figured the book would cause much more outrage than it did.

"My life with women has been paradise," he adds. "And I have never suffered from going too low with one. So, all the screams and yells and protests empty pretty fast once you find the nerve endings. I wanted petitions. I wanted [protesters] marching around the building. I got nothing."

He did, however, get his friend Helen Gurley Brown to buy an excerpt to run in the November 1970 issue of *Cosmopolitan* (coverline: "The Compleat Witch: Time-Tested Ways to Cast a Spell Over a Man!").

"I jumped up and down on their heads until they took it."

With membership requests regularly flooding the house whenever he popped up on radio and TV or in newspapers and magazines, LaVey sensed he might be attracting unwanted attention and soon began avoiding public appearances. He assured friends that he wasn't being paranoid, just realistic. Right before *The Compleat Witch*'s publication, he wondered about his image, whether he was going to be considered a benign advisor to women interested in the occult or a diabolical fiend. And if the latter, would some self-righteous religious fanatic be compelled do away with the Devil?

These concerns motivated him to issue a form letter directed at those who expressed interest in visiting San Francisco to meet him, insisting that the building that once held ceremonies was now used exclusively for administrative purposes and was closed to all but staff: "Dr. LaVey resides in various locations and is rarely in San Francisco." It went on to discourage aspirants from coming to the city to join the church, increase their involvement, volunteer their services, or hope to find a Satanic haven ("We operate no missions, half-way houses, or opportunity centers").

Before embarking on the *Compleat Witch* publicity tour, LaVey had already filmed a few things for Canada that appeared right around the book's release.

On Tuesday, February 2, 1971, the Canadian Broadcasting Corporation aired *The California Movie,* a documentary about the state of the thirty-first state, which had been shot over five weeks the previous summer. It didn't take much for Martyn Burke to convince his bosses at the CBC to let him make the film, for which he'd interview celebrity lawyer Melvin Belli, Jefferson Airplane singer Grace Slick, and some Manson followers, among others. It was a time when being in your early twenties and having long hair often worked to your advantage as a culture reporter.

"The idea was that the craziness going on in California was absolutely predictable if you take the idea that Americans had always been moving west," Burke says. "First, they moved west physically through Manifest Destiny. Then at some point you couldn't move any further west physically. It became a psychic moving. And that's why California came up with all these new fads, ideas, and trends."

Anton LaVey appeared to him as an outlier, a character born of the counterculture but disconnected from it. Right from their introductory phone call, Burke recalls, LaVey seemed anxious to be a part of the show but also dogmatic about what he wanted to discuss: lust, indulgence, vengeance, and why Satanism makes sense in modern times.

The filmmaker had gone in with no agenda or preconceived notions, and upon meeting LaVey at the Black House, he immediately detected a "hucksterish" quality about him, someone not only extremely friendly, but also very persuasive. "I thought I was in the hands of a master salesman," Burke says. "And what he was selling was his view of life and his aura, and they were almost inextricably combined."

For the interview, Burke and his cameraman and sound person, just the three of them, entered the ritual chamber where LaVey sat elevated on an ornate chair, resembling an emperor on his throne, surrounded by Diane and some half-dozen acolytes. "The people around him were not impressive at all," Burke says. "He was clearly the star."

And he was a star willing to take direction. For the filmmaker, who had yet to begin his decades-long career in narrative features, that meant a subject who was eager to please so long as he was being presented in the most effective, convincing light. The LaVey segment, replete with a theremin-heavy spook-show score, amounted to just a few minutes of the high priest philosophizing ("California shows itself to be a goal-oriented area, and Satanism is a goal-oriented religion"), along with Diane offering that *Rosemary's Baby* "was based largely on the Church of Satan."

"He had a gaze that could cut through steel," Burke recalls. "And he was staring at me as if I was a fish on a hook." And partway through the interview, the filmmaker came to believe he was there to be recruited. "LaVey never said this [explicitly], but toward the end, he and the blonde next to him did say: 'Join us.'"

Burke suspects that LaVey was working him for his media connections. "I guess if he could get the Canadian Broadcasting Corporation in as part of his group, he'd have a mole who'd be pumping out Anton LaVey *Satanic Bible* stuff."

It was a sales pitch disguised as an interview. "He talked about how what is called 'the Devil's work' is not really evil. It is a form of enlightened self-interest that can benefit the world."

And he admits LaVey's technique was having an effect. "When you're in your early twenties, you think you know more about the world than you really do," Burke says. "At one point, my mind was reeling. I'd never heard anything like this. . . . It was so seductive and presented beautifully with this mellifluous voice."

Burke describes LaVey as a "situational raconteur" who didn't linger on specifics of Satanic doctrine or personal philosophy, instead telling him whatever fit the particular moment. "He was very smart," says the filmmaker. "Like a trial lawyer, he didn't go outside what he already knew the answers to. He could handle himself if he was challenged. . . . He was very careful not to [say] anything he couldn't safely defend." Burke recalls other subjects of his film, major figures, crumbling when challenged.

At one point during the six or so hours he spent in the house, Burke felt the baiting take a carnal turn. "Nothing that would stop you in your tracks," he says, "but it was 'anything goes.'" With Anton and Diane exchanging glances and offering, "You can join us," Burke detected a come-on that was flagrantly sexual without being erotic. "It was practical sexuality being dangled in front of somebody whom they were hoping to either curry favor with or recruit."

Burke had been in what he called flagrantly sexual situations that same week in San Francisco—interviewing pioneering topless dancer Carol Doda, for one—where he knew exactly what was being said. LaVey's skill was to couch his temptations in plausible deniability.

"I had the impression that they were polyamorous," Burke says. "'Anything went' was what he said to me at one point. He said something that indicated that they don't abide by conventional strictures of morality."

The filmmaker left the house with an admiration for what LaVey was achieving. "It was so beautifully choreographed and staged that I thought, 'This guy's going to have a future.'"

In one of the more bizarre LaVey sightings, later in February he appeared on *Man Trap*, a talk show—more like an argument show—

hosted by Alan Hamel and coproduced by Dick Clark, shot near Vancouver, British Columbia. A production of Canada's CTV, it was also syndicated to some fifty-five American markets. The premise of the show—which was aimed squarely at the with-it, liberated *Cosmo* crowd—was certainly in line with what the high priest was selling: a kind of verbal battle of the sexes, a high-concept he-versus-she rhetorical throwdown. The premise: a male guest faced a panel of three female celebrities—in LaVey's case, actresses Phyllis Kirk, Jan Sterling, and Margot Kidder—and had to defend himself and his positions against their cutting remarks. The topics addressed on the provocative series—which featured the comedians George Carlin and Nipsey Russell, actors Raymond St. Jacques and Forrest Tucker, and even Little Richard—included marriage, divorce, alimony, abortion, gay liberation, and child-beating.

The writer Harlan Ellison, who occupied the hot seat on one episode, described it as "merely a distaff-oriented *Joe Pyne Show*." "The concept," he elaborated, "is that a 'good' show can only emerge from a vitriolic and bitchy confrontation between a male and females." But he also called *Man Trap* "genuinely fascinating," despite its being based on an unhealthy premise that would only serve to widen "the artificial gulf between men and women."

After a February 10 stop at San Francisco's Channel 7 for a chat with news radio pioneer Jim Dunbar's morning TV show, LaVey began his *Compleat Witch* promotional tour in earnest, flying to Los Angeles on the twelfth for *The Virginia Graham Show*, *A.M.*, *Tempo*, and *The Steve Allen Show* (this time with actor Jack Palance and cohost Charles Nelson Reilly). Then to Pittsburgh for some local shows, then Chicago and Washington, DC, then New York City, then Philadelphia, then back to New York City—where he stayed at the swank Waldorf Astoria on Dodd, Mead's dime—then to Detroit, and then back home to San Francisco on March 2.

Having established his bona fides with *The Satanic Bible,* and with a classy hardcover—featuring the LaVey Personality Synthesizer depicted in gorgeous, full-color endpapers—under his Baphomet-buckled belt, for *The Compleat Witch,* LaVey was getting reviewed right out of the gate. And some of the notices were very favorable.

Calling the book a "frank and oft-times funny bible of bewitchery," Martie Kazura, in the *Cincinnati Post & Times-Star,* suggested "an even better title": *How to Be a Woman for Pleasure and for Profit.* "If you are a woman and don't know quite what to do with all you've got," she concluded, "then listen to LaVey."

The *Detroit Free Press's* Bobby Mather fixated on the author's own personal fixation: "It's fun to read in kind of a simple-minded way, but I'm afraid all you'll end up with is Anton LaVey's idea of the perfect woman."

And his perfect woman just might have been Isabel Edwards at the *Minneapolis Tribune.* "The demonic lore on which he bases his advice to would-be sirens is worth at least that half-hour you have been spending on *Dark Shadows,*" she wrote, name-checking a popular gothic soap opera. "As for the advice, I've read nothing more comforting in years. . . . LaVey advances a game plan that requires only that you accept your real self and dig out some outdated high heels, nylons, your oldest undies, and that dress that never quite fit."

Robyn Rickard of the *Honolulu Advertiser* opined, "While some of the work is bewildering, much of it is just plain boring."

Larry Harmon of the *El Paso Times* begged to differ: "More delicate readers may be repelled at certain passages, but no reader will be bored by this book."

While *The Compleat Witch* failed to become the hardbound blockbuster Lipscomb had hoped (neither, for that matter, did Arthur Lyons's *The Second Coming*), Dodd, Mead at least made its money back. "As a publisher, that's what we care about," he says. "Because one in five books makes money. [For the] original edition, I tarted it up with a lot of color and graphs and stuff. I made it look pretty damn good. Since I was selling horseshit, the packaging was going to matter."

That "horseshit" was repackaged as a paperback by Lancer Books the following year. Around the same time, author Michael Mooney listed "Dr. Anton LaVey" in the acknowledgments of his book *The Hindenburg* about a commercial passenger dirigible, the pride of Nazi Germany, that became engulfed in flames while attempting to dock in New Jersey in 1937. Lipscomb, who was also Mooney's editor, introduced the author to LaVey. "They got a kick out of each other as I thought they might," he says.

Looking back on his association with LaVey, the editor remembers him being perfectly reasonable and great company. "And he was one of the most remarkably balanced people I've known," he says. "He knew he was zooming us. He didn't mind if we knew we were being zoomed or not. We were all just going down the road together. He also had, for some delusional rich San Francisco people, pretty good advice."

In 1972, as LaVey ceased all regular public rituals at the Black House, Lipscomb brought over a woman he was hoping to impress. "I had my hooks into a widow with a fortune who was madly in love with me," he recalls. "We're out in San Francisco, doing the town, in all the fancy places. So, my move was to take her out to California Street to speak to Anton LaVey. And Anton immediately got it. He knew his job was to astonish her, and boy did he do it. He played the organ in calliope mode. Then he started telling stories about him versus fifteen man-eating tigers in Clyde Beatty's cage, when something went wrong and he couldn't get out. I'm just sitting there with my jaw open because his creativity was so high. Meanwhile, she's getting all wet listening to this terrific story of derring-do, and her lover knows this incredible person."

Wayne Chonicki was seven years old when he discovered his grand-father was a Luciferian Satanist. The old man ascribed to a philoso-phy that interpreted Lucifer as the literal bringer of light, as a symbol of human progress, potential, and self-determination. While the rest of the family went to their Roman Catholic Church in Pittsburgh on Sundays, he stayed behind. "He belongs to a different religion" was all Chonicki's grandmother would say.

As a kid in the late 1950s, Chonicki would revel in the horrific plea-sures of Saturday matinees at the Arcade, Rex, and Liberty, the local theaters presenting movies starring giant spiders and gargantuan apes as well as more down-to-earth frighteners, like the vampires, werewolves, and witches of England's Hammer studio. When he got his first library card, he began to read voraciously about occult topics, eventually find-ing his way, as a young teen, into a ceremonial magic lodge in the Pol-ish steel mill town of McKeesport. There, he apprenticed under the grand master who showed him how to summon and apply the ambient energy, or chakras, the human body can create.

"We are coming to this weird point," Chonicki says, "where you have an intersection between science, with the [physicality] of what's going on, as well as the philosophy, the occult belief, and the demonstrable, manageable, actual phenomenon. That energy, in and of itself, is nei-ther good nor bad. It's like a firearm, it's simply a tool. How you use it is determined by another's perspective, whether it's viewed as positive energy—good magic—or black magic."

Though Chonicki attended Catholic school, his interests lay else-where, and he became a junior Luciferian Satanist. By eighteen, he was initiated into the lodge as a full-fledged member. It was 1969.

When *The Satanic Bible* came out soon after, he immediately iden-tified with the secrets LaVey was disclosing. Chonicki experienced the hypocrisy of the Catholic Church firsthand: "Do as I say, not as I do"; "Be a good sheep, don't ask questions." The worst of it could be found in what Chonicki calls "the control mechanism of the sacrament of confession, when the parish priests basically have their finger on the pulse of the congregation, knowing where the sheep are heading." He found himself drawn to LaVey's observations about human nature, the perspective of the organist who played for the same men at a carny striptease show as he did at church on Sunday.

When Chonicki discovered he could contact the Church of Satan and acquire a basic membership, he decided to reach out. He eventually took the exam that promoted him to warlock. The church was just beginning to franchise grottos, and he was being considered to lead one in Western Pennsylvania.

He began receiving *The Cloven Hoof* in the mail. In one issue, he read an article that featured an English translation of a diabolical incantation. "Now keep in mind," Chonicki says, "this is going out to all the members, including the newbies, who are taking everything they read as gospel. And [the writer] is suggesting that the members use this as a meditation mantra. The purpose of a mantra or incantation is to act on our subconscious to think on this imagery, and this is one of the most dangerous of the incantations." One, he said, that could summon demons.

Chonicki wrote to the Central Grotto requesting that it publish a correction in a subsequent edition, to warn church members. He received a terse response, chiding him for lacking a sufficient understanding of Satanic philosophy.

"I wrote back, 'You're talking about fucking over your own membership. . . . This is not misinformation to your adversaries. You're looking to force something upon newbies who are trusting you.'" In other words, Chonicki says, the Satanic philosophy amounted to "If you're foolish enough to trust us without independent verification, then you deserve what happens to you." It was a way of thinning the herd. He wrote back and referred jokingly to "Uncle Anton."

"Apparently they felt that was disrespectful," Chonicki says. After he was asked to write an apology to the contributor of the translation, he responded, "That ain't happening."

Around ten days later he received a letter from Michael Aquino, advising that Chonicki's interests would best be served outside the Church of Satan and that his membership was being terminated.

"That," Chonicki says, "was my letter of excommunication."

In the spring of 1971, LaVey received an interview request from a fellow named Jack Fritscher, a thirty-two-year-old assistant professor at Western Michigan University who taught writing, literature, and film. At an American studies convention three years earlier, Fritscher had met Ray Browne, a Bowling Green State University professor who was starting up the first academic association devoted to the study of popular culture. It was the year before the Stonewall riots in New York City birthed the gay rights movement, and Fritscher, an activist and an out homosexual, insisted that there be a gay plank in the association's pop culture platform. After some discussion, Browne agreed.

Soon, Fritscher, who attended seminary for eleven years at the Vatican-affiliated Pontifical College Josephinum in Ohio, pitched Browne a book about witchcraft, an idea he'd hatched with a colleague at WMU, a retired English vicar's widow. When she balked at including Satanism in the mix, he went solo and was given a contract to write the first book for Browne's Popular Press imprint.

He began contacting witches through the mail after scouring ads in the back of tabloid papers, which in the late '60s and early '70s were big business—with the *National Enquirer* and its even scurvier ilk, such as the *National Insider* and the *National Tattler,* bringing scandalous grotesqueries to newsstands everywhere. The occultists would eagerly respond to questions he'd send. "My colleagues at the university, and everybody else I talked to thought, 'That's very nice,'" Fritscher says. "It was sort of a pat on the head. Because at that time, in American culture, witchcraft and Satanism were dismissed as simply Halloween—something like Hallmark Cards art."

Fritscher, who had studied Thomas Aquinas and Søren Kierkegaard, wanted to use his intellectual prowess in the service of interpreting pop culture, while still making the book entertaining. LaVey, he thought, would be a perfect subject since the culture was currently welcoming in the era of "radical chic." New Journalist Tom Wolfe coined that phrase to describe the concept of upper-class elites associating with people and ideas then considered revolutionary—as when composer Leonard Bernstein hosted a fundraiser at his Manhattan apartment in January 1970 for members of the Black Panther Party.

"San Francisco began to take LaVey in, in terms of the radical chic that he would represent to them," Fritscher says. "Among gay people, he was a little bit of interest. They didn't really know that much about him, but what they did know, they liked, because he offered an alternative. He seemed to be spitting in the face of Christianity, of the religions that had oppressed gay people." To those in San Francisco's gay community who were aware of him, Fritscher says, "LaVey was this camp figure who embodied all kinds of things that were considered both good and bad."

In fact, LaVey had been toying with the idea of Satan as a hermaphroditic deity, both female and male in one figure. He believed ritual transvestism could lead to men and women functioning more easily in public. Simply wearing fashionably androgynous clothing (trousers on women, beads and blouses on men) was not working. He encouraged men to wear a woman's wig, dress, stockings, and heels, and understand why they were doing it, a far healthier approach.

In those heady San Francisco days, Fritscher watched as pop culture evolved around him. It had begun earlier, when a gang of veterans showed up in the '40s after World War II, had a good time, and didn't want to leave. "They were basically the first bikers that started up in the East Bay," he says. Then in the '50s came the Beats, followed by the hippies in the Haight, and the gays on Castro and Folsom.

"The city began to fall in love with itself and with its diversity," says Fritscher. "Anton LaVey helped build that diversity, because once you've invited the high priest of the Church of Satan to your cocktail party, the social [scene] and Herb Caen and every place else begins to approve of him too. In a celebrity-hungry culture, he was ready to be launched into stardom, and he was already a star."

Intrigued by the academic's proposal, LaVey wrote Fritscher back, and after a couple of months of further correspondence, he agreed to meet. Fritscher, who by then was commuting between Kalamazoo, Michigan, and San Francisco, arrived at the house at the appointed time: midnight on Wednesday, July 28, 1971, as it turned into Thursday.

Standing in front of 6114 California Street, he was immediately struck by the singular blackness of the Black House. "When the gay people came into San Francisco," he says, "we painted all the Victorians, which had been beiged-out into white and gray, paling the colors of the Victorian woodwork." Those flamboyantly hued "painted ladies" are still visible all over town.

Diane opened the door and invited him to have a seat in Rasputin's sleigh chair in the red-ceilinged black parlor lit by candles, its windows obscured by black curtains. He took it all in: the animal heads, the fireplace mantel, the Baphomet wall hanging. "The whole room was done up like the set of a Vincent Price horror movie," Fritscher recalls, "very American International [Pictures]. But it worked."

He had seen his share of occult palaces, having interviewed Frederic De Arechaga, founder of the Sabaean Religious Order, at El-Sabarum, the warlock's Chicago store. "His church was disguised as an incense shop for hippies," Fritscher says, "but in the back it looked like a temple from a Rhonda Fleming movie about Simon Magus."

Satan's HQ wasn't anything like that. No, it was much more refined and meticulous. Fritscher was impressed by what he called the Victorian "collectorabilia"—the kind gay men would accumulate.

"It had a certain elevated taste you wouldn't have expected from an ordinary straight man," he adds. "But then LaVey was no ordinary straight man. He was a very liberated straight man who was into the finer things."

Fifteen minutes passed. "I was left alone to cool my heels," Fritscher says, "which I think was part of the whole drama, because this was a piece of wonderful performance art." Suddenly a bookcase opened up and out lumbered the stocky six-footer, wearing a clerical collar and red-lined vampire cape.

To signal his own otherness to his host, Fritscher, five foot ten, 150 pounds, was clad in a black cotton dress shirt, opened to expose his chest, as well as a leather vest and jacket, with black motorcycle chaps over his beat-up Levi's dungarees. "LaVey was very imposing," Fritscher says. "But I'm a leather top. I can be imposing too."

Immediately he felt welcomed by the couple. "They didn't blink," he says. "I really appreciated that, because out of the hundred or so witches I interviewed by mail, a large proportion didn't want to have any gay association. They were merchandising themselves to women and straight people. They didn't want to sully their reputations, because back then we were dirty people."

Fritscher sensed LaVey's intense charisma and had a specific interview approach that he knew would serve him well. "LaVey had a very definite power, because he was an alpha male who knew how to take over a room," Fritscher says. "I only deferred to him because I was asking the questions and he was the authority. But I approached the questions from an alpha point of view. I was not sucking up to him or subservient or wanting something from him. I challenged him and he liked that."

For one thing, Fritscher didn't want the interview to come off as adversarial. "I wanted to be his collaborator in terms of getting him to come up with new material: 'Don't tell me the old shit. Let's go somewhere fresh.'"

And go somewhere fresh they did, Fritscher furiously capturing it all on a yellow legal pad.

Right at the start, LaVey clarified his position on the existence of Satan: "I don't feel that raising the Devil in an anthropomorphic sense is quite as feasible as theologians or metaphysicians would like to think."

Then he tore into what he saw as Christian hypocrisy, citing the letters he received from "good Christians" condemning his church. "What is far worse than making war is making war . . . and saying it's 'waged under the auspices of God' or that 'It's the Christian thing to do,'" he inveighed. "Most Christians practice a basic Satanic way of life every hour of their waking day and yet they sneer at somebody who has built a religion that is no different from what they are practicing, but is simply calling it by its right name."

Of the various Protestant interpretations of the Bible, he told Fritscher, "Why the hell didn't the writers mean what they said or say what they meant when they wrote that stupid book of fables . . ."

Three hours after beginning their discussion, LaVey invited Fritscher to partake in a ritual, which involved a shirtless Fritscher kneeling before the fireplace, a Baphomet amulet dangled over his head, an invocation, and a bunch of "Hail Satan"s.

In the resulting book, *Popular Witchcraft*, Fritscher featured many other occultist interviews and surveyed devilry in films and music, among sundry other topics. "But LaVey was the star attraction," Fritscher says. "I knew then, and it proved to be true."

After Fritscher sent him a copy of the book, LaVey wrote back to say how much he liked it. "But I did not send it to him for his approval before I published it," Fritscher says. "And I thought, 'Am I violating something here?' I also didn't want to have a curse put on me." (The author later self-published the complete interview as a standalone book called *Anton LaVey Speaks: The Canonical Interview.*)

LaVey's influence would later surface in the author's three-year love affair, from 1977 to 1980, with the iconoclastic photographer Robert Mapplethorpe. Fritscher says Mapplethorpe had his own genuine interest in black magic and Satanism. "Robert appreciated the kind of humanism and materialism that LaVey taught," Fritscher says. "A lot of that LaVey imagery ended up in Robert's photography."

One photo, called "Cock and Devil" (1982), depicts a Mephistophelian figurine threatening to jab his pitchfork into a penis bound by a knotted leather cord. Another, a 1983 self-portrait, has Mapplethorpe posed as a different San Francisco icon, kidnapped heiress-turned-revolutionary Patty Hearst, holding a machine gun while standing in front of an inverted pentagram. And in the 1986 book *A Season in Hell*, for which he contributed photographs to accompany the prose poem by Arthur Rimbaud, Mapplethorpe, in another self-portrait, wears on his head a pair of comical devil horns similar to those beloved by LaVey.

"He was looking in all that for the dark side of sex and race and gender," Fritscher says. "Not that he joined the Church of Satan or read much LaVey, but he was aware of the pop culture surrounding LaVey. I was part of that to him, and we would discuss it. I called Robert 'the Prince of Darkrooms.'"

Looking back more than fifty years after his interview with LaVey, Fritscher is aware of some of the high priest's seemingly dubious claims—his possibly exaggerated résumé—but is not bothered by them and doesn't find them all that dubious anyway. "I swear to you on a stack of Bibles, stories I can tell you that seem like fantasy are real," he says. "I mean, I ended up in places with names that would shock people today. And everybody else I knew was having affairs with movie stars.

"I stay critical about it, but I believe Anton LaVey, whether he was a lion tamer for two nights or not makes no difference. If he only necked with Jayne Mansfield, I'll take that as a truth. Because it's more than other people did.

"With some people, you don't have to fuck them. All you need to do is kiss them to get their truth."

One foggy and drizzly Friday in late August 1971, when LaVey had Jacques Vallée and his wife, Janine, over for coffee, the scientist was alarmed at the sight of an eight-foot chain-link fence topped with barbed wire that had been newly erected in front of the old Victorian. LaVey, the local celebrity, was currently appearing both on the cover of *Look* magazine as well as inside *Newsweek*, both of which enjoyed circulations in the millions. A story in the latter linked murderers and Nazism to what the magazine called "his cult" (and featured a photo of Zeena's baptism). He was now attracting even more unwanted attention than usual.

"We had barely begun a discussion about hauntings when we heard the crash of glass breaking against the house," according to Vallée. "Anton and I rushed to the front. Diane was already there, gun in hand. Two men had tried to climb the fence." After sweeping up, Diane showed the others the shrapnel she recovered, shards of a Fanta Orange bottle.

"These people have no taste," Vallée told his host.

"Unfortunately, they rarely throw Château Lafite at us," LaVey responded. "I'm a threat to their mediocrity."

But there were few laughs to be had when, a few weeks later, the Department of Public Works, calling the barbed wire a danger to passersby, declared it had to go. Diane appeared before the Board of Permit Appeals to make the case that the spiky deterrent couldn't possibly hurt anyone "unless they were doing what it's there to prevent them from doing." Her appeal was denied. Quipped Herb Caen in his column, "You'd think he could just cast a spell."

By December, LaVey was finishing up a book of Satanic rituals for Avon, a companion volume to *The Satanic Bible*. In it, he laid out in scrupulous detail how to perform a number of ceremonies, including a few inspired by Lovecraft's Cthulhu mythology, H.G. Wells's *Island of Dr. Moreau*, and Fritz Lang's *Metropolis*. Its dedication page would end up rivaling that of LaVey's first book, with shout-outs to sixty-seven extreme, obscure, and often downright puzzling characters, including Nazi-adjacent naval officer and poet Bogislav von Selchow, composer Irving Berlin, film noir director Hugo Haas, avant-garde filmmaker and pal Kenneth Anger, actor Paul Robeson, bullfighter Juan Belmonte, blonde actress Kim Novak, head of Amsterdam's Church of Satan Maarten Lamers, Nazi commander Joachim Richter, film star Charles Chaplin, Nazi-adjacent race-car driver Rudolf Caracciola, and Tiny Tim. That last personality held particular appeal to LaVey, who had called the album *God Bless Tiny Tim* one of the most bizarre and magical things he had come across in a long time, as he praised the fish-voiced, tulip tip-toeing ukuleleist's ability to combine sentiment with wonder as few artists could.

When *The Satanic Rituals* was published just in time for Christmas in December 1972, one reviewer called it "a kinky gift for a kinky enemy. But nevertheless extremely amusing."

LaVey spent the evening of May 1, 1972, Walpurgisnacht, at home in the company of friends and church members. It was a night of revelry that featured a masterful organ performance of national anthems, including "Deutschland über Alles" and "La Marseillaise," which prompted one guest, Jacques Vallée, to write, "When he sits at the keyboard, Anton is a true magician, deliberate and smart under pretense of overt buffoonery. His group isn't a real church or sect, although he relishes scaring everyone with that notion. Its real purpose is to provide entertainment for himself and a steady supply of stimulating people to relieve his boredom."

A few weeks later Vallée brought over to LaVey's an older Frenchman named Aimé Michel, a UFOlogist and psychic experimenter and someone with whom the high priest was familiar. Like Vallée on his first visit, Michel expected to at least be entertained by his quirky host. "But," according to Vallée, "once he saw the genuine depth of the man he had first regarded as just another amusing charlatan, he changed his attitude and argued in earnest about psychic realities." The gathering became something of a mutual admiration society, with LaVey retreating to his keyboard to play for hours as his white bull terrier Typhon, who he claimed was the great-grandson of the dog in the film *Patton*, ran around banging into the furniture.

But Michel was not resistant to LaVey's ominous pull, later telling Vallée, "Either he has no powers, other than those of his strong personality, in which case he is not interesting except as a distant friend; or he does have powers and they are maleficent for those he touches, because he puts strength and personal realization above everything else. His system anticipates nothing except using others for his own profit."

One night in early December, Vallée returned to the house, and after they shared cheese and crackers, LaVey led his friend to the basement to show off some of his favorite books. "There we spoke of Patton, one of his heroes, and discussed *The Satanic Rituals*," Vallée wrote. "He launched into a dazzling series of anecdotes, literary references, circus lore, movie trivia, unknown musical traditions, exploits of espionage."

LaVey read aloud from the work of eighteenth-century Scottish poet James Thomson; the surrealistic fantasy *The Circus of Dr. Lao* by Charles G. Finney; and *The King in Yellow*, a collection of short horror stories by Robert W. Chambers. "People need someone to scare them," he told Vallée. "That's why they love those UFOs of yours. All animals are conditioned by fear, humans included. Their God scares them, and the Devil scares them, and now ecology, too, and flying saucers. You and I are different. We know that there is nothing to fear, ever."

People are afraid of their repressed side, LaVey reasoned, which is why they loved him—even as he stared at them while clutching a skull on the cover of *Look*. "I supply them with that fear without which they wouldn't exist," he said. "That fear defines them, makes them real."

Richard Lamparski, author of a popular series of books called *Whatever Became of . . . ?*, became intrigued when he first saw LaVey on the cover of *Look*. Though he specialized in reporting on the current lives of faded stars, the Los Angeles–based writer wanted a chance to meet this bright new one. He was on a book tour in San Francisco when he called the Black House to set up a dinner—his treat.

"Is it all right if I bring my wife along?" LaVey asked him.

"I won't know that until I meet her," Lamparski responded.

"He was very cheap, right from the beginning," the writer says more than fifty years later. "It tells you a lot about people. They're looking for something and they're not going to pay a dime. But it's all right. It's their time and they can price it however they want."

Despite, or perhaps because of, their playful combativeness, the two grew very close, spending hours discussing old and obscure Hollywood figures, like showgirl Toby Wing, character actor Dan Seymour, and

Maila Nurmi (a.k.a. horror hostess Vampira), as well as literary favorites like William Somerset Maugham.

"We clicked immediately—and by 'clicked,' I mean I was interested in him, and he was interested in me," Lamparski says. "I knew more people than he did, and he was dying to meet celebrities. But not everyone wanted to meet him. He didn't seem to understand that." LaVey often asked him to bring over autographed photos of movie stars, which his friend never did because, Lamparski says, "some of them knew who he was, and they thought he was a creep."

Even though LaVey did most of the talking, Lamparski, who admittedly played to his ego, considered him wonderful company. "He's laughing most of the time," the writer says. "It's often at someone else's expense, but that's better than someone who's gloomy all the time. The thing is—I learned this very early in life—you keep the ball in the air or you won't be asked back." And LaVey kept the ball in the air.

Unlike Vallée, Lamparski had no interest in the Church of Satan. "[LaVey] thought that I was a follower of his," he says. "There's nothing to follow. It's just, do whatever you please as long as it's legal, and who cares what the bourgeoisie thinks? And the thing is, he and [Diane] were so bourgeois. He would laugh if you told him that. But it was true."

Lamparski saw the church simply as a moneymaking opportunity— "the clubhouse of a grade-school boy"—that LaVey was so invested in because he had nothing to fall back on. "He really had no profession. People would go out and give him money, and he wanted money from everyone."

The writer acknowledges that fear was a key motivator for LaVey. "He wanted people to be afraid of him," Lamparski says. "For a lot of people— Hollywood people, particularly—it's like they want to find out where your chink is. Like all people with ego, he wanted to scare people.

"But I didn't think he was scary at all."

VIII.

The Wham of Sam

AND now, ladies and gentlemen, a man who needs no introduction. Please put your hands together for Mr. Sammy Davis Jr.!

In his 1989 memoir *Why Me?*, the most famous publicly acknowledged early supporter of the Church of Satan wrote of his fascination with the occult, admitting, "I wanted to have every human experience." For Davis, by any measure one of the most accomplished entertainers ever, those experiences also included snorting bowlfuls of cocaine, drinking heavily, having extramarital affairs, and appearing on *Celebrity Bowling*.

Born to Christian parents in 1925, Davis converted to Judaism in 1961, a few years after he lost his left eye in a car accident. He was introduced to the dark side during a 1968 visit to a Satanic orgy with a group of young actor friends, each of whom sported one red-painted fingernail, which Davis understood to be a sign Satanists used to recognize one another. "I was curious. Evil fascinated me," he wrote. "I felt it lying in wait for me. And I wanted to taste it."

At this old house in the Hollywood Hills, he saw a nude Young woman, splayed out and chained to a velvet altar. It didn't take long for Davis to suss out the scene. "I'd read enough about it to know that they weren't Satanists," he wrote, "they were bullshit artists and they'd found an exotic way they could ball each other and have an orgy." And, Davis reasoned, so long as she wasn't getting "anything sharper than a dildo stuck into her," he was game. As Davis enjoyed the evening's erotic delights, the identity of one of the ritual's hooded leaders surprised him. It turned out to be Jay Sebring, his (and Warren Beatty's and Frank Sinatra's and Jim Morrison's) hairstylist and friend, then a huge presence on the Hollywood scene and known to Davis as someone with a dungeon in his basement.

The following year, Sebring, who for a time was actress Sharon Tate's lover, would be shot, then stabbed repeatedly, killed alongside Tate and three others by members of the Manson Family, including former LaVey associate Susan Atkins. "Everyone there had at one time or another been into Satanism or, like myself, had dabbled around the edges of it for sexual kicks," Davis wrote, adding that he had run with Tate and Roman Polanski's crowd, and if he'd been in LA at the time of the gathering at 10050 Cielo Drive, he would have attended. "But something had saved me. The evil had missed me. But how close I'd come."

Indeed, Tate was no stranger to the occult, having been coached for her first film, *Eye of the Devil*, by British Wiccan high priest Alex Sanders and his wife, Maxine. In an interview for the podcast *The Last Bohemians*, Maxine recalled that as they became friendly, Tate told her something about being into "the craft."

Christopher Jones, an actor who claimed he had an affair with Tate when she was pregnant, said that once when he looked her way and asked what she was thinking, she suddenly exclaimed, "The Devil is beautiful. Most people think he's ugly, but he's not." At the time Jones thought the comment strange, but since Polanski had just made *Rosemary's Baby*, he shrugged it off.

Davis wrote that a week after the Hollywood Hills orgy, while in San Francisco for a concert, he met Anton LaVey, who warned him, "Don't get involved with this unless you really want to commit yourself to something." The entertainer, who says he returned to Los Angeles with a red fingernail—that high sign for the devilishly inclined—had apparently compressed this Luciferian chronology. He was actually introduced to LaVey a few years later.

On Wednesday, February 14, 1973, some five years after Davis's first brush with Satanism, NBC aired *Poor Devil*, a feature-length TV comedy pilot in which he starred as a bumbling, overeager junior demon named Sammy who's been shoveling coal in Hell's furnace for 1,400 years and thinks it's high time he got a promotion.

With the reluctant permission of his superior, Lucifer himself (played by British horror icon Christopher Lee), he ascends to San Francisco to bargain for his first earthly soul, one belonging to nebbishy department store accountant Burnett Emerson (*The Odd Couple*'s Jack Klugman), who wants to exact revenge on his unctuous boss (*Batman*'s Adam West). Throughout the telefilm, Davis, resplendent in primary-colored, wide-lapeled polyester suits, mugs ferociously for the camera, for his costars, for anything and anyone in sight.

The pilot was a big deal for Davis. Arne Sultan and Earl Barret, who wrote a weekly show for Sandy Duncan—another popular '70s entertainer with sight in only one eye—had the idea for a sitcom about a Devil's minion at the same time Davis pitched a similar concept to NBC, so the network put them together. Davis said he was "104% sure" *Poor Devil* would go to series. "Things couldn't be better as a singer, but it gives you a good feeling to find the right vehicle to be in people's homes every week." Calling the show "uncontroversial," Davis defended his *Poor Devil* character as a person "who can't do evil. . . . Everything he does turns out good." Besides, he said, "the Devil never wins: The church should like it!"

A mix of silly *I Dream of Jeannie*–style antics with garish *Batman* production design and bug-eyed vaudevillian shtick, the pilot failed to get picked up for a series. Word had it that NBC was displeased that church groups were writing in to the network complaining that the show depicted an associate of the Devil's in a positive light. With a hip-looking Lucifer and wall-to-wall pentagrams in its depiction of Hell, the film was seen as a sympathetic portrayal of LaVey's movement and even featured a shout-out to his church. In one scene Emerson tries to reach the Devil's emissary and says aloud to himself, "How am I supposed to get in touch with him when I need him? The Church of Satan downtown— they'll know how to reach him!" And when he dials the phone, Sammy indeed appears.

Two days after *Poor Devil* aired, Michael Aquino, tickled to see all the inverse pentagrams on network TV, drafted a letter to LaVey, informing him that the movie was "beautifully done . . . a magnificent commercial for the Church." He proposed that either he himself or LaVey reach out to Davis and offer him an honorary warlock degree. Aquino wondered if the connection could even lead to the producers offering LaVey a guest spot or using the Black House as a location. LaVey suggested that Aquino make the initial outreach and if Davis was amenable, the high priest himself could mail him a letter with a certificate and a pendant.

LaVey also sent copies of *The Satanic Bible* and another of his books to Davis's costar Christopher Lee, who later expressed doubts about LaVey's sincerity with regard to the occult: "Obviously, if it was true and complete Satanism, it wouldn't admit it." Lee said one of these books was inscribed by the author, "To Christopher Lee, a fine actor and a perfect devil, Anton Szandor LaVey."

"I took that as a compliment," Lee said, "and I don't think that's intended to be taken too seriously. . . . But the real thing is something which I wouldn't be prepared to discuss. . . . I would not even begin to discuss what actually takes place during a Black Mass because it is so appallingly blasphemous and so repulsive . . ."

In mid-March, Aquino received a response from Davis. The star would be thrilled to accept the honorary title and was thankful that the film hadn't caused offense. He also invited Aquino and LaVey to make the presentation during his engagement the following month at the San Carlos Circle Star Theater in San Mateo County, an hour's drive south of San Francisco, where he was booked to appear from April 10 to 16 with singer-actress Diahann Carroll. Before the show on Friday the thirteenth, Aquino, accompanied by Karla LaVey, bestowed upon the poor devil a warlock certificate, a Church of Satan membership card, and a Baphomet medallion, which the entertainer wore during that evening's performance.

"The original idea of the presentation as a simple gesture of appreciation—to be 'accomplished and filed' by both the Church and Sammy—began to seem quite shortsighted," Aquino later wrote. "Here was someone who was genuinely interested in Satanism—and not just in its public image, but in the deeper philosophies and concepts involved.

"On the other hand," Aquino added curiously, "Sammy Davis was one of the world's 'celebrity Jews.'"

While at the theater, Aquino and Karla were also welcomed by two members of Davis's entourage, publicist David Steinberg and road manager Murphy Bennett, who Aquino claimed expressed their own interest in Satanism and asked for copies of LaVey's books. "Sammy always enjoyed meeting people from different walks of life, if they had some kind of an interesting story," says Steinberg. "He was a sponge for information." This particular meeting, in Steinberg's recollection, was totally uneventful. "And, quite frankly, I found these people fairly silly."

The following month, according to Aquino, LaVey reached out to Davis, thanking him for accommodating the pair while also inviting the entertainer over for a tour of the Black House next time he's in town.

But then in June, Aquino claimed to have received from LaVey a sort of epistolary wrist slap. LaVey, pleased that his associate had charmed the entertainer, was nevertheless reconsidering how loudly he wanted to trumpet Davis's association to the church's members. He also told Aquino not to get too squishy over Steinberg's purported interest, suggesting, fairly astutely, that it was the publicist's job to feign enthusiasm for his star's diversions.

According to Aquino, in the letter LaVey called Steinberg a "professional Jew" who would not be happy with someone else wresting his authority over his client. In LaVeyan jargon, a professional Jew— or Catholic, for that matter—was one who grew up in a stifling, herd-like environment. "Some people that come from Jewish backgrounds, where Judaic traditions were really emphasized in the home, are the most rabid anti-Semitic people I know," he wrote. "And I don't blame them." Anyone he'd ever met who accomplished something "had a real disdain for his own 'people.'" LaVey suggested that whatever interest Steinberg might have in Satanism, public relations and Judaism were his true faiths, and he'd want Davis to remain devoted to the latter. In other words, Steinberg knew on which side his challah was buttered.

By August, Aquino wrote, LaVey and Diane enjoyed "a most memorable evening" with Davis at the entertainer's estate at 1151 Summit Drive in Beverly Hills. The three of them had another get-together, in October, only this time some friction appeared to have marred the meetup.

When Aquino visited Davis's wife, Altovise, in the hospital the following February, she dished that at the October gathering her husband introduced LaVey to Christopher Lee and the two didn't quite get along—possibly because Lee, who made a career out of playing sinister figures in dozens of horror films (even Satan himself in 1963's *Challenge the Devil*) and took a genuine interest in the occult, had no time for its practitioners. After Aquino let slip to Diane that Altovise had told him of the meeting, it was information he came to regret he knew.

LaVey wrote to him insisting that, from then on, Aquino clear with the high priest any contact he was to have with celebrities—and their spouses—lest there appear to be any confusion or disorganization within the church. Aquino wouldn't want to impede Satan's inroads into Hollywood now, would he? (Years later, Zeena, who, with then-husband Nikolas Schreck, produced an album of Lee's singing, refuted the claim that Lee and her dad even met. "Lee said Sammy was nuts about my father, but Lee saw my father as a 'Johnny-come-lately opportunist and con man' within the occult," she said. "Lee expressed that he had no intention of ever meeting LaVey.")

Anton, Diane, and Michael were all in attendance when Sammy returned to the Circle Star Theater for a nine-show engagement beginning March 29, with support by *Laugh-In* comedian Johnny Brown and the legendary dancing Nicholas Brothers. Davis, who had been hospitalized for chest and abdomen pain the previous month, recuperated in time for these shows, where, accompanied by a full orchestra, he sang such hits as "I've Gotta Be Me," "The Candy Man," and "Mr. Bojangles." Aquino would later recall Sammy flashing them the sign of the horns from the stage as he performed.

In a lavish display of post-gig largesse at Davis's hotel suite, the performer gave his three guests eighteen-karat gold bracelets as a sign of friendship. Playful snapshots were also taken. In one, LaVey, clad in a dark suit and light tie, rests his left arm around the diminutive Davis, who comes up to the high priest's shoulder, while a slick, sideburned Aquino in a hip turtleneck/jacket/Baphomet-medallion ensemble beams to Davis's right. In another, Davis, in a garish plaid jacket, wraps his arms around a similarly dressed Diane. "Anton and Sammy settled down to talk about Satanism," Aquino later wrote, "which both of them agreed was the wave of the future."

Aquino, who had apparently become a glutton for admonishment, managed to incur LaVey's wrath yet again after contacting Davis, without permission, to see if he'd agree to meet with Lilith Sinclair. She was "a true star of the Church of Satan," Aquino believed, and one with whom he was smitten. The New York–area witch was coming to the West Coast to visit Aquino in Santa Barbara and was a big fan, so could he maybe bring her around to the Davis mansion sometime? Aquino later learned from Diane that an angry Anton feared that Sammy might run off with the woman the high priest himself called a "stunner."

While he claimed his dalliance with the church was short-lived, Davis sure got a kick out of parading around with that red fingernail. "It was a turn-on," he wrote. "The chicks loved it." He defended his affiliation with these words: "However bizarre the subject, I don't pass judgment until I have found out everything I can about it. People who can put up an interesting case will often find that I'm a willing convert."

Davis wrote that his association with Satanism came to an end one morning after he experienced "a 'coven' that wasn't quite fun and games," but his attraction to dark spirituality apparently did not diminish. "Sammy told me he worshipped the Devil," the comedian Eddie Murphy, a friend of the entertainer's, said in 2019. "Sammy was like, 'You know, Satan is as powerful as God. . . . Why do you think there's so much anger in the world and killing and murder?'"

Despite *Poor Devil*'s failure, in late 1973 *The Cloven Hoof* was happy to mention that "Mr. Davis is now starring in the new *NBC Follies*, a series recalling the best of vaudeville to the screen. Those who extend the hand of friendship to Our Lord Satan rarely regret having done so."

Thirty-three years after Davis's death, David Steinberg was still doing damage control for his late client, insisting that the entertainer dabbled in the occult purely out of curiosity: "I'm telling you, Anton LaVey was a non-event in Sammy's life."

The writer Jack Boulware recalls once asking LaVey about the extent of Davis's involvement. The high priest gave a typically cryptic reply.

"He was one of our best recruiters."

IX.

Hell Ain't a Bad Place to Be

THE Reverend Adrian-Claude Frazier had a change of heart and, by March 1973, he was back leading Denver's Plutonian Grotto. And he had lots more to grumble about. He was once again writing, this time to Magister Michael Aquino (carbon copying LaVey), to report on a bad morale problem at the grotto, where doctrinal discussions turned into arguments and some of the men didn't respect the leadership of women. He also cited a lack of communication between the Central Grotto and local membership: renewals and orders were getting ignored, defective amulets were going unreplaced, calls to the church were being rudely dismissed.

Diane wrote back with an apology, claiming she and LaVey rarely stayed at the house anymore, having moved the family and most of their belongings to Sonoma County, north of the city. The bricks, bullets, eggs, spray paint—even a bomb—drove them out and away. In February 1974, trouble once again plagued the Denver grotto. Frazier, at Diane's suggestion, turned in the membership cards of three members. One, an apparent cocaine addict, slashed her wrists in a suicide attempt. The others were smoking pot in the open and snorting coke in the bathroom.

Another grotto leader, this one in Detroit, was suspected of pocketing money intended for church memberships and merchandise. The Stygian Grotto of Dayton, Ohio, had its share of problems as well. In addition to internal power struggles, two of its leaders were excommunicated when they were accused of dealing stolen goods. LaVey was glad to see these and other troublemakers exit. After they left, new organizations would crop up—the First Occultic Church of Man, the Church of Satanic Brotherhood—then fade away as quickly as they came, like some teasing apparition.

LaVey eventually felt embarrassed by members who took their Satanic cosplay to extremes. "I'd step off the plane and there they'd be, all huddled together to meet me in their black velvet robes and capes with huge Baphomets around their necks," he sniffed. "Many of our grass roots people didn't know much about subtlety then, or decorum. I was trying to present a cultured, mannered image and their idea of protest or shock was to wear their 'lodge regalia' into the nearest Denny's."

With *Rosemary's Baby*'s urbane cultists, comedian Flip Wilson's ubiquitous catchphrase "The Devil made me do it," Marvel Comics' Satana and Son of Satan characters, and the head-turning success of *The Exorcist*, both the novel and movie—the Devil, by 1974, had become a domineering presence in mainstream pop culture, infiltrating seemingly every genre of entertainment, as well as advertising. LaVey predicted a huge contingent of preadolescents and teens would swell the ranks of the church overnight and that the glamorous Lilith Sinclair's appearances on TV and in magazines on behalf of the church would have every American girl with an interest in gothic romance following her lead. About *The Exorcist*, LaVey may have tut-tutted, "This film allows failing priests a new role, whereby they can become heroes instead of useless poseurs." But he also called it "good, dirty, effectively photographed horror cinema" and envisioned that it "will bring many allies into the Satanic camp who had previously remained mute."

Then there was *The Devil's Avenger*, a vainglorious hagiography of the high priest, written by former church member Burton H. Wolfe, which Pyramid Books was about to publish as a paperback original. (The author, a close friend of LaVey's, would later lament that the book contained "inventions" and "fabrications" fed to him by his subject.)

But on this day, the Black Pope was in a blue mood.

An article in the *Santa Barbara News-Press* on November 14, 1974, found LaVey striking an atypically somber pose. Fed up with the endless parade of annoying looky-loos at his home and echoing Diane's concerns about harassment and vandalism, he said he had taken steps to secure the structure from the public, fortifying it with closed-circuit TV cameras and a ten-foot electrified fence. Though the building was still being used for church administration, to flee the anticipated Halloween hassles he decided to move his family temporarily into an associate's house in Montecito, 330 miles down the Pacific coastline.

Around that time, he also told Marcello Truzzi he was maintaining alternate addresses on South La Cienega Boulevard in Beverly Hills (an office building that also housed B-movie studio Crown International Pictures) and Heritage Court in Las Vegas. He said he had grown to prefer the honest kitsch of these other locations to San Francisco, which he felt had come to resemble New York City, replete with phony culture and exaggerated tradition concealing a dull provincialism. Still, the world saw San Francisco as a place of brash bohemianism, which ultimately was where his church belonged.

To the leader of the Church of Satan, LaVey told the *News-Press*, Halloween was "like New Year's Eve to a bartender." "Being indulgent and selfish," he added, "I don't want to become a martyr to my own cause, to be besieged on the equivalent of a sanctified day to Satanists."

He also announced he was essentially done with performative Satanic rituals. "The new type of Satanist is not the ostentatious or garish type," he said, "but a substantial, responsible citizen. Many new members prefer Satanism inside rather than on the sleeve." What he didn't mention was that in September he essentially dismantled the church's grotto system, after lamenting that a majority of the more public ones couldn't sustain themselves due to rivalries, misunderstandings, scandals, and prevailing coffee-klatsch atmospheres.

The article concluded with the news that LaVey was leaving Montecito imminently and heading down to Durango, Mexico. Producer Sandy Howard, who was making a movie about a cult of devil worshippers that takes over an Arizona town, had come knock-knock-knocking on Hell's door. He wanted to hire LaVey as a technical advisor to make sure the chanting sounded legit, the altars looked right, and the human sacrifices appeared, well, realistic. The film's irresistible title: *The Devil's Rain*.

With the success of *Rosemary's Baby*, which opened just two years after he established his church, LaVey continued to propagate the myth that he consulted on that film's Satanic shenanigans and appeared onscreen as the Devil. (*Polanski*, British journalist John Parker's 1993 biography of the director, features a long, unsourced section on LaVey's purported participation, which reads as if it came directly from the high priest himself.) "Since that film with Roman Polanski," LaVey said in

1971, "I am constantly confronted with scripts by thick-skulled exploitation producers who want me either to be technical advisor or play the role of the Devil or the Satanic doctor in their new films."

The Devil's Rain wouldn't be LaVey's first legitimate danse macabre with Hollywood. In 1969, he came in contact with Anthony Wilson, a writer and producer working as a story consultant for the TV Western *Lancer.* Wilson asked LaVey to vet the occult details in an episode titled "A Scarecrow at Hackett's," which centered on an enigmatic stranger who comes to town to secure a parcel of land where the Devil buried souls of the dead before he was ready to harvest them. In a letter to Kenneth Anger, LaVey went into great detail about a cameo he shot dressed in a Victorian frock coat with a silver cravat and black hat, as he assayed the Devil himself. The appearance, for which LaVey anticipated credits as both a technical advisor and "special guest," was touted in an issue of *The Cloven Hoof.* He must have been deflated, then, when he failed not only to make the final cut, but also to receive any credit whatsoever. Still, LaVey worked with Wilson again, advising on the script for the 1973 TV movie *The Horror at 37,000 Feet,* starring William Shatner, about an airline flight haunted by the ghosts of druids. (A few years later Wilson wrote and produced *Look What's Happened to Rosemary's Baby,* a made-for-TV sequel—this time with no input from LaVey.)

In 1970, director Paul Wendkos asked LaVey to consult on *The Mephisto Waltz,* a thriller based on a novel by Fred Mustard Stewart, which he was preparing for Twentieth Century Fox. Wendkos hoped that the film, about a dying Satanic piano virtuoso (Curt Jurgens) who transfers his soul and talent into the body of a younger man (Alan Alda), would "tear away many of the misconceptions about Satanism and the mystical world." He also said LaVey even offered the use of his home for location shooting. While the high priest's specific contributions to the movie remain unknown, the film does feature a few LaVeyan touches: a pentagram scrawled in blood on a floor, a room painted red, and a gaggle of randy Satanists wearing animal masks at a New Year's Eve party. Stewart admitted the success of *Rosemary's Baby* inspired him to write the book, and in an eerie coincidence, *Mephisto Waltz* costar Barbara Parkins, who plays a Satanist with an incestuous connection to her father, served as maid of honor at Sharon Tate's wedding to Roman Polanski.

Gauzy and overheated, *The Mephisto Waltz* is the kind of movie with so little feel for the way real human beings interact that it gives the best death scene to a dog. "That film still has the old elements of witchery," LeVay lamented. That's okay: Alda, who claimed he always had been interested in the occult—or what he characterized as the "powers of the mind"—had no use for LaVey's brand either. "I really don't want to get mixed up with Satanism," he said during production.

Though LaVey, who received no credit for his participation, flaunted his association with *The Mephisto Waltz*, in a 1971 *Cloven Hoof* article, Michael Aquino panned the film, calling it "a bomb, a cop-out, a flaming bore" and complained about its lack of "good ritual scenes" and "demonic manifestations."

LaVey claimed to have consulted on the script for the trippy 1971 feature *Simon, King of the Witches*, which he said had been researched from *The Satanic Bible*. With its unclothed sex-magic-ritual participants, the naked living altar who says, "Don't touch me, I'm a religious object," and the histrionic warlock on a quest for godhood, it's no stretch to believe that LaVey, whose contributions again went uncredited, had something to do with it.

Michael Aquino, then at Louisville's Nineveh Grotto, himself worked on the 1972 regional horror flick *Asylum of Satan*, providing costumes, props, and script suggestions, as well as coaching the film's demon character and pretend Satanists. For this one, "The Church of Satan" actually received an end credit.

LaVey also consulted on *Svengali the Magician*, an art-damaged exploitation picture by San Francisco director Paul Aratow, whose background in pornography, academia, and haute cuisine made him something of a Renaissance man. "The producers felt that [LaVey] might lend some information or credibility to the project," Aratow later said, before adding, "He was one weird dude. I do not think much of his advice was incorporated into the final film." Regardless, LaVey finally received acknowledgment in the credits. After a brief, unsuccessful run in San Francisco in 1974, *Svengali* was rereleased in 1977 as *Lucifer's Women*. And with the addition of new footage shot by schlock-movie maverick Al Adamson, it was later Frankensteined into a whole 'nother picture: 1983's *Doctor Dracula*.

But Sandy Howard was a different breed, a veteran player making some serious moves in the industry. Starting off as a director of TV's *The Howdy Doody Show*, he went on to produce the hit 1970 Western *A Man Called Horse*. That film starred Richard Harris as a white man among Native Americans, who as part of a Sun Dance ritual gets strung up by piercings through his chest, an image luridly and lovingly depicted on the movie's poster.

It was with this same dedication to verisimilitude—and his carny's instinct for ballyhoo—that Howard sought LaVey's guidance. The producer had done well with his two previous films—the cut-rate undersea disaster epic *The Neptune Factor* and the blaxploitation thriller *Together Brothers*—and like so many other showbiz machers, he wanted to chase the blood-and-bile-spattered dollars recently levitated by *The Exorcist*.

And he was on a roll, announcing in November 1974 that he had ten films in development, among them *Embryo* (a sci-fi shocker to star Rock Hudson) and *The Devil's Rain*. For the latter, Howard had originally teamed with Canadian producer Harold Greenberg to shoot in either British Columbia or Alberta for $1.2 million. But then he was approached by Bryanston Pictures, an independent distributor that had recently caused a stir with Andy Warhol's X-rated *Frankenstein* and *Dracula* films and made a mint with *The Texas Chain Saw Massacre* and Bruce Lee's *Return of the Dragon*. Bryanston offered to increase *The Devil's Rain*'s budget to $2 million ($12.5 million in 2024 dollars).

A seasoned pro like Howard had to have done his due diligence, so he must have known about Bryanston's unsavory reputation. The company was formed in 1972 by Louis "Butchie" Peraino, a member of New York's Colombo crime family who made his first killing in the movies with *Deep Throat*, the notorious porn flick made on a minuscule budget that went on to become one of the most profitable movies of all time. That same year, Peraino backed his first Devil-themed feature, *Legacy of Satan*, directed by *Deep Throat*'s Gerard Damiano, a troubled production that lurked on a shelf for two years before getting barely released.

With *The Devil's Rain*'s decent budget, Howard figured he could really put on a show. To direct, he enlisted Robert Fuest, who had recently found success with the stylish Vincent Price vehicles *The Abominable Dr. Phibes* and *Dr. Phibes Rises Again*, blackly comic Grand Guignols whose protagonist—a pipe organ–playing esoteric researcher, biblical scholar, and ex-vaudevillian with the first name of Anton—bore something of a resemblance to LaVey himself. Which, of course, led to its permanent inclusion on LaVey's résumé. Fuest, however, insisted there was no connection between the two, as did the character's creators. "I never met nor spoke to Mr. LaVey," said one screenwriter, William I. Goldstein. "I've never even heard of the guy," said the other, James Whiton.

For *The Devil's Rain*, *The Neptune Factor*'s Ernest Borgnine, who won an Oscar for 1955's *Marty* before breaking big on TV in *McHale's Navy*, was cast as Jonathan Corbis, the leader of a witch's coven seeking vengeance on the Preston family for something one of its ancestors did three centuries earlier. *Green Acres*'s Eddie Albert, another genuine small-screen star, would play a paranormal scientist on his trail. Film noir actress and pioneering director Ida Lupino signed on as the

Prestons' matriarch, after Mercedes McCambridge, who gave voice to the Devil's vile expletives in *The Exorcist*, decided to pass. As for the three other leads, William Shatner, Tom Skerritt, and Joan Prather had all just made *Big Bad Mama* for B-movie giant Roger Corman.

LaVey, who understood this movie could be a big deal for him, was impressed by the talent behind and before the camera, and was especially eager to meet the cinematographer, Álex Phillips Jr., who shot one of the Satanist's favorite films, *Yanco*. The 1961 Mexican drama concerns a boy, supersensitive to sounds, who meets a hermit who teaches him the violin. After the old man dies and the boy begins to surreptitiously play his instrument, the haunting music unnerves the townsfolk, who believe a diabolical force has been unleashed. At the time, LaVey had just finished an essay collection titled *The Devil's Notebook* and was working on a book called *Hell on Reels*, an investigation into movies with Satanic themes, of which *Yanco* was a prime example. (The former wouldn't be published for nearly twenty years, and the latter would never be.)

Michael Aquino later characterized the high priest's participation in *The Devil's Rain* as an attempt to legitimize and monetize his notoriety right at a time when the church was beginning to lose some momentum and luster. "It seems reasonable to conclude," Aquino wrote, "that Anton LaVey saw it as a vehicle which would move his 'center of gravity' from being the leader of a disappointingly imperfect Church of Satan to becoming the czar of Satanism in Hollywood films."

LaVey himself admitted that money was a motivating factor, at a time when he attempted to deemphasize the supernatural elements of Satanism but felt he had to indulge in them out of popular demand. "The remuneration was enticing and I'm a Satanist, you know," he said. "I don't have to be pious. I don't have to deny myself anything." Further justifying his participation, he explained that the movie "will deviate from the usual potboiler of good vs. evil. . . . The possessed people come out looking very sympathetic. They come out as being innocent victims of fanatical Protestants."

Still, he cautioned, there was only so much he could do. "What a shame that this film can't eliminate the idea that Satanists are bad and the other guys are good," he said. "That's still a hard nut to crack—that Satan has to be bad." He did, however, believe the movie could serve to spread the word about the concepts of the church, which at the time he claimed counted some twenty thousand members and more than two and a half million followers worldwide.

And that, for Anton LaVey, was enough.

Thirty years after its release, Robert Fuest called *The Devil's Rain* "a terribly difficult picture to shoot." From the start, the pinky-ringed iron fist of Bryanston slammed down hard on the production. "There was a cloud hanging over the financial situation," said Fuest, who claimed to have never even seen a budget.

Howard had decided to film in Durango both to approximate the story's American Southwest backdrop and take advantage of locations he used for *A Man Called Horse* a few years earlier. Right before filming was set to begin at the start of 1975, Fuest was immediately ordered to shave fourteen days from the schedule; what was originally an eight-week shoot had shrunk to six. There were also language difficulties with the largely Spanish-speaking crew, not to mention the director's refusal to communicate with his production and location managers.

Tom Burman, who worked with his brother Ellis on the movie's special effects, recalled New York gangsters being an overbearing, if occasionally helpful, presence in Durango. "The Mafia were there on the set," he said. "That was their money." At one point, Burman recalled, he had no oil to heat the house he was renting in the chilly Mexican winter. When one member of the production team, whom he described as "a movie thug," refused to supply any, Burman asked a facilitator named Vinnie. "Within an hour, we had a fifty-five-gallon drum of heating oil."

Once ensconced at the Hotel Campo Mexico Courts, LaVey set to work putting his cloven imprimatur on the ghoulish proceedings. This fan of old Westerns felt right at home on the windswept set in the wide-open spaces of this Central Mexican cowboy capital. It was, after all, John Wayne country, where the rugged American icon shot many films and even owned a ranch. Thrilled to finally exert some authority outside of his own highly circumscribed world—which could sometimes seem oppressively, hermetically sealed—LaVey relished sitting in his director's chair beside Borgnine, Lupino, and Shatner, eating meals with the actors, and sharing a bottle of Early Times whiskey with a wild-haired Fuest, in whom he found a compatriot. "Terribly nice guy," Fuest said later, adding, "and he was really one of the most normal people there. The whole Church of Satan thing, of course, was a total front, which Anton freely admitted to me. It was just a good idea that made him a lot of money."

Asking LaVey for input, Michael Aquino later wrote, "was rather like inviting Sylvester the cat into Tweety Bird's cage." In LaVey's hands, "the anemic coven became transformed into the most sinister of Satanic grottos, the singsong chants became blood-and-thunder incantations of sizzling power, and the 'witchy' decorations in the coven's meeting hall and canyon-hollow metamorphosed into black and silver Satanic Art Deco—with geometric trapezoids, stylized beast-heads, and fiery Baphomets."

Among his other contributions, LaVey wrote the Satanic congregants' chants, using the occult-constructed language of the Enochian Keys, ritualistic hymns taken from *The Satanic Bible*. He even crafted phonetic cue cards for the mostly Mexican day players to read slowly and spookily, stuff like OD-VARBAY-ZODIREY GA MAY LEEAXA OD BA HALA-NE-EE-SO. Corbis's initial incantation begins with the "Invocation to Satan" from *The Satanic Bible*, and he later recites bits of "Ceremony of the Nine Angles" from *The Satanic Rituals* and "The Eighteenth Enochian Key" (this one in English: "O mighty light and burning flame of comfort, enter this body and cleanse it of its unworthy soul!"). Without LaVey's guidance, Borgnine likely wouldn't have known how to bend his fingers into the sign of the horns and slice them through the air in the shape of a pentagram, a Satanic version of the sign of the cross.

Still, nearly fifty years after the movie's release, LaVey's contributions were in dispute. "Anton LaVey really had nothing to do with the movie," says coscreenwriter Gabe Essoe. "I believe I spoke with him on the phone once, but don't remember the conversation, not one bit."

Even coproducer Michael S. Glick, hired by Sandy Howard to oversee the shoot, had no memory of LaVey's participation, despite acknowledging that, yes, his name does appear on the poster. "I was there for four months, from the beginning to the end, and I never met him," he says. "He might've helped with the story, but I didn't see him on the set"—photographic and cinematographic evidence to the contrary.

LaVey himself appeared briefly in the film, playing Corbis's unnamed ritual assistant, though a golden helmet embossed with a goat's head obscured the top half of his face. His one line had two words. In response to Corbis's query, "Has a soul been prepared to receive a new body?" LaVey sneers, "It has." Diane also had a small speaking role, as Corbis's wife in a flashback sequence. "She was very exotic-looking, very striking," says script supervisor Ana Maria Quintana. "She had that typical Satan kind of look."

Quintana recalls the couple being particularly transfixed during the sequence in which Corbis's church burns down. "I do remember that they were acting very strangely," she says. "I don't know if it meant something to Anton and Diane. They really kept to themselves. They sort of just always watched."

Perhaps not surprisingly, LaVey's presence on set provoked among the cast and crew some soul-searching and contentious discussions about religion. Lupino admitted to having misgivings at first. "I was dreading meeting LaVey," she said during production, "because there's a lot of Satan in and around us. That's why I've been wearing this crucifix all the time I've been here." (In the end, she said she found Anton and Diane to be "very charming people.")

And despite his history with Sandy Howard, Borgnine had a few reservations about starring in the picture. "I wondered if my image could take it," he said. "But then the challenge of the role got to me, and I figured if Spencer Tracy and Fredric March could do those kinds of parts, why not me?" In a strange coincidence, one of the actor's previous roles, on the TV series *Little House on the Prairie*, was a guardian angel who also happened to be named Jonathan.

For *The Devil's Rain*, Borgnine immersed himself in literature about Satanic practices. "But once the film ended, those books went right back to the library shelves," he insisted.

"I believe in getting very close to the part I'm playing," he said, adding that LaVey saw his approach to the role as an indication that the actor was interested in the Church of Satan. "In any event he asked me to join his congregation. But I couldn't go that route. I explained that though I was playing the Devil, I'm really a God-fearing man. I was raised a Catholic and I've fallen away. But I couldn't go as far away as that."

Still, the actor said he was thrilled by LaVey's offer to make him an honorary priest in the church. "Of course, I'm going to accept it," Borgnine said. "He's for every man having his own religion. I think that's a fine way to be in a world where many people wear blinders."

Eddie Albert, on the other hand, was not buying the hoodoo that LaVey was peddling. "This current fascination with the Devil intrigues me," he said. "I consider it some kind of peculiar wart on the current face of our culture. I'm trying to figure out what vacancy exists that would create such a need." He supposed it was the result of some rampant, widespread tension or anguish, the grasping for some kind—any kind—of spirituality. "I think this little aberration of Satanism is . . . a rip-off, for God's sake." Even on set, he didn't keep his disdain to himself. Tom Burman remembered Albert asking him one day in the makeup chair, "What the hell am I ever doing working on a piece of crap like this?" Albert, soon to embark on the TV series *Switch*, did, however, accept Marcello Truzzi's phone number from LaVey, who recommended the actor ring up the professor to prepare for his role as a detective who uses con artist tricks to bust criminals.

For his part, Shatner didn't have much contact with LaVey during the shoot. "I suppose that is not surprising," the actor later wrote. "What would I have asked him, 'Is this the way Satan holds his fork?'"

Whether it was reality or just some public-relations bunk, Shatner did, however, recall a few odd occurrences when he took a hunting trip with some locals. "Things went wrong that apparently had never happened before," he said. "People cut their hands. The oars of our canoe broke, the pattern of birds was impossible to follow. Finally, the canoe tipped over. And these people were sure it was the presence of the devil in Durango."

That wasn't his only bad memory. A photographer from *Playboy* had been sent to the set to shoot actress Lisa Todd in the scene where Shatner's Mark Preston, wearing nothing but a loincloth, was being offered up to Satan. While his hands and feet were secured to the altar, Todd, playing the seductress Lilith, began touching him: first his arm, then his chest, then his abdomen. "Untie me!" the actor yelled, a line not in the script.

"I was grappling with a photographer who had taken partially nude pictures of me being groped by an almost-naked starlet, while being sacrificed by Ernest Borgnine, as the founder of the Church of Satan looked on dispassionately," Shatner recalled. His effort to reclaim the film was apparently unsuccessful; in November 1975 *Playboy* published a photo of the buxom Todd, in a see-through, blood-red negligee, fondling the actor.

Dressed as he was in dark shirts, a turtleneck, jeans, leather car coat, and cap, LaVey cut quite a striking figure on set—"like a sort of failed U-boat captain or something," recalled Fuest. LaVey, however, didn't make the slightest impression on one of the stars, despite their having been photographed together. Once asked about LaVey's participation in the film, Tom Skerritt responded, "I have no idea who he is" before figuring he must have met the guy at some point.

Odd man out among all these veterans was a young actor named John Travolta, making his feature film debut. He had arrived in Durango depressed that for his first movie he'd be playing an eyeless cult member mostly hidden beneath a robe. He'd also have only one one-word line of dialogue—actually, one word screamed twice: "Blasphemer! Blasphemer!"

Noticing Travolta's distress, Joan Prather, one of the production's few English speakers close to his age, handed him a copy of *Dianetics*, a book purporting to offer the secrets of the modern science of mental health, written by L. Ron Hubbard. "He glommed on to me from day one," Prather said of Travolta. "He was extremely unhappy and not doing well." She told him about how much the practices and techniques of Hubbard's Church of Scientology had helped her.

"She gave me some auditing sessions and applied some basic principles," Travolta said. "That was when I became involved in Dianetics— because it worked."

Not to be upstaged, LaVey, who was photographed with his arm around Travolta while wearing a T-shirt emblazoned with the words "Bates Motel" (the site of carnage in Alfred Hitchcock's *Psycho*), claimed to have performed a success ritual for the actor, who turned twenty-one during the shoot.

Upon returning to Los Angeles, Travolta visited Scientology's Celebrity Centre to begin training and auditing, a process intended to rid a person of negative influences from past events. "My career immediately took off," he said, "and I landed a leading role on the TV show *Welcome Back, Kotter* and had a string of successful films." He has since become one of that church's best-known and most vocal supporters. (LaVey was acquainted with Hubbard, with whom he had a mutual friend in monster-magazine editor Forrest J Ackerman, the Scientology founder's erstwhile literary agent.)

One week before LaVey was set to wrap, his time on the film came to an abrupt end. "You may simply say that a situation arose where I felt I was being minimized," he told *Argosy* magazine writer Dick Russell, who'd visited Durango. "I was able to crystallize and direct the energy of some people who felt the way I did. The results were rapid. Extremely rapid. I found I was soon blamed for all kinds of things. They were glad to get rid of me. And I was delighted."

Russell asked crew members about LaVey. The responses: "A bent Billy Graham." "A stimulating conversationalist." "A true connoisseur of the arts." "Just say his brand of Satanism began to clash with the director." Not exactly. Apparently, LaVey instead had butted heads with associate producer and coscreenwriter Gerald Hopman, who Essoe said "wasn't a talented individual at all."

"I resent it when people place me in that position," LaVey told Russell. "Nothing angers me more than *that*, and when I retaliate it's not because I want to. I've just been pressed too far, that's all."

The movie wasn't even opening for another three months, and it was already being ridiculed. One syndicated newspaper column in March 1975 had this report:

Another disaster: Down in Durango, Mexico, a bunch of old-timers headed by Ida Lupino, Ernest Borgnine, Eddie Albert and Keenan Wynn have all but been washed away in a tidal wave for a new disaster epic called *The Devil's Rain*. Anton LaVey, high priest of the Church of Satan in San Francisco, is also on hand, playing a part and acting as technical adviser. His contract called for him to remain true to life and never commit a good deed.

The last bit no doubt referred to a hyperbolic press release issued by the production, which read in part, "[LaVey's] evil commitment is insured by the strangest contract in entertainment history which binds him to total unChristian behavior and forbids him to commit any but inhuman acts."

After a brief postproduction period, Bryanston got the movie into theaters by June 1975, just as the Vatican publicly asserted its belief that Satan was a literal being, not just a metaphor—reaffirming Pope Paul VI's controversial pronouncement in 1972 that the Devil was in fact a fallen creature of God, not merely a representation of evil. It was a claim shared by Michael Aquino, who wrote in *The Cloven Hoof*, "Indeed Satan exists. Not as just a myth, nor as a mere psychological archetype, nor as just a colorful figure of speech—but as an essential, intelligent entity."

Certain he had a blockbuster on his hands, Butchie Peraino pumped a bundle into promoting the film. Below the bold and puzzlingly ungrammatical tagline "Heaven help us all when THE DEVIL'S RAIN!" the garish newspaper ads blared, "With the Special

Participation of ANTON LAVEY, High Priest of the Church of Satan." And they positively bellowed, "ABSOLUTELY THE MOST INCREDIBLE ENDING OF ANY MOTION PICTURE EVER!"—hyping the ten-minute sequence in which the titular meteorological anomaly causes the coven members' bodies to explode, melt, and drip into gloopy, burbling, rainbow-hued puddles.

In perhaps the film's biggest promotional splash, Forry Ackerman ran a six-page, photo-filled *Devil's Rain* feature in his popular magazine, *Famous Monsters of Filmland*.

Roger Ebert, in his *Chicago Sun-Times* review, had kind words for Ernest Borgnine, writing that the star "works up a fine fiendish cackle and a passable growl," but panned the movie as "painfully dull." In the *New York Times*, Richard Eder wasn't nearly as nice, calling the extended orgy of liquescense "as horrible as watching an egg fry." *Variety* labeled the film "very commercial" but dismissed the screenplay as "amateurish" and the performances as "pedestrian." According to Rex Reed in the *New York Daily News*, it was "inane gibberish" and "ludicrously unconvincing."

One interested party, Michael Aquino, was very impressed with what he saw, claiming the film featured "the most striking and authentic Satanic ritual sequences ever brought to the screen." His one gripe: "The *only* Satanist with any character, initiative, power, and vitality was Borgnine himself. All of his followers were mindless robots, waxen-faced zombies capable only of carrying candles and chanting."

LaVey himself ultimately had this to say: "Robert Fuest . . . really had no concept of what this picture was all about, and it was really Borgnine's demonic personification that saved it. He gave the role, and the picture, power and stature."

Having eventually earned a reported $6 million, the film was deemed a disappointment relative to Bryanston's expectations. Long after it had been revived and reconsidered as a flawed yet atmospheric time capsule, critic Michael Adams wrote what is probably the most fitting epitaph for *The Devil's Rain*, which he called "the ultimate cult movie": "It's about a cult, has a cult following, was devised with input from a cult leader, and saw a future superstar indoctrinated into a cult he'd help popularize."

In June 1975, just as *The Devil's Rain* was hitting theaters, Michael Aquino sent a letter to certain church members revealing that he was resigning from the editorship of *The Cloven Hoof* and severing his ties with the Church of Satan. At issue: his disagreement with LaVey over an article scheduled to appear in the May/June edition, announcing that financial and material donations to the Central Grotto at 6114 California Street will enable the donors to advance to the degrees of witch and warlock (II°) and priest or priestess of Mendes (III°). LaVey previously had awarded honorary titles to the likes of Sammy Davis Jr., but Magister Templi IV° Aquino, whose rank was one grade below Lavey's, characterized this new shortcut as prostitution and a corruption of the church's values. "Since the founding of the church, elevation to all of the degrees has been only through personal intelligence, dedication, and accomplishment," he wrote, before declaring that the organization "no longer carries the true sanction of the Prince of Darkness."

He had also been dismayed earlier in the year after seeing Tony Fazzini, Anton's longtime driver and bodyguard, sporting a blue Baphomet medallion signifying IV°, making him a Satanic priest. Aquino told LaVey it was a "slap in the face" to church members who had worked hard to earn theirs. He did not resign his own IV° status, however, since he claimed to have stripped the LaVeys of their ranks and was now authorized to carry what he called the "Infernal Mandate." Satan himself told him so. In fact, he compelled Aquino to write a document called *The Book of Coming Forth by Night*, which was to be the basis of the magister's new religious society, one that he promised would be sanctioned by the Prince of Darkness.

The firestorm set off by Aquino's initial letter led to the exodus of a number of other officials—including the Lilith Grotto's Lilith Sinclair, priestess of Mendes III°, and the Asmodeus Grotto's Robert Ethel, priest of Mendes III°—and a few dozen members. It was a schism from which the Church of Satan would never fully recover.

LaVey responded to Aquino's abdication with a letter of his own, writing to those same recipients that the magister had "become too large for his trousers" and "if others reinterpret my organization and philosophy into a fundamental kind of supernaturalism, it stems from their needs to do so." In other words, Aquino had turned into what the high priest mockingly called an "occultnik," and LaVey had no time for that mindset. "If you want to split, go ahead," he wrote. "I won't soft-soap you into thinking that there are no hard feelings, because there sure as Hell will be. But I'll soon get over them. I have too much to do."

As he dealt with the crisis in the church, LaVey escaped *The Devil's Rain* unscathed—coscreenwriter Gabe Essoe even had him contribute to his 1981 *Book of Movie Lists*—but for some of the movie's other principals, the film must have seemed cursed. Robert Fuest's career never recovered from the disastrous notices. Not long after the film's release, production manager Terry Morse Jr. was arrested and Sandy Howard was detained in Greece for several weeks after an explosion on the set of their subsequent film, *Sky Riders*, killed a local electrician. While there, Howard also received a threatening phone call from Bryanston regarding a financial dispute. "I did feel a certain amount of hot Sicilian breath on my neck," he said. "Let's say my nose was being threatened, and my ears, etc."

By 1976, the mobbed-up movie company had been rubbed out. Then, in 1977, Peraino received a one-year prison term and was ordered to pay a $10,000 fine after being convicted along with seven others of conspiracy to distribute obscenity across state lines—in this case, his original cash cow, *Deep Throat*.

In what is perhaps the cruelest of ironies, *The Devil's Rain*'s box office might have fallen short due to the success of a similarly Luciferian exploitation film that had recently been released; *Race with the Devil*, starring Peter Fonda and Warren Oates, went on to gross $12 million. And what may have smarted the most: that film featured in a supporting role Clay Tanner, the actor who—LaVey's boasts to the contrary—actually played the Devil in *Rosemary's Baby*.

LaVey claimed to follow up *The Devil's Rain* with another advisory role, on a 1977 movie called *The Car*—about a customized Lincoln Continental that runs people over in a Utah desert town. He did receive credit, but it's on the screen-filling quotation from *The Satanic Bible*'s "Invocation Employed Towards the Conjuration of Destruction" that opens the movie: "Oh great brothers of the night, who rideth upon the hot winds of Hell, who dwelleth in the Devil's lair; move and appear!" That seems to have been his sole contribution. "I know nothing about LaVey's participation in the production or postproduction," says Michael Butler, one of the screenwriters. He and his partner, Dennis Shryack, initially wrote the film as a landlocked riff on *Jaws*. "There is no theology in there whatsoever," Butler says, adding that the picture's occultic elements were so unspecific, LaVey's input would have been entirely unnecessary.

X.

Anton's Inferno

IN April 1976, Jacques Vallée met with LaVey to discuss a recent development that had cast a bad light on the church—a report by Donald Flickinger, a special agent with the US Bureau of Alcohol, Tobacco and Firearms, that claimed a nationwide network of Satanists was responsible for a spate of cattle mutilations and was incorporating the animals' blood and genitals in rituals. According to Vallée, LaVey dismissed the report as "a fabrication by the hippies at the *Berkeley Barb*." It also warned that the cultists planned to target government leaders for sacrifice at the start of 1976. "I'd have known about it, if the SFPD had uncovered serious evidence," LaVey told Vallée. "I work closely with their Intelligence unit. They call on me when they have a crime that involves witchcraft or cults . . ." To buttress his point, he took out his wallet and showed his friend a badge purportedly issued by the San

Francisco Police Department. That LaVey would have such connections made perfect sense to Vallée.

The report was discredited after law enforcement sources said the agent had been misled by two prisoners who fabricated the stories. "It may make good reading, but ninety percent of it's pure hogwash," Flickinger was forced to admit.

Some fifty years after first meeting LaVey, Vallée says he became interested in the high priest while conducting a survey of major sects and cults gravitating around new age themes related to UFOlogy, ranging from what he considered the sinister—like LaVey's church—to the escapist, frivolous, and pseudoreligious. In the early 1970s, Vallée says, other researchers were concerned with such sects' influence, including their mutual friend, Marcello Truzzi.

"My own research," Vallée says, "has no such academic credential but it included half a dozen other groups or UFO churches I observed for periods of a few months, including the Two, which became Heaven's Gate.

"I reported on it," he continues, "and published a stern warning against joining that group with the potential to meet a tragic end, which indeed took place about ten years later." In March 1997, cult leader Marshall Applewhite and thirty-eight members committed suicide under the impression that their souls would then be lifted up, board a spacecraft traveling behind the Hale-Bopp comet, and relocate into alien bodies.

For all of the Church of Satan's cynicism, Vallée was never concerned about it wading into this kind of apocalypticism. "[The church] was not so much an esoteric school as a social experiment, mixing literary and poetic imagery with some of the themes dear to Hollywood at the time," he says. "It maintained a healthy sense of humor, at least in those early days."

In his contemporaneous journals, Vallée wrote, "Among the fakeness of the current 'revolution' he is saving a little piece of weird creativity. Behind his charlatan's front, Anton has built a mind cathedral, not to an obsolete Satan as he wants his followers to believe, but to that major power of our time, the secret goddess of Absurdity.

"To the chagrin of his followers who worship a Halloween devil," he continued, "Anton is an intelligent cynic who looks with detached humor at the fakery of pompous academe, the vacuity of politics, the silliness of the media, and the pretentiousness of the righteous."

Vallée was, however, critical of his friend's avowed misanthropy. "Anton fails," he wrote, "because he has no interest in humanity in a broad sense, no empathy for the downtrodden, the real greatness of the Earth." Vallée rejected LaVey's philosophy of self-deification because "the man who is concerned with his own power and well-being only achieves a hardening of his unconscious, the sclerosis of his dreams."

In the end, Vallée—who, in a long, distinguished career helped NASA map the planet Mars, inspired the Claude Lacombe character in Steven Spielberg's flying-saucer epic *Close Encounters of the Third Kind*, and assisted in the development of the proto-internet ARPANET—decided that since LaVey and his church members showed little interest in his main area of study, UFOlogy, he would keep his distance. "His opinion about UFO reality was openly skeptical," Vallée says, "and he also treated parapsychology mostly as occasion for entertainment."

Still, throughout his life, LaVey held much appeal to intellectuals. In 1978 he was offered $125 to speak over the Labor Day weekend at Asilomar 13, the thirteenth annual conference of a local Mensa group. The event's theme humorously embraced witches, warlocks, and magicians. Enough members of the high-IQ society knew of his philosophy that LaVey was assured they'd be receptive to what he'd have to offer. For reasons unknown, he did not appear.

To the Devil, a grandchild.

On January 18, 1978, a fourteen-year-old Zeena gave birth to a boy she called Stanton Zaharoff LaVey. His first name echoed both Anton's original middle name and the protagonist of *Nightmare Alley*; his middle name honored one of Anton's heroes, arms dealer Basil Zaharoff. The family has never revealed who the father was, and as an adult, Stanton himself claimed to not know the man's identity.

Zeena would later say that becoming a young mother was inevitable. "My father taught me how to crack a bullwhip at nine," she wrote in the 1989 introduction to *The Satanic Witch* (a retitling of *The Compleat Witch*), adding that at eleven she already had the power to manipulate the opposite sex, owing to the witchiness that surrounded her at home. "Seeming much older than my years and going out with guys who were older still, it should come as no surprise that I became pregnant at thirteen . . ." One of her father's friends, biographer Burton H. Wolfe, made Zeena's appeal explicit in a letter he wrote to her when she was eleven, ostensibly praising her potato salad. In it he volunteered that, as Anton foresaw in her baptismal ceremony, with her looks and ability to cook, any man she desires will be an easy target.

"I viewed the lifestyle of other teenagers with disenchantment," Zeena wrote. "Consequently, with the responsibility of raising my son came a freedom my peers were not privy to. I was now a woman." Relatives tried to discourage her from keeping the baby, she claimed, saying it would only bring hardship and prevent her from eventually attracting other men. For Anton's part, he told Marcello Truzzi that becoming a grandfather had a positive effect, making him feel very patriarchal, despite remaining as misanthropic as ever.

"[As] 'the devil's daughter,' a teenager with living proof of her carnal knowledge," Zeena wrote, "I put the formulas of *The Satanic Witch* to good use." She found ways to tempt various types to get what she wanted—"everything from married lawyers and policemen twenty years my senior to juvenile delinquents and bikers who volunteered to kill anyone who bothered me."

She told a different story to the City College of San Francisco's student newspaper in 2016, saying the school's free tuition rescued her from a dysfunctional family. Claiming her parents forced her to move two weeks after delivering her son, without providing any financial support, she said she "was desperate to find a way out of a hopeless situation." Stanton, however, maintained that Diane co-parented him until age five, when Zeena left home and took him with her.

As 1979 turned to 1980, LaVey attended a party at the home of the hotelier, real-estate developer, and Democratic contributor Donald Werby, and his wife, Willy, a daughter of the founder of Chock Full o'Nuts coffee, in Hillsborough, a wealthy town south of San Francisco. Also in attendance was nineteen-year-old UC Berkeley student Don Frew, a friend of their son Christopher. Frew had enjoyed *The Satanic Bible* and *The Satanic Rituals* in junior high, but the spiritual path he followed bent toward Wicca, a modern pagan religion whose devotees worship nature, observe the cycles of the seasons and the moon with ritual, and practice magic to enhance their lives. "The Nine Satanic Statements were something I could get behind," he says. "Most modern progressives could get behind most of it." He was excited at the prospect of meeting the author. At one point during the evening, Christopher took Frew over to LaVey, who was standing alone, enjoying a cocktail. "This is my friend Don. He has disagreements with how you translate Enochian."

Explaining away the awkward introduction, Frew says, "I'd commented to [my friend] at some point that the Enochian [Keys] in *The*

Satanic Bible were not really translated the way most people would translate them. They're translated in a way that favors Satanism."

Left to fend for himself, Frew ended up chatting with LaVey for an hour. The following month Frew had his first meal with his new, older friend. Then came others. The young man always showed up at the house after sunset and usually left around 7:00 a.m. He took copious notes on those meetings, hoping to catch whatever magical morsel LaVey might proffer. "He'd be telling stories," Frew recalls, "and often you'd have to listen carefully for the twist, where the actual teaching was."

At their first dinner, after Frew inquired about joining the Church of Satan, LaVey told him, "Don't worry. I'd be very proud to have you in our group. I think you'd be a worthy and worthwhile addition."

"That struck my ego to no end," Frew says.

One of the few times Frew saw LaVey away from the house, in daylight, was when they both attended a March 1980 screening of *Freaks* at the UC Berkeley Art Museum. Both LaVey and Willy Werby had a personal attachment to the controversial 1932 film, which starred real-life sideshow performers. Werby was one of the founders of San Francisco's Camera Obscura Film Society, and in the late '50s, at LaVey's insistence, she searched for a print of *Freaks* to screen in a program of horror classics. She contacted a producer and distributor named Dwain Esper, who had acquired the rights from MGM and played it on the lowdown exploitation circuit. After Werby bought the rights, she began circulating intact prints of the film—which over the years had been recut and censored—bringing it to new, appreciative audiences and turning the spotlight on a dark, misunderstood masterpiece.

When LaVey had Frew over for dinner one night, he told the young man a story about his time with Marilyn Monroe. "It was a Tuesday and there was a storm going on," Frew recalls. To add to the melodrama,

LaVey said that when he met her, "it was a rainy Tuesday, just like tonight." This was before she became a star, and LaVey said that they had hooked up at a theater where they both were working.

"She gave him some sheet music," Frew says, "and he said it was some 'very slow, sensuous, and languorous striptease'—those were the words he used." Marilyn had really milked the performance, which greatly impressed her accompanist. Right after she got offstage, the venue's manager came up to LaVey. "Don't ever play that crap again," he spat. LaVey and Monroe went out for a drink afterward, which began an affair that he told Frew lasted about a month.

The conversation shifted to the upcoming 1940s-themed costume party LaVey was throwing for his fiftieth birthday. Frew, who had long hair at the time, was struggling to figure out what he was going to wear. LaVey suggested he come as eden ahbez, a lowercased, bearded eccentric who lived under the Hollywood sign in the '40s and dressed, Christ-like, in robes and sandals. Adding to his mystique, ahbez also wrote "Nature Boy," which became a number-one hit for Nat King Cole in 1948, as well as other songs recorded by such artists as Eartha Kitt and Sam Cooke. LaVey thought the garment should look like a boxer's robe, with a name emblazoned on the back: "Serutan Yob," "Natures Boy" in reverse.

"I didn't really get it," Frew says, "but if LaVey thought it was funny, fine, I'll go with it."

When it came time for LaVey to decide what he himself would wear, he opened the bookcase and entered the red-walled room where he kept his collection of knives, costumes, and ritual gear. As LaVey donned a '40s suit jacket, he noticed something crinkling in one of the pockets. "He reached in, pulled out an old wadded-up piece of paper, opened it up, and it said, 'Tony, ran down to the pharmacy, back soon. Love, Marilyn,'" recalls Frew, who adds that this surprising synchronicity immediately prompted LaVey to choose that outfit for the party. It also prompted Frew to consider that maybe, just maybe, magic followed LaVey after all.

"I've always thought, 'That would be a lot of setup if this was all just to convince me that he knew Marilyn,'" he says.

At the party on April 26 (two weeks after LaVey's birthday), mingling among church VIPs and local celebrities, Frew realized he was just about the youngest person there, which led him to believe that LaVey was beginning to think of him as something of a protégé. "He was very disappointed when I made it clear that my interest is in Wicca," he says. "But it seemed like he was . . . 'grooming' means something totally different nowadays. He seemed to be trying to set me up in that direction, especially when he was introducing me around to the higher-ups."

Among the people he met were a Soviet diplomat and his wife. Frew, who knew a little Russian from his university studies, introduced himself. "He took this as a cue to start [speaking] in Russian," Frew says. "And as I did this, I noticed that his wife was peeking up my robe, which was cut high on one side, and [trying] to see what I had on underneath. I excused myself, but I always thought, 'Okay, Church of Satan people. That was a little weird.'"

LaVey's fondness for the young man became even more pronounced when he appeared at Frew's own twenty-first birthday party on May 9, 1981. "I didn't really expect him to come, but a lot of local occultists, especially pagans like Isaac Bonewits, were there," Frew recalls, perhaps forgetting that LaVey himself wrote in *The Satanic Bible*, "The highest of all holidays in the Satanic religion is the date of one's own birth." As the evening grew late, the pagans began clearing out of his Berkeley apartment, leaving Frew and some friends behind. At around midnight, a black limousine pulled up to the house, and out stepped Anton, Diane, and Tony Fazzini, along with two big men in dark suits. LaVey was dressed in all black, save for a silver lamé tie, and Diane wore a black skirt and red blouse. The other guests were agog.

"I don't remember who the two guys were, but Anton said they were the heads of the church in Europe," Frew says. "They were visiting, and he wanted them to meet me." LaVey proceeded to hold forth, while the men, who didn't speak much English, stood around awkwardly. In a move that might have killed at a comedy club in the less-enlightened 1950s, LaVey began to run through a list of derogatory terms that was breathtaking in its comprehensiveness. "I'm not a racist," he announced. "I just hate [N-words], wops, chinks, dagos, honkies, blah, blah, blah—*if they're stupid!*"

At one point, Frew was standing in a corner of his bedroom talking to Diane, when a martial-artist friend began to engage with Tony: "I understand you're LaVey's bodyguard."

"I've sometimes performed that function" was the terse response.

"I was wondering what kind of training you had to do that job?"

Diane quickly looked away from her conversation and said, "We don't talk about Tony's past."

"She turned back to talking to me," Frew says, "and continued right where she'd left off. That was pretty weird."

Fazzini, around ten years younger than LaVey, had been devoted to the high priest since the '60s and at times lived in the Black House. "I got the impression that Tony had been in a situation of need, had been attracted to the Satanic philosophy, and had thrown in his lot with the forces of darkness as a path to extricating himself," says Blanche Barton, LaVey's final longtime companion.

Sometime early on in their friendship, LaVey gave Frew an application to join the church, already approved, which Frew never filled out. "But after my birthday party, the next time I saw him, he said, 'By the way, consider yourself a member,' and he just tossed me a card."

"If my father had a religion," Frew says, "it was capitalism." His dad, an executive at Georgia-Pacific and then Louisiana-Pacific, had a flexible view of morality. "If it was legal," Frew recalls, "it was ethical." And it was this perspective that put his father in a number of strange business situations and led to a few near brushes with the law. "In his divorce from my mother, he pulled a bunch of shady deals that were skirting around the law as best he could to his own advantage," Frew says, "even to the detriment of the rest of his family." But because what he was doing was legal, he didn't consider it wrong. If life is all about survival of the fittest, then of course whatever it takes to become the fittest is, by definition, ethical. "That was sort of how LaVey saw it," Frew says, "and to a great extent how my father saw it."

At one point after the divorce, Frew's dad wanted to see what his kid was getting up to, so when he came to town, they arranged to have dinner with LaVey. "He and my father hit it off famously," Frew recalls. After returning to the house, they descended to the basement. It was the first time Frew would behold the humanoids of the Den of Iniquity.

"There was somebody playing a pinball machine," he remembers. "There was somebody slumped in the corner next to him, masturbating. There was the sailor at the end of the bar. There was another figure that was trying to pick up a woman at the bar. If you put your glass in the right place, the bartender would pour you a drink. And there was a drum set and a keyboard." LaVey sat down at his favorite instrument and began playing a medley of songs from the '40s, which prompted Frew's dad to jump behind the kit. "That was the first time in my life I'd ever known my father to play drums," Frew says. The duo jammed for forty-five minutes while Diane and a dumbfounded Frew hung at the bar.

"It was later that I was putting together a little radio program and I wanted to interview LaVey," Frew says. "He said, 'You should just talk to your father. He's the most Satanic individual I've ever met.'"

Frew recalls that one night at LaVey's the older man delighted in showing him a print of *The Creeping Terror*, the Z-grade horror film from 1964 notable for featuring little dialogue (but lots of narration) and a monster resembling a giant Venus flytrap covered in ragged quilts. Only the movie that unspooled had been reedited, Frew supposes by LaVey himself, to include graphic moments from stag films. "In Anton's version, whenever an actor made any remark that could possibly be construed as sexual innuendo, the scene immediately cut to a couple going at it with vigor. He found this hysterical. I found it amusing, but it got old quickly."

The younger man was protective of his friendship with LaVey and would often test people who claimed they'd been invited into his home. "I'd say, 'What's the first thing you noticed when you stepped into the house?' And the correct answer is 'the overwhelming stench of dog.' If you didn't notice that immediately, you had not been there."

He and LaVey saw each other regularly until around 1982, when their interests took them elsewhere, Frew becoming very prominent in the Wiccan community. They got back in touch a few years later under most unfortunate circumstances.

On October 31, 1980, agents from the Federal Bureau of Investigation and the Secret Service appeared at the door of 6114 California Street. But they weren't neighborhood kids dressed in dark suits out trick-or-treating. LaVey, who had just returned from a trip to Los Angeles the night before, knew they were real and why they were so eager to speak with him: he had been implicated in a plot to kill Senator Ted Kennedy.

The politician, who lost two brothers to assassins, had been in San Francisco the previous few days to stump for President Jimmy Carter, who was running for reelection against Ronald Reagan. Two months earlier, Kennedy, who had challenged the incumbent in the primaries, lost the nomination at the Democratic National Convention and decided to back him.

The FBI became alarmed when, on October 20, someone reached out to the Chicago office claiming to have received a phone call at home from LaVey, who was looking for a favor. LaVey, the informant relayed, was going to send him eight kilos of hashish as well as some cash to deliver to a reputed Mafia boss on Chicago's South Side, payment for a hit on the senator. According to FBI records, the informant expected to introduce federal agents to LaVey as potential assassins, "then planned to instigate a gunfight resulting . . . in the death of LaVey and his bodyguards." The informant, whose name was redacted in the files, would walk away with the hash and the cash, and a new leader would take over the church.

LaVey was no stranger to the bureau. FBI files indicated that, in September 1973, he was "listed in a computer printout list of those described as 'interested' in the NSWPP"—the National Socialist White People's Party, formerly known as the American Nazi Party. Two years later, an informant told the FBI that the church had recently acquired property in Ukiah, California, and purchased handguns, a double-barrel shotgun, and a rifle. In March 1977, someone threatened to bomb the church and shoot and stab a member, but the state's attorney declined prosecution due to the age and mental history of the accused.

FBI, Secret Service, and Drug Enforcement Administration agents met all incoming flights at Chicago O'Hare International Airport on October 27 to determine if LaVey would indeed be bringing in drugs. He never showed.

Anton LaVey plays with a five-month-old Togare on November 18, 1964, a year and a half before founding the Church of Satan.
San Francisco Chronicle/Polaris

On January 31, 1967, LaVey officiated the marriage of John Raymond and Judith Case, the event that thrust him onto the world stage.
© *Walter Fischer Estate/Courtesy of Alf Wahlgren*

An adult Togare, with LaVey in 1967, usually stayed in a cage in the backyard.
© *Walter Fischer Estate/Courtesy of Alf Wahlgren*

With his partner Diane's assistance, LaVey baptized their daughter Zeena into Satanism on May 23, 1967.
© *Walter Fischer Estate/Courtesy of Alf Wahlgren*

LaVey and Jayne Mansfield hammed it up at her Pink Palace on Sunset Boulevard in June 1967. He later claimed they had been lovers.
© *Walter Fischer Estate/Courtesy of Alf Wahlgren*

LaVey and Mansfield with her daughters, Jayne Marie and Mariska, and Sam Brody just a few weeks before the actress and her lawyer/boyfriend died in a car crash.
© *Walter Fischer Estate/Courtesy of Alf Wahlgren*

On a 1967 visit to magazine editor Forrest J Ackerman's Ackermansion in Los Angeles, LaVey admired his friend's vast collection of horror, sci-fi, and fantasy memorabilia.
© *Walter Fischer Estate/Courtesy of Alf Wahlgren*

On the syndicated *Joe Pyne Show* that same year, the high priest remained unflappable against the combative interviewer.
© *Walter Fischer Estate/Courtesy of Alf Wahlgren*

LaVey recorded *The Satanic Mass* on Friday, September 13, 1968.
Collection of Adocentyn Research Library

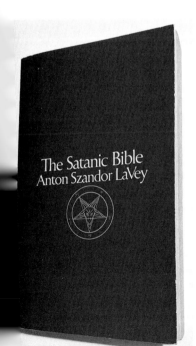

The Satanic Bible, first published in 1969,
has sold more than one million copies.
Collection of the author

The 1970 documentary *Satanis*, which began as a student film, explored the nascent Church of Satan.

Contrary to the advertisement, the Italian shockumentary *Witchcraft '70* depicts LaVey conducting a wedding ceremony in a chamber filled with bosomy naked acolytes.

For a two-dollar-and-fifty-cent admission fee, the curious could hear LaVey lecture on such topics as ritual magic, love potions, and cannibalism.
© *Walter Fischer Estate/Courtesy of Alf Wahlgren*

LaVey also taught a Witches' Workshop from his home on California Street. The blonde was his longtime companion Diane LaVey.
© *Stanton and Sharon LaVey family/Courtesy of Alf Wahlgren*

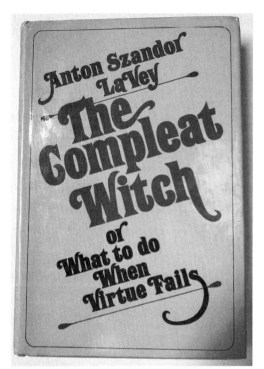

In *The Compleat Witch*, LaVey posits that men are "quarry" and "looks mean everything."
Collection of Adocentyn Research Library

In the early '70s, when LaVey was arguably at his most productive.
© *Stanton and Sharon LaVey family/Courtesy of Alf Wahlgren*

LaVey served as technical advisor on the 1975 horror film *The Devil's Rain* and had a speaking role.

LaVey's friend Kenneth Anger would typically mail him bizarre clippings from newspapers and magazines. *Collection of Adocentyn Research Library*

Diane gave LaVey's friend Don Frew this Baphomet pendant as a gift.
Collection of Adocentyn Research Library

LaVey and his firstborn, Karla, at San Francisco's Presidio Park in 1989.
© *Nick Bougas/Courtesy of Alf Wahlgren*

LaVey, Blanche Barton, Nikolas Shreck, and his wife, Anton's daughter Zeena, in the early '90s.
© *Nick Bougas/Courtesy of Alf Wahlgren*

For a *Nose* magazine fashion shoot, LaVey was photographed in March 1993 in his garage with his beloved Cord and a model named Tari.
© *Jay Blakesberg/Retro Photo Archive*

Looking suave among his artificial human companions in the Den of Iniquity.
© *Jay Blakesberg/Retro Photo Archive*

Gregg Turkington, who released LaVey's music and reissued *The Satanic Mass*, became a close
friend and edited the posthumous essay collection *Satan Speaks!*
© *Cathy Fitzhugh*

The lifelong admirer of weaponry handles a gun from his collection.
© *Cathy Fitzhugh*

Readying for an organ recital in 1994.
© *Cathy Fitzhugh*

At a press conference announcing her father's death, Karla
grabbed the hand of an ersatz Anton on loan from the San
Francisco Wax Museum.
Brant Ward/San Francisco Chronicle/Polaris

In January 1998, a year after LaVey's death, the house on
California Street stood in a terrible state of disrepair.
Deanne Fitzmaurice/San Francisco Chronicle/Polaris

A multifamily dwelling
now stands on the site of
6114 California Street,
although that house
number no longer exists.
© *Doug Brod*

Agents arrived in San Francisco to interview LaVey two days later. The woman answering the door at the Black House—whose name was redacted in the file but was likely Diane—informed them that he was away and wouldn't be home for a few days. They told her that there was reason to believe an attempt may be made on LaVey's life and that he should contact the FBI ASAP.

During the Halloween interview, LaVey told agents that he had "the highest regard" for Kennedy and his family. He also denied any involvement with drugs, adding that he was morally opposed to them. LaVey also said he had not visited his hometown in a while and had no intention of going there anytime soon. After checking his latest phone messages, he saw that he had indeed received two unidentified calls from Chicago that he had no intention of returning. He also told the agents that, owing to his association with the church, he himself had been the victim of verbal and physical attacks. But, he assured them, any folks who traveled with him were neither armed nor bodyguards.

"LaVey stated that he was well aware that most people associated with the Church of Satan are in fact 'fanatics, cultists, and weirdos,'" according to the FBI file. His interest in the church, he told the agents, was "strictly from a monetary point of view." The San Francisco Police Department earlier had advised the FBI that LaVey was no longer "personally active in the Church of Satan, having become disillusioned, and now devotes his time to writing books." Agents concluded that LaVey appeared candid during the interview and didn't present any threat.

The bureau, which found irregularities in the informant's interviews and polygraph results, concluded that the potential hit on Kennedy was a hoax. Though he was not charged with any crime, the source, who never revealed why he had concocted the conspiracy, was placed on a "quarterly," meaning his whereabouts and actions would be monitored by the Secret Service every three months. The investigation was officially dead.

Congdon & Lattès, a brand-new publishing outfit distributed by St. Martin's Press, had a hot little number on its hands.

"*Michelle Remembers* is the biggest piece of nonfiction I've ever had," publisher Thomas Congdon crowed to the *Washington Post*. "It's about a little girl whose parents gave her to a Satanic church, where she was made part of the rituals. She buried it all in her subconscious and, when she was grown, a psychiatrist pulled it all back out again, bit by tortured bit. . . . Gosh, what it feels like to have a great, big trembling piece of commerce on your plate!"

More like a great, big steaming pile of commerce.

Filled with grisly anecdotes detailing ritualistic torture, sexual assault, dismemberment, and human sacrifice at the hands of Satanists, including her own mother, the book purported to be the memories of a young woman from Victoria, British Columbia, named Michelle Smith, as dredged up during hypnosis sessions by her therapist (and coauthor), Dr. Lawrence Pazder.

Smith and Pazder claimed that the Satanists involved in her torment belonged to an organization with a name that would have sounded familiar to most everyone with the slightest awareness of Satanic thought in North America.

"The only group I know about that fits your description is the Church of Satan," reads page 117 of the first hardcover printing in 1980.

"In this mausoleum, members of the Church of Satan performed a ritual in which they attempted, unsuccessfully, to give Michelle a 'rebirth into evil,'" reads a photo caption in that same edition.

Once he became aware of the book, LaVey was appalled to see the Church of Satan being connected to these atrocities. So in 1981, he retained a young lawyer named Stuart MacKenzie to sue Smith and

Pazder, and their publishers and distributors, for libel. MacKenzie, who at the time knew nothing about LaVey and only recently had been admitted to the bar, took the case on contingency, hoping he'd make his money from whatever settlement might be offered or if he won the case. And besides, he found LaVey himself intellectually interesting.

LaVey gave his new attorney a copy of the book with passages underlined and annotations scrawled in the margins. In one instance, Michelle was remembering a Black Mass called "the Feast of the Beast" that allegedly occurred in 1955. A footnote on the page states that "according to experts on Satanism," the next feast would be due "five years after Satan's return to earth in 1977," where the dark lord would reveal his new "Master Plan." Underneath this, in pencil, was scrawled, "We, the Church of Satan, are the acknowledged experts on Satanism. National + international law enforcement agencies and every type of school and library consults us. Why didn't they? 'Master Plan' + 'Feast of the Beast'—nonsense!"

Adjoining a reference to one Len Olsen, who said he was a member of a witches' group belonging to the Church of Satan of Canada, was the notation "We have never had a member by the name of Len Olsen. If he has a membership # we can easily check."

In the complaint, LaVey claimed the passages citing the Church of Satan were actionable because, during the period Smith said she was abused, his organization had not yet been founded. "I find it inconceivable that any expert in the field of occult or religion would have been ignorant of my existence relative to the Church of Satan," an incredulous LaVey asserted, later adding, "For us to harm a child or animal, physically, emotionally or mentally is unthinkable. The heinous acts attributed to the Church of Satan by *Michelle Remembers* are profoundly misleading and damaging . . ."

The court ruled that some of the Church of Satan mentions were used generically and since "[o]ther references clearly place the church in the British Columbia area of Canada or, at most, in the Pacific Northwest and at a time several years before the California origination and incorporation of plaintiff church"—nor did the book make any mention of Anton or Diane—it clearly wasn't referring to LaVey's church.

In LaVey's defense, Marcello Truzzi submitted an affidavit reading, in part, "I don't see how anyone could confuse your organization with any that existed before your own." Nevertheless, on March 4, Judge Marilyn Hall Patel of the US District Court for the Northern District of California dismissed the lawsuit.

"Typically, in libel cases, because they're very difficult to establish, the defendants will not go through trial," MacKenzie says. "They'll just file a motion at the very outset to get the whole case dismissed. And that's what happened." It came as a surprise, then, when in subsequent paperback printings, publisher Pocket Books did excise a few, though not all, mentions of the Church of Satan. MacKenzie had not stated a cause of action, which would have specifically asked for such adjustments, so he doesn't know why Pocket Books administered this bit of recompense on its own.

But the damage had been done.

Spurred by widely read stories in *People* magazine and the *National Enquirer* as well as the authors' appearances on TV news and talk shows, the book became a bestseller.

In its wake, unsubstantiated conspiracy theories popped up like mushrooms in a dark, dystopian garden of evil. More reports of mass animal mutilation were once again being linked to Satanists. Dangerous messages hidden in rock 'n' roll records would be revealed when played backward (and not only those by allegedly Satanic acts like Ozzy Osbourne and AC/DC). Accusations flew—even popular role-playing games like Dungeons and Dragons were said to be indoctrinating youth into Devil worship and other Satanic activity.

The book, and the hysteria surrounding it, sparked a widespread moral panic that would last more than a decade and ruin thousands of lives. The Devil, apparently, lurked in every corner.

First came the McMartin preschool case in Manhattan Beach, California. In 1983, a mother alleged that a teacher there sodomized her son, leading to administrator Peggy McMartin Buckey, her son Raymond, and five others being accused of more than three hundred counts of child abuse involving forty-eight children. Charges were soon dropped against five of the defendants due to weak evidence. Ultimately, the number of students who said they had been abused swelled to 360. Smith and Pazder, who eventually got married, even met with some of the parents and children involved in the case. Prosecutors, armed with outlandish claims extracted during highly suggestive interviews with impressionable children—teachers molesting them in Satanic rituals, shooting pornographic films, and slaughtering animals—won no convictions, though Raymond Buckey spent five years in jail. At a cost of $15 million, the case, which lasted seven years, became the longest and most expensive criminal prosecution in US history.

More than a hundred other cases involving the rumored sexual abuse of children at day-care centers followed the McMartin affair.

Mary deYoung, professor emerita of sociology at Grand Valley State University in Michigan, says three shifts in American culture led this insanity to snowball so quickly. One was the change in the family. "More women were working," she says. "We had more anxiety about the care of children. It was very hard to find affordable public day care that was safe and healthy for a child." "Latchkey kids" became the buzzword to describe children who would come home from school unsupervised while their parents worked. "All of that was very symbolic of concerns about gender-role changes: [Many] men, perhaps because we had been going through a severe recession, lost their jobs and took on home-care responsibilities."

The second factor was the rise of the evangelical religious right, with its enormous infrastructure of television programs, radio shows, and publishing houses. Its desire to influence politics led to its obsessing over many of the era's social problems, deYoung says, "one of which was whether the family was losing its force as a kind of moral foundation of society."

Third was the sexual victimization of children becoming an emerging issue. "We had people coming forward talking about child sexual abuse in their histories," says deYoung, author of the book *The Day Care Ritual Abuse Moral Panic*. "As people began saying, 'Yes, this happened to me,' you realize that the family that lived next door, or maybe somebody in your own family, has experienced something that's been secret forever."

But the methods used to extract those histories contained serious flaws. In typical therapy for trauma, patients don't provide coherent, linear narratives of their experiences. "You have to interact, pull it out, interpret, feed it back," says deYoung. "And that, of course, leads to all kinds of problems about whose story it is in the end."

As a clinician during that era, deYoung had been primed to look at all the ways children could be harmed, not just by family members, but by people and institutions they were familiar with and trusted. "Take even one step further in that continuum," she says, "and children could be not just sexually abused within day care, but by forces that were unique to that particular period of time.

"By a Satanic influence."

In the day-care cases that popped up across the country, the alleged Satanists were rarely tied to an identifiable, systematic, religious body. "The words 'Church of Satan' sometimes were used without reference to that entity," deYoung says, "but meaning, in general, a group of people probably out in a forest somewhere invoking Satan and [practicing] rituals."

Having gone relatively quiet in the late '70s, LaVey reacted to this Beelzebub hubbub by not reacting much—at least publicly. He refused to defend the church on TV, not wanting to lend legitimacy to the accusations of those he considered "delusional psychotics." "In *The Satanic Bible*," says Blanche Barton, who, after meeting him in May 1984, became LaVey's lover and partner, "LaVey specifically honors children and animals as revered by Satanists because they are closest to their natural state, full of joy, unsullied by social constraints and free of institutionally imposed guilt."

But the church's detractors didn't care to read anything LaVey wrote, she says. "They were happier just waving his book around to get an emotional reaction from television audiences. If there were ill-educated kids fashioning themselves as Satanists who were sacrificing animals, Dr. LaVey said the bodies of those victims should be laid at the doorsteps of the talk show hosts who claimed that's what 'real' Satanists did."

LaVey told one interviewer in 1986 that he took some comfort in knowing that whatever damage he unleashed by opening a demonic Pandora's box, killings in the name of Satan would "never catch up with the Christians. We have centuries of psychopathic killing in the name of God."

In her father's stead, Zeena took the lead and to the airwaves—making TV appearances with Sally Jessy Raphael and Ted Koppel, among others—to articulately defend the honor of the church against these scurrilous attacks. "I contacted him and asked what his plans were to address the situation," Zeena later said. "I learned that he had no plans because he no longer had anyone to help him and there really wasn't a Church of Satan anymore." She decided to become a temporary spokesperson, a role she said lasted five years.

"I knew these TV shows were a disaster," she later said of her appearances. "This is a public relations disaster. My next thought was, 'I have a child. This is dangerous. These people are crazy. They're using children to buttress their insanity. What are they gonna do to me and my child?'" At the time she feared Child Protective Services could take her own son away from her.

"[Anton] lived in a dream world where absolutely nothing to do with social issues was of any importance," she said. "We were targets of a nationwide witch hunt and all he wanted was for me to talk about Marilyn Monroe and Jayne Mansfield."

To explain this mass hysteria, this disassociation from reality, deYoung recalls that when the book was first published, "if you were to say, '*Michelle Remembers* makes incredible claims that require incredible evidence to treat them as being credible,' the [counseling] community would circle around you very quickly and say, 'You don't believe. And if you don't believe, you're part of the problem.' And so, we get caught in that trap between belief and reason, belief and thinking."

Human beings have a need for the world around them to make sense, and the more complicated it gets, that need strengthens. "So, if you tell me that this happened, even though you can't prove it, and I skeptically say to you, 'But you have no evidence,' and you respond, 'That's because the people who have more power than I do have taken away the evidence'—we now not only have a conspiracy theory that's going to grow and grow, but we have evidence getting further and further out of reach, and belief strengthening at the same time."

Coincidentally, a few years before releasing *Michelle Remembers*, Thomas Congdon, as a senior editor at Doubleday, was responsible for publishing another book that helped to trigger a widespread public panic. Only this one, the debut novel by a magazine writer named Peter Benchley, kept people away from beaches.

A book called *Jaws*.

Don Frew rekindled his friendship with LaVey when he started working on a project connected to the Satanic Panic. *Satanism in America:
How the Devil Got Much More Than His Due*, published in 1989,
was a guide to the hysteria, essentially for law enforcement. Its main
authors, Shawn Carlson and Gerald A. Larue, belonged to the Committee for Scientific Examination of Religion, an organization that
investigated the claims of fundamentalist religions and institutions.
The book, Frew says, was the first study of "Satanic" crime to conclude there was no evidence of organized, practicing Satanists perpe-
trating these misdeeds. "What there is," he says, "is evidence of wacko
individuals sometimes roping a couple of their buddies into committing crime, people who were clearly disturbed before they ever even
heard of Satanism."

While doing research, the writers spoke with LaVey as well as
Michael Aquino, who, after breaking from the Church of Satan,
claimed to invoke Satan in a ritual. This encounter led him to establish
the Temple of Set, an occult order centering on Set, the name ancient
Egyptians gave to Satan. "We heard some of the stories from each side,"
Frew says, "and just knowing the people and the way things shook out,
I tended to side with LaVey."

In one of his early conversations with LaVey, Frew told the high
priest, "You know, with all that's going on, I'm afraid your image and
the Church of Satan and everything else is turning off more people
than it's attracting, and you're attracting the wrong people."

"You're right," LaVey responded, "but what can I do? I'm the Black
Pope."

This, Frew believes, was LaVey acknowledging that he might have
felt trapped in the persona he crafted for himself, one that, despite
becoming toxic to many, he really couldn't abandon. "So I think he

withdrew," Frew says. "He really seemed downcast after that. I don't think there was regret. I think he was just bummed."

Frew recalls Aquino being very helpful in providing information, but when it came to one of the book's appendices, he and the writers hit an impasse. They intended to list authorities they could recommend as well as those they couldn't. "It was usually that the people we didn't recommend had demonstrably lied," Frew says. "In terms of the material we were talking about, we hadn't found that LaVey had lied to us."

Aquino, however, was adamant that they include him, but not LaVey, as a credible expert. "Then I'll tell everybody how wonderful this book is and how everyone should be using it," he said. "But you can't list Anton because he's this carny guy and you can't trust him, whereas I'm the authority on Satanism."

The authors told him they couldn't oblige. If people wanted to find out more about the Church of Satan, the book was going to direct them to LaVey.

"Aquino got furious," Frew remembers. "He said, 'Then I'm going to tell everyone that this book is crap and no one should use it or pay attention to it.' We're like, 'You're saying that the book is good or not depending on whether we list LaVey and how we list you?' He basically threw a fit. We decided to list him as a nonexpert, because we couldn't trust him."

Diane had had enough.

In April 1984, she fled the house on California Street, her home for twenty-two years, after accusing LaVey of abuse and obtaining a restraining order. She claimed he caused her to lose consciousness after locking her arm behind her neck and lifting her off the floor.

It was no secret that LaVey had a temper, but the public allegation of violence was something new. "I have no idea what possessed him to become aggressive with her, especially so late in their relationship, but it is nonetheless what happened," according to their grandson Stanton, who added that, when he lived at the Black House, on a number of occasions Anton told Zeena to take him upstairs. "[That] was code for 'Me and Grandma are going to start yelling at each other.' It wasn't all the time, but it was often enough to be not-cool."

In the lawsuit that followed, Diane—now using her birth surname, Hegarty—had Anton agree that they had been equal partners in the creation, promotion, and operation of the Church of Satan for the duration of their union, and wrote and edited his books together. Though they never married, she took his last name, and they acted as husband and wife, filing joint tax returns for more than two decades.

They ended up signing a property agreement in 1985 that awarded Diane the couple's 1967 Jaguar and LaVey the Cord, Datsun, and Cadillac. The settlement also stipulated that Diane was entitled to royalties from *The Satanic Bible, The Satanic Rituals, The Compleat Witch* (later reissued as *The Satanic Witch*), and *The Devil's Notebook*, and that LaVey couldn't sell off or dispose of any community property. Anton also agreed that by January 1, 1986, he'd build a second entrance at 6114 for Diane and run additional gas and electric lines to the top floor so that they could share the residence without running into each other. He never made those adjustments, so Diane never went back.

Blanche Barton became a member of the Church of Satan at fourteen, after having read *The Devil's Avenger* and *The Satanic Bible*. At the time, she was known in her hometown of San Diego as Sharon Leigh Densley, and his philosophy was potent stuff for this self-described "smart, weird kid" just beginning to explore her own abilities. And it led to her becoming both productive and wily. "I was always . . . drawn to darker aspects of humans and to the supernatural and inexplicable shadow realms," she says. "What I appreciated—still appreciate—about Satanism was that it blended the mythic with reason, gave us avenues to ritualize, dramatically calling forth the dark gods, but always emphasizing that the power to attain our goals ultimately came from within us."

While in college, she wrote LaVey a letter. She had been invited to join the honors society Phi Beta Kappa on what turned out to be his birthday, and she wanted to acknowledge what she saw as magical serendipity. In return he invited her to visit the Black House. She expected to see Diane there—she knew nothing of their split—and ended up taking him out to dinner. He later played his keyboards for her, and on the next night they kissed. "I only found out later that the woman he'd been with for twenty-some years walked out on him that Walpurgisnacht," Barton says, "the day before we met."

As she got to know him—this person whose picture she slept with every night under her pillow—Barton, thirty-one years his junior, found LaVey to be "deeply committed to what he'd written, what he'd started, and reflected that in everything he was."

For the high priest of the Church of Satan, lust and lasciviousness were part of the job description and nothing that Barton discouraged. "Anton had always been fit and had a vigorous sexual appetite," Barton says. "He allowed me to explore aspects of roleplaying and BDSM [bondage and discipline, domination and submission, sadism and masochism] I'd never shared with anyone before, or since. I satisfied certain fetishes for him. We were magically compatible and found each other sexually exciting."

That excitement sometimes included bringing other consenting adults into their activities. "LaVey intuitively practiced advanced sex magic from an early age," she says, citing his Witches' Workshops and

The Compleat Witch as venues where he put his knowledge into practice. "He helped shape a woman into a mesmerizing witch, fulfilling a potential he saw in her manner of dress and presentation, much as a director or artist would. It was a sensual dance.

"These transformations sometimes involved sexual contact of one sort or another," Barton continues. "I was certainly aware of it, as we talked quite frankly about such things. We'd usually spend a significant time together first, going to dinner or maybe working in the office, long before anything further would evolve. If a sexual relationship emerged, I was either initiating, participating directly, or taking on an appropriate role outside the scene. Many of these contacts didn't last more than a few weeks, as Anton would grow bored or frustrated. We both found it fun for as long as it lasted."

Barton never became jealous in these scenarios since she knew LaVey considered her his primary love. "And [he] would never betray that," she says. "He wouldn't actively hurt me or make me feel excluded." (By 1991, it appeared he had grown disinterested in sex. "I've been around women all my life," he said. "It takes more than a lot of nude female bodies to move me now. I'd rather be reading an old book.")

In 1988, Diane filed a complaint in San Francisco Superior Court claiming that LaVey reneged on the 1985 agreement and petitioning for their community property to be liquidated with half the proceeds going to her. Among the items on the list were the tombstone coffee table, a shrunken head, several medieval torture implements, three pinball machines, a Rock-Ola jukebox, an antique leopard chair, a gun collection, a Tesla coil, and a bed of nails. LaVey's lawyer, Owen Mayer, who was also his stepbrother—his father had remarried a few years after Gertrude died in 1984—claimed Diane was just trying to capitalize on

Anton's success. Her suit, he said, sought "rights that would be the envy of everyone without the institution of marriage."

Diane amended her complaint in December and sued for damages, alleging that Anton breached multiple terms of their contract, acted fraudulently and deceitfully, and intentionally inflicted emotional distress. She aimed to dissolve their partnership, divide their property, and recoup her legal fees. In her suit, she said that she left the house fearing for her life and renewed the restraining order against LaVey in 1985 and 1986.

The following June, in a response to the complaint, LaVey denied her allegations, insisting that he was never violent or abusive nor was the property jointly owned.

The court sided with Diane. On August 5, Judge Ollie Marie-Victoire ruled that Anton was in default and ordered him to sell the house and its contents and share with Diane the estimated half-million dollars in proceeds. The judge also awarded Diane $205,000 in punitive damages and legal fees. Anton's new lawyer, Kent Russell, asked for both another hearing and a reduction in damages, pleading that serious illness prevented his client from appearing and that his previous attorney had quit, leaving LaVey literally defenseless. "He has a continuing and worsening heart condition, a blood disorder, and he suffers from hypertension," Russell said, adding that out of concern for his well-being, Blanche hadn't informed LaVey of the deposition dates and other legal matters. "He just didn't know what was going on."

On September 27, 1991, more than seven years after Diane initially filed suit, the case came to a close. Judge Marie-Victoire denied LaVey's request for a new hearing and to cancel the default. She didn't buy his excuses.

LaVey filed for Chapter 11 bankruptcy less than a month later, subsequently telling the court that his average net income each year from

1989 to 1991 was $10,406. In 1992, the case was eventually converted to Chapter 7, which required a sale of assets to pay creditors.

"On the platform he was king; the marks in their anonymous mass were below him and his voice held them, but down on their level, jammed in among their milling, collective weight, he felt smothered," William Lindsay Gresham wrote in his 1946 novel *Nightmare Alley*.

Movies that ranked high in LaVey's lair included *Rosemary's Baby, Metropolis, M, The 5,000 Fingers of Dr. T, The Black Cat, The Cabinet of Dr. Caligari*, the *Dr. Phibes* films, and *Freaks*. But if there's one that can be said to have made the strongest impact on LaVey, and perhaps revealed more about him than any documentary could, it's the 1947 adaptation of Gresham's book. It tells the story of Stanton Carlisle, an enthusiastic barker at a traveling carnival who through a fatal mishap comes to assist the resident mentalist, Mademoiselle Zeena. Having learned her act's secrets and become adept at duping the rubes, he takes the show out of the tents and into high-society nightclubs, where he performs to great acclaim as "The Great Stanton." Eventually greed enters the picture—it is film noir, after all—and Carlisle gets done in by a femme fatale, and a psychologist at that.

The similarities between Carlisle's story arc and LaVey's are so uncanny, it's almost as if he traced the outlines of his persona from this fictional character. In the book, Carlisle, the unrepentant carny, transforms into a spiritualist minister who founds the nondenominational Church of the Heavenly Message. He makes money presenting lectures on Tarot cards, molds a human hand out of rubber for one of his hustles, and is ultimately ruined by a bewitching woman named Lilith.

A poster of the movie—star Tyrone Power, cigarette dangling from his mouth, glancing sidelong at the three dames who aid in his degradation—hung in the LaVey kitchen like a totem of a desirous identity, right next to his wall painting of a red, pitchfork-wielding devil, mouth agape, sucking on the stove's exhaust pipe. LaVey named his second daughter after Zeena—"the Woman Who Knows," a seeress married at seventeen—with whom Carlisle hones his act. The former Howard Levey coincidentally, or synchronistically, shared his middle name with the protagonist, which is also what Zeena called her child.

It was a film Anton would push on his friends and church members alike. "What was strange is, when I saw *Nightmare Alley*, it was really like LaVey going, 'Hey, look at me!'" Don Frew says. "You're laying yourself bare for everybody when you recommend this film."

LaVey's former son-in-law Nikolas Schreck had the same reaction. "Why would you base yourself on a phony medium who becomes a circus geek?" he says. "Why would you make that your prototype?"

XI.

Re-Animated

NOT long after Pope John Paul II met with the Dalai Lama and Mother Teresa in India in February 1986, the *Washington Post Magazine* put a much different spiritual leader on its cover. It was Anton LaVey's first major profile in nearly a decade. Among the "revelations": LaVey, who charged one hundred dollars a session for Satanic counseling and ate breakfast at the fast-food chain Jack in the Box, had "several luxurious homes and a 185-foot yacht at his disposal," and a follower paid his medical insurance.

The LaVey that reporter Walt Harrington encountered over five evenings spent at the house was pleasant, welcoming, and missing teeth. He went so far as to open the church's membership files with the caveat that the writer not name names. The applicants included a Beverly

Hills office manager, an Indiana plumber, and a middle-aged lesbian former nun.

At one point, LaVey, clad in a black shirt and lavender tie, along with Blanche and a female friend, startled Harrington with a misanthropic outburst so casually cruel the writer characterized it as seeming "evil." Having encountered an apparently disturbed man at Jack in the Box, LaVey wondered that if somebody blew his brains out, would anyone care? "They're not even zombies!" Blanche said. "Because they never had a life in the first place. They're just zeros! It's frightening."

Later, the high priest was flipping through *Time Frames*, Michael Lesy's book featuring the autobiographical commentary of family members—mostly first- and second-generation immigrants in the postwar Midwest—as they looked at snapshots of their lives, a concept LaVey labeled "very Satanic."

"You know why?" he told Harrington. "Because the average person thinks that his life means something, that people give a crap about it. This guy has taken real nonentities, people who nobody would give a crap if they ever lived or died. It's Satanic because it comes full circle. It's not just dignifying them. It's like putting the microphone in front of the drunk. It's really being sadistic."

This man who couldn't care less about those who had less, Harrington surmised, his religion is egotism.

"Let's give me a little credit for having moved society," LaVey told him, "up or down—but for at least having moved it."

His mission was to make a difference. "In a world where it's hard to matter," Harrington says nearly forty years later, "he struck a chord with many people who felt, alas, the same way: they wanted to matter."

LaVey told Harrington that he got so angry one night in July 1984—after being summoned to appear in court when Diane had a restraining order issued against him—that his pounding at his keyboard unwittingly caused a man to shoot up a San Diego McDonald's, killing twenty-one and injuring nineteen others. Another time, he provoked an earthquake in Mexico City.

"Did he really believe that?" Harrington says. "I thought he did believe it, but again it could have been shtick, because he'd been doing shtick for a long, long time."

That was a fact LaVey freely acknowledged. "I started out like Edward G. Robinson in *Night Has a Thousand Eyes*," LaVey told him, referring to the 1948 supernatural film noir. "A carny mental act, a fraud. I believed everything was fixed, gaffed. Then, like Robinson, you start to get real flashes. Only if your life isn't full of miracles can you recognize the real miracle."

Harrington, who called his subject "a junkyard intellectual," posits that LaVey was someone who came to believe things a faithless person might regard as serendipitous or coincidental were actually causative. "Could I have had something to do with this stuff," the journalist recalls LaVey considering out loud, "and am I responsible?"

"Could he have been scared?" Harrington says. "To me, he genuinely seemed a bit—I don't want to say worried—but maybe he had done some stuff that led to lousy, bad outcomes."

Ultimately, Harrington was pleased to hear that LaVey agreed with the conclusions he drew. "You've really come to understand me," he told the reporter.

Almost forty years on, Harrington couldn't recall what compelled him to pitch the story, published two decades after the church's founding, although he supposes it had something to do with a reaction to the Satanic Panic. "It was a freewheeling time," Harrington says. "We were able to do a lot of weird stories that a newspaper wouldn't normally do, and we had quite a bit of freedom in terms of writing style and interpretation."

One of Harrington's interpretations involved thinking maybe, just maybe, there was some blackened kernel of truth to what LaVey was going on about. "Anton came to really wonder whether what he had plugged into was not something real," Harrington says, "that it was perhaps a real force. . . . Maybe he really had uncovered some powers that actually existed."

Soon after the piece ran, Harrington received a surprise phone call. It was Diane, who was in the process of suing LaVey. She had read the piece. "I don't know how you did it," she told Harrington. "But that was Anton."

Harrington never heard from LaVey himself post-publication, but he did get a memo from the paper's executive editor, Ben Bradlee, attached to a letter from a concerned mother. "This is absolutely awful," she wrote. "Why are you running a story that encourages people to join this guy's church?"

"How do you answer this woman?" Bradlee asked him.

Harrington proceeded to compose a long response to her and a note to Bradlee, explaining that the story was intended not as a glorification of LaVey, but as an attempt to understand why people were susceptible to him, to examine what made him so appealing. Harrington admits the mother's letter was "heartfelt, sad, and emotional," and took the grievance seriously because he thought Bradlee, who legendarily oversaw the paper's Pulitzer Prize–winning coverage of the Watergate scandal, probably wasn't too excited about running this story in the first place.

With the arrival of grunge, industrial-strength noise, and Satan-centric death metal, music in the mid-1980s took on a decidedly gloomy and portentous countenance, which only served to help breathe new life into the old Devil.

Along with these new sounds came new words, as fanzines— small-circulation newsletters or journals devoted to their creators' obsessions—sent out sometimes toxic smoke signals eagerly sucked up by the latest countercultural constituency jonesing for out-there info, way before the internet had all the answers. And in the worlds of low-brow art, indie film, and photography, transgression ruled the day (and night). From Tod A to Beth B to Tesco Vee to Nick Zedd and all the wicked characters in between, it was an exhilarating, degenerate, and deeply weird time.

Eugene S. Robinson was a student at Stanford University when he started *The Birth of Tragedy*. The tabloid-style newsprint zine, named after a book by Friedrich Nietzsche, was one of the first indie publications to document this nascent culture. Essays about pedophiles and S&M butted up against Charles Manson comics, interviews with Matt Groening (before *The Simpsons* was a thing), Beat poet Lawrence Ferlinghetti, and busty stripper-actress Kitten Natividad, not to mention advertisements for SST Records, home of sound collagists Negativland and SoCal punkers Black Flag.

But when Robinson approached Anton LaVey to be on the cover of his fourth edition, "The God Issue" (dated November 1986), little did he know he'd be partly responsible for the high priest's rebirth in the counterculture. Like Jack Fritscher in 1971, Robinson went into the interview not as a dispassionate investigative journalist or curiosity seeker, but as an inquisitor who kinda, sorta agreed with a lot of this stuff.

At their first meeting, Robinson spoke with Blanche for a bit before LaVey crept up behind him. "I realized it for exactly what it was," Robinson says. "I just started laughing. I shook his hand—this big meaty handshake—and he smiled. He understood immediately that, one, I appreciated his theater, but that, two, I'm not likely to be swayed by the woo-woo scary shit."

"Evil is what doesn't feel good," he remembers LaVey saying during their conversation. "I go, 'A root canal is what doesn't feel good. I don't think it's evil.' And that's when he said, 'Look, I'm just trying to make the rent. I'm an atheist.'"

So Robinson changed the subject. "It never seemed to me that he was well-situated," he says. "I never had the sense that, 'Wow, LaVey's got it made.' I got the sense that LaVey had a hustle going, and it either paid or didn't.

"It's a good shtick, it pays the bills, it brings him some women that he probably wouldn't have access to ordinarily," Robinson continues. "Cool. I'm not gonna shake a man's hustle." Robinson later released an audio offshoot of his zine, called *Fear*Power*God*, a compilation (on cassette, vinyl, and CD) that features LaVey reciting a particularly violent passage from *The Satanic Bible*'s "Infernal Diatribe."

For all his magisterial bluster, LaVey, in the *Birth of Tragedy* interview, did manage to offer a moment of what for him surely resembled vulnerability. "I do lapse into states of melancholia," he said, "but it's not because I'm an unhappy person. It's because I'm a very happy person in a compulsively unhappy world."

"That interview," said Boyd Rice, himself a polarizing underground figure, "was literally like the shot heard 'round the world. Not only was it hard-hitting, funny, blasphemous, and intelligent, it served notice that LaVey was still very much alive and kicking and a force to be reckoned with. . . . People who had grown up on LaVey's material began to come out of the woodwork, anxious to pay homage to the man and acknowledge their gratitude for his early influence."

Rice, who edited the RE/Search book *Incredibly Strange Films* with Jim Morton and was himself the subject of an interview in the RE/Search book *Pranks!*, became an important catalyst in bringing LaVey further into a scene that was becoming progressively more outré—where serial killers, extreme exploitation movies, body modifications, and button-pushing performance art ruled. RE/Search Publications evolved out of the San Francisco–based punk fanzine *Search & Destroy*, which editor V. Vale launched to cover such artists as Patti Smith, Iggy Pop, the Ramones, and the Weirdos, as well as local bands like the Avengers, the Dead Kennedys, and Chrome.

LaVey had seen *Incredibly Strange Films*—containing interviews with such maverick directors as Russ Meyer and Herschell Gordon Lewis and essays on disreputable genres like women-in-prison and mondo movies—liked it, and invited Vale and copublisher Andrea Juno over to the house. When Morton finally met LaVey, they bonded over their obsession with B-movies of the '40s. "It was one of his great loves in life," Morton says.

The man Morton clicked with was congenial and unpretentious, a shrewd guy who knew just how to act with each person he allowed into his circle. "When he did public appearances, he would put on something with more stature and gravitas," Morton says, "which he knew he didn't really need to do around me."

LaVey understood pretty quickly that Morton was not going to be joining the Church of Satan anytime soon. But film noir—that was a topic they could go on about for hours. "He really knew his stuff," Morton says. "It's a shame he didn't write a book about cinema." LaVey turned Morton on to *Yanco*, the film shot by Álex Phillips Jr., the cinematographer on *The Devil's Rain*. "Almost nobody I've ever met has ever heard of this movie. And yet it's this weird, haunting, lyrical little film."

They watched movies in the front room, where LaVey would set up a screen and run his sixteen-millimeter projector or pop a VHS tape into his VCR. By that time, the air in the house was so thick with dust that often after a night of fun, the asthmatic Morton found himself puffing vigorously on his inhaler. "I think that probably affected his health as well," he says. "It was pretty musty."

When they would talk about the characters and actors and actresses from the '40s, Morton got a sense that LaVey longed for something that was similarly satisfying. "There's a certain amount of inevitable nostalgia that comes as you get older, whether you want it to seep in or not," he says. "And he generally didn't—he wasn't one for that kind of nostalgia. But sometimes I would get that impression that the '40s was the best decade as far as he was concerned."

At other times, their rap would revolve around evangelists, fake psychics, and other grifters—the *Nightmare Alley* multiverse. "I understood cold reading," Morton says, referring to a mentalist technique. "I understood how easy it is to completely fool people. So we got along well."

It was before a RE/Search-sponsored screening of *The Corpse Grinders* and *The Doll Squad*, films by polyamorous psychotronic auteur Ted V. Mikels, when Boyd Rice first met LaVey. "He walked over to where I was standing and said, 'Is your name Boyd? I think we share some mutual interests,'" Rice recalled. Rice was soon invited to spend time at the house, of which he wrote, "LaVey's personality was so thoroughly imbued in every square foot of the place that it seemed almost an extension of him. . . . It was like a work of art that he'd created over the course of a lifetime."

The interview in *The Birth of Tragedy* may have marked his first foray into contemporary indie culture, but what arguably put LaVey over in the underground was his appearance in the 1989 RE/Search book *Modern Primitives*, a survey of the burgeoning tattoo and piercing scenes, in which the high priest offers historical and philosophical perspectives.

Not everyone who visited LaVey left dazzled and entranced. Bobby Neel Adams accompanied Vale to the house to shoot LaVey's portraits for *Modern Primitives*. After they knocked on the door, LaVey himself answered dressed in all black. "The stench that wafted out of the house was pure death," Adams recalls. LaVey had mentioned that his dog was dying of cancer, which Adams inferred was the reason for the odor. "Obviously LaVey had become immune to the smell of death, and perhaps Vale and I were being polite by not bringing it up."

"Get me out of here," the photographer thought as he lugged his lighting case into the kitchen and began setting up. He moved quickly, wanting to leave as soon as he was physically able. During his time inside, LaVey spoke of palling around with Sammy Davis Jr. and meeting Richard Ramirez, the Southern California serial killer known as the Night Stalker. "It could have been me, but it sounded like LaVey thought it was cool that a serial killer had come to pay a visit," Adams says.

"But I was totally disgusted."

"It's hard to imagine a time when everyone didn't wear black, everyone didn't love horror movies, and everyone didn't know their serial killers," says a guy who calls himself Evil Wilhelm, the cofounder and drummer of the Los Angeles goth band Radio Werewolf. He met caterwauler-lyricist Nikolas Schreck in the early '80s, and the two bonded over their love of "dark fact or fiction."

"Things that were considered shocking appealed to both our sense of humor and aesthetic," Wilhelm says. Those things included not only the macabre, but also the fascistic. "Schreck had a real fascination with Nazis. I thought Nazis were interesting, certainly, but I didn't *admire* them." Radio Werewolf, which Schreck also called a terrorist organization, was named after Joseph Goebbels's Third Reich propaganda outlet.

With their over-the-top onstage ghoulishness—undead makeup, frilly Victorian costumes, dangling skeletons, funereal organ, fog machines—the group attracted a following at clubs like the Roxy, Whisky a Go Go, and Scream. After he and Schreck put together a press package, Wilhelm suggested they send one to Charles Manson, who was serving a life sentence in San Quentin State Prison. "We'd had no contact with Manson, but we both had John Wayne Gacy paintings," he says. "We both had these things before they were in vogue. You know, 'We can get this killer clown to do a painting for us. We can write to [Hillside Strangler] Kenneth Bianchi, and he'll do a drawing for us.'" Wilhelm got Manson's address from one Nick Bougas, who was big in these circles.

Not long after, Wilhelm's bandmate told him they had a press agent in San Quentin and were getting responses from underground figures like Boyd Rice, the publisher and editor Adam Parfrey, and the painter Joe Coleman: *hey, Charlie said to check you guys out!*

"This hub of communication became this Anton LaVey fan group," Wilhelm says. "It became sort of a network." When Schreck moved up to San Francisco with his girlfriend to be nearer to it, Wilhelm made him fly back to LA to attend band meetings.

Schreck, a lifelong occultist who was certain the Devil was real, became close with LaVey soon after meeting him. Early in their friendship, LaVey asked Schreck and his girlfriend to appear on a local TV show with Arthur Lyons, who was promoting his 1988 book *Satan Wants You.* "We were young and stupid, and we looked very dramatically Satanic, so he wanted us to be there to represent the Church of Satan," Schreck says. "In retrospect, I see that he was using us for his purposes—not in any harmful way."

As they spent more time together, Schreck soon came to doubt many of LaVey's more extravagant biographical details. "He claimed to be a lion tamer," he says. "You would think if you're a lion tamer, there are photographs of you taming lions." He pressed LaVey on his carnival work, his crime photography, and his viewing of Nazi occult films, and he remained unconvinced.

"He's interesting enough on his own," Schreck recalls thinking. "Why does he have to embellish everything?"

The Strand Theater, a repertory movie house on Market Street, five miles east of the Black House, was beloved for its hip double bills of gems like *Pink Floyd: The Wall* and the animated cult classic *Heavy Metal*, as well as Alfred Hitchcock triple features. But on the night of August 8, 1988, the marquee announced a different kind of program, one that would add a serrated edge to an apparent celebration of industrial culture. The organizers—Schreck, Rice, and Parfrey—called it a renaissance of Satanism.

Flyers touted "An Evening of Apocalyptic Delight" with a lineup that would feature, among other things, a rare Manson docudrama; Rice's noise project, NON; Zeena LaVey reading excerpts from *The Satanic Bible*; and a short film by Jonathan Reiss and Survival Research Laboratories called *A Bitter Message of Hopeless Grief*, depicting destructive robots and machines in gore- and pyro-filled scenarios. (The SRL film ended up not being screened.)

Schreck had invited Evil Wilhelm up for what he was promoting as a Radio Werewolf appearance, but it wasn't even close. The drummer reluctantly agreed, and upon seeing the billing, became genuinely pissed. "I said, 'I would've never taken this minor booking,' because—I had an ego, you know—we would've headlined this thing." One of his arguments was "I'd rather be the Addams Family than the Manson Family." Schreck, he says, held the opposite opinion.

The band members were currently on movie theater screens nationwide, purveying their peacocky death rock in the schlock comedy *Mortuary Academy* and, according to Wilhelm, "were in a position to become a different thing." The film's tagline, "Where the dearly departed meet the clearly retarded," accurately bullhorned the coarseness to be found within. Legendary rock DJ Wolfman Jack played the band's manager who introduces their literally undead performance at a big-money bar mitzvah.

The night before the Strand event, they all went to hang out at LaVey's. "They say I'm going to like this guy, but I can't imagine it," Wilhelm says. Walking past his dog, the fellows took their seats in the living room. "They all call him Doctor," Wilhelm says. "Doctor, Doctor, Doctor—everyone's calling him Doctor, and I'm calling him Anton." To his surprise, he and LaVey became fast friends, going deep into their shared obsession with classic cars like Stutzes, Cords, and Grahams—bulbous, tanklike, beautiful—much to the dismay of the others.

Conversely, Wilhelm recalls, everyone else was telling stories about how they were picked on when they were young. "LaVey was saying, 'You know, the guys in the raccoon coats and straw hats used to beat me up.' I'm looking around the room, saying, 'I was six feet tall in fifth grade. I don't remember anyone ever picking on me.'" The whole crew reminded him of *Revenge of the Nerds*. "It was this striking back at everything that represented good. . . . 'Let's get revenge on the populace.' . . . 'We have to kill all the subhuman scum.'"

The Strand's main event the following evening was going to be the San Francisco premiere of *The Other Side of Madness*, an obscure 1971 exploitation flick also known as *The Helter Skelter Murders*, particularly notorious for including two of Charles Manson's songs.

The program was to commence with a recreation of the destruction ritual targeting the hippie movement that Anton LaVey claimed he performed on that date nineteen years earlier, the night Sharon Tate and four others were murdered at 10050 Cielo Drive. The current date's numerals, 8/8/88, arguably had an even more sinister association: H being the eighth letter of the alphabet, to neo-Nazis 88 represents "Heil Hitler."

Schreck and Rice previewed the event in a radio interview with Berkeley's KPFA a few days before. Rice called it "a celebration" of the murders, which he said brought an end to an era. "The '60s was just for us a disgusting decade," he said. "It was like the culmination of two thousand years of Judeo-Christian rottenness."

The two men said they were introduced to each other through Manson, after both had been corresponding with the prisoner Schreck called "one of the more important thinkers of the twentieth century."

Schreck had been in contact with Malcolm Barbour, a producer working on a special about devil worship for the sensationalist TV talk show host Geraldo Rivera, who brought along a crew to capture the action.

The theater was packed. "It was a very noisy audience," Jim Morton remembers. "Some people were there to denounce the whole thing, and some people worked to champion it."

"I don't remember there being any seats available," says attendee Harvey Stafford, who admits to rubbernecking to catch glimpses of San Francisco countercultural superstars, like performance artist Monte Cazazza, and would go on to become a close friend of Rice's and LaVey's. Stafford was a fan of Parfrey's book *Apocalypse Culture* as well as Rice's work, and was excited to finally get to see them in the flesh. He describes the evening as "one of the most delicious moments of my entire life."

But even before the show began, there was tension behind the scenes. "Shortly before we went on," Zeena recalled, "we learned of a call-in threat from someone with the intention of stabbing the participants on stage with syringes filled with AIDS-infected blood."

Morton says that it was Mark Spainhower, a gay activist who also did some writing and editing on *Incredibly Strange Films*, who threatened to inject Parfrey. "Parfrey was understandably freaked out by that," Morton says. "[Mark] didn't do it. And I don't think he would've either."

Rice later said it was he who was Spainhower's target. "He had a crush on me, and was devastated that I might not like homosexuals," he said.

The show went on. At the start of the program's final section, a black-clad honor guard crossed the stage hoisting a flag emblazoned with the Nazi Wolfsangel symbol. Rice, darkly handsome in a dress shirt adorned with that same emblem, walked up to the podium and began his spiel: "We're gathered here tonight to celebrate this day in history. . . . A day of purification, a day of truth and vengeance, a day of tar and feathers." He closed his rant with "Murder is the predator's prerogative, and there is no birth without blood!"

Parfrey followed, attempting to play the theme from *Valley of the Dolls*, a film that costarred Sharon Tate, on an oboe.

Soon came Schreck, his short bottle-blond hair framing the wart-like bumps where his right ear should have been. (He lost it the previous year, after being assaulted while posting anti-gay flyers, which he characterized as a "prank.") Schreck managed to take the evening's violent messaging even further, working himself up into a spitting, oratorical frenzy as he railed against "psychedelic vermin," a phrase LaVey himself used.

"Musically, the event was a travesty, since we'd had no time to practice or even do a soundcheck," Rice later wrote. "But the audience didn't know and they loved it."

Evil Wilhelm, who was the percussive accompaniment for the entire rally, doesn't disagree: "It was musically horrible. I struggled valiantly to try to tie it together."

Zeena later recalled Rice's stage fright during his speech, which she was scheduled to follow to recite passages from her dad's book. "When the time came for my part, Boyd just stood there," she said. "I kept looking around, wondering when he'd get it, his part was finished, but he stood there an interminably long time, just sort of zoning out." Having noticed Rice and Parfrey's nervousness during dinner, Zeena figured it was the presence of TV cameras that caused the jitters. "They weren't yet used to that level of national attention."

According to Wilhelm, "Nothing could be further from the truth. Adam was grinning from ear to ear."

But then, maybe nervousness was the appropriate response. In the midst of a mass hysteria over a Satanic child-abuse conspiracy and brutal murders committed in the name of the Devil (and, by association, Anton LaVey), a group of miscreants and pranksters—all hovering around thirty years old and fashioning themselves as the Church of Satan's next generation—decided to throw a hybrid debutante ball/ Nuremberg Rally, inviting a production team from Geraldo Rivera, whose daytime talk show, then just a year old, was already attracting millions of viewers.

Aligning the Church of Satan with the burgeoning industrial and goth scenes was one thing. But adding the fascist frippery, with some audience members clad in swastika T-shirts and a few actual Nazis hanging around backstage, took the punkish co-opting of the symbol a decade earlier to much more nefarious extremes.

And what about the Final Solution speechifying at the event that, in 2021, the news website *SFGate* called "the Church of Satan's last gasp in the mainstream"?

"I think it was just to take the piss and unnerve people," Stafford says. "I don't think you could get away with that sort of experimentation these days. Even then, it was really unsettling, and I was trying to have an open mind and see it as a performance."

Parfrey said years later that Rice saw it "as a way of making people anxious and putting across his own love of [Hitler]."

"I could rant and rave about Parfrey and Rice and their lack of sincerity, but it was all a joke to them," Schreck says. "They were just being provocative for its own sake. And that is not anything I or Zeena have ever done. We felt like we are taking a risk going on this stage." Looking back, he has second thoughts about having mixed Manson with LaVey. "Another thing is Anton hated Charlie, and Charlie hated Anton," he says. "Anton went along with this because he saw this is going to be good PR for the Church of Satan."

A few weeks after the rally, LaVey didn't have much to say about it except, "I could have perhaps provided some advice for cohesiveness, and some kind of helpful direction that it could have taken." He told the British experimental musician Genesis P-Orridge, whose band Psychic TV had a gig in San Francisco the following evening, "Zeena, I think, was a little dismayed, more than anything else, about the lack of organization. . . . Although obviously the audience didn't seem to mind. It went over very well."

Backstage, the likes of Nick Bougas and Bob Heick lurked. The following year, Bougas, an associate of the church, would release *Death Scenes*, a documentary composed of vintage gruesome crime-scene photos, narrated by Anton. A photo of Heick, the founder of the San Francisco–based white supremacist group American Front, and Rice, both in full uniform and brandishing knives, would later appear in the book *Blood in the Face: The Ku Klux Klan, Aryan Nations, Nazi Skinheads, and the Rise of a New White Culture.*

"I was not at all comfortable with the atmosphere immediately after the show and wanted to immediately leave, as was the original agreement," Zeena said decades later. The car that was supposed to pick her up never came, so she found herself, she said, "stuck in the backstage area with a bunch of dips wanting to ape for the camera."

That night, Evil Wilhelm made the decision to leave Radio Werewolf, the group he helped form four years earlier, "even though I'd worked so hard and the band was actually doing very well, with legitimate record companies saying, 'Lose the singer, we'll sign you tomorrow.'"

Nearly forty years later, Schreck stands by his performance as well as his inflammatory rhetoric. "People often would say, 'He was being a troll—he was just trying to be provocative.' But no, I meant what I said. I was being more offensive than I needed to be, because I took a kind of sadistic joy in seeing how much it bothered people."

After the show, the core group reconvened at Schreck's apartment in the Tenderloin district, where Rivera's producers conducted individual interviews. The image of a soft-spoken Rice sitting in a big rattan chair, clutching a cane, managed to evoke both Black Panther revolutionary Huey P. Newton and white goth goddess Morticia Addams—only this guy had a Nazi flag and Baphomet statue as part of his backdrop.

It didn't take long before he dropped the name on everyone's lips. "Anton was saying the other night, 'Satanism is coming out of the ritual chamber and into the mainstream.'" Picking his teeth and tripping over his words, Rice explained that the goal was a return to social stratification: "We need to bring power back to the powerful" and "We need the slaves to be enslaved again."

And what about those people killing in the name of Satan? They're "nitwits," he said, but they're helping out by "thinning down the population."

When asked what appealed to him about Nazism, Rice replied, "Order. Bringing things back to order. . . . If you work with nature and work in its will, you're all powerful. But if you work against its will, it'll step on you, and you'll never get anything accomplished."

After clarifying that he was speaking for himself and not LaVey's church, he offered that Hitler, an occultist who disdained the Judeo-Christian ethic, was trying to give rise to a pagan revival. Tonight's ritual, he said, was "the start of a renewal process."

Schreck, during his interview, waxed even more hyperbolic, remarking, "It's important to recognize National Socialism as one of the few times in the twentieth century that humanity's full potential has been unleashed: the predatory instinct, the beast in man."

Evincing an impressively dead-eyed thousand-yard stare, he intoned without affect, "We would like to see most of the human race killed off. It is unworthy of the gift of life."

Among his grandiose claims, Schreck said he and others like him were forming a master race. But then he also had some really cool stuff to promote: he and Rice were collaborating with LaVey on the high priest's first recording since *The Satanic Mass*. On it, LaVey was going to perform invocations, the ritual "Die elektrischen Vorspiele" ("The Law of the Trapezoid") from *The Satanic Rituals*, and "Psychopompos," an epic poem by H.P. Lovecraft that appeared in the September 1937 issue of *Weird Tales*. He also plugged his own forthcoming book, to be published by Parfrey's nascent Feral House imprint, titled *The Demonic Revolution*, the first "to summarize from a Satanic point of view what's going on in the world today." (The book, like his new master race and the LaVey CD, never came forth.)

Sitting beside him throughout the interview was Evil Wilhelm— elegant in a dark tuxedo with a white bowtie, hair tied back, fingers intertwined on his knee, the monocle encircling his left eye adding a maniacally goofy touch. He rarely interjected as the frighteningly artic- ulate Schreck pontificated. "If I had a little thought balloon by my head," Evil Wilhelm says nearly forty years on, "it was just, 'I'm outta here. These guys are all losers.'"

As for Parfrey, in *his* post-rally interview, the pompadoured cherub also couldn't ignore the opportunity to engage in some blatant plugola, getting in a mention of Feral House's fall 1989 reissue of *The Compleat Witch*, now titled *The Satanic Witch*.

Zeena—brilliant red lips, B-movie-blonde coif, rouged cheeks, tri- umphantly arched eyebrows—said in her interview that she moved away from home for around three years to try to live a "normal life" in anonymity, but became miserable and practically suicidal. Was she brought up in a very loving home? "Yes, I feel like I was raised in a very caring environment."

After echoing her dad's views on sexual freedom, she was asked about the public conception of Satanic orgies. Is it total bullshit? "From my experiences, it's bullshit," she answered with a shrug. "I've never witnessed any orgies."

At around three that morning, after the interviews were done, someone knocked on the door. "There's this old wino standing at the door, this old bum," Wilhelm remembers. "He comes walking in, they close the door, and just like in a movie, he peels the paper-thin mask off, and it's LaVey. He'd walked past Geraldo's crew unnoticed."

"How was the performance?" he asked Wilhelm, who didn't say a word.

He turned to the others.

"Oh, it was glorious!"

"This will go down in history!"

"Fantastic!"

"We changed the world tonight!"

Says Evil Wilhelm, "I just thought it was a travesty."

More than thirty years after the rally, the promoters' antisocial antics, put-on or not, were still being felt in the city. "When the lines of parody and reality are blurred and distorted to such hateful, nefarious ends, what they actually think doesn't matter," Joshua Bote wrote on *SFGate*. "That these views, racist, anti-Semitic and white supremacist in nature, were potentially shrouded in multiple layers of irony belies the fact that on this night, Radio Werewolf and their supporters brought these ideas out into the world to be shaped and molded into genuine hate."

Harvey Stafford, who was twenty when he attended and spent some time that summer printing Charles Manson T-shirts in his parents' basement, takes a more nuanced view. "This was a pre-internet edge-lord competition between a lot of people," he says. "It has all come back to haunt us now with the Republicans owning the libs. But for a kid it was pretty exciting. And it seemed like an interesting place for an alternative, punk-rock goth subculture to go—one that was rooted in literature and philosophy. It wasn't simply screaming angrily against the establishment. There were some pretty erudite arguments made. I don't necessarily agree with all of them. And, in hindsight, a lot of them are clunky or a little too close to fascist for comfort.

"But it scared the shit out of straight people, which ultimately is the goal of the underground."

Stafford, who had been attending art school at the time, was used to seeing his peers test the limits of acceptability. "Students would try to provoke a response and a critique by using a Christian cross or a swastika. I mean, there's four or five no-brainer, piss-a-bunch-of-people-off images you can throw into a picture," he says. "Which is not to say that they can't be used in a way that will provoke genuine critique and discourse, but most art students are pretty ham-fisted in their deployment of them."

The 8/8/88 event could be considered a clumsy handling of those symbols and their associated philosophies, Stafford says, "which is me basically saying it's not good art."

The night also augured a turning point in the relationships among the ringleaders, most of whom would never again work together. After having romantic dalliances with both Rice and Parfrey, Zeena soon became entwined with Schreck. "It's important on a human level to understand the degree of hatred that was then levied against Zeena," Schreck says. "The hatred of our relationship and how much we loved each other created this—we joked about it—*Satan Place*, like *Peyton Place*. It was a soap opera."

A little more than two months after the Strand performance—and just in time for Halloween—NBC aired *Devil Worship: Exposing Satan's*

Underground, Geraldo Rivera's alarmist "investigation" that claimed to rip the lid off the torture, murder, and child sexual abuse that devil worshippers were currently inflicting on the nation. He trumpeted this foulness with the same vigor he hyped the opening of gangster Al Capone's vaults just two years earlier—an undertaking that turned up bupkis.

For better or worse, *Devil Worship* would go on to deliver to the Church of Satan the biggest mainstream audience in its history. During primetime—those magic weeknight hours when viewers sat glued to their sets—it aired footage of Anton LaVey from *Satanis* within the first minute, the 8/8/88 rally and Nikolas Schreck within the first two, and the Satanic wedding and LaVey's appearance on *The Joe Pyne Show* (not to mention a shot of the cover of *The Satanic Bible*) within the first three. All before the opening credits. Even though sponsors didn't want to go anywhere near it, the program became the network's highest-rated two-hour documentary, seen in nearly twenty million homes.

As expected, the show trotted out a dubious assortment of subjects: parents who insisted their kids suffered extraordinary abuse at the McMartin preschool, "breeders" who claimed they gave up their babies for human sacrifice, and young convicted killers who said the Devil made them do it.

And then there were the usual associated bugaboos: Charles Manson, heavy metal music, supposed demonic possession.

For this mix of pretaped segments and a talk-show format, Zeena was on hand in front of the studio audience to defend her father's Satanism as a legitimate religion with thousands of adherents all over the world. Seated to her left was her father's former right-hand man, Michael Aquino, representing the Temple of Set, looking every inch the caricatured Satanist (or, in his case, Setian): preternatural jet-black hair combed forward to approximate Vulcan bangs, and profuse, winged eyebrows that suggested at any moment he might take flight. He told

Rivera that the evildoers showcased on the show weren't true Satanists but "the failures of a conventional religion." Later, after the host called *The Satanic Bible* "the handbook of devil worshippers everywhere" and falsely claimed that Anton LaVey and Sammy Davis Jr. worked on a film together, a photo of LaVey on the set of *The Devil's Rain* with John Travolta and Tom Skerritt flashed on screen.

Rivera announced that Aquino himself had been implicated in allegations of child abuse but that no charges were ever leveled against him and that, presumably, he had been exonerated.

Why were there no charges, he asked? At the time of the purported events in San Francisco, Aquino responded, he was working out of the National Defense University in Washington, DC.

But wasn't it a fact that a three-and-a-half-year-old girl identified him as her alleged molester? Well, her stepfather—an army chaplain—made an accusation on behalf of the child, Aquino countered, before pointing out that in the original FBI interview she denied ever being molested. Aquino, who was now based in St. Louis, said the girl had been subjected to therapy that developed her claims. (Along with a two-volume history of the Church of Satan, Aquino would go on to self-publish a five-hundred-page defense of his molestation case called *Extreme Prejudice: The Presidio "Satan Abuse" Scam.*)

Later in the program, in a pretaped segment, Nikolas Schreck launched into an impassioned defense of Manson and flaunted the clump of Charlie's hair he kept framed in his apartment. Footage flashed by of Boyd Rice intercut with Manson and serial killers Henry Lee Lucas, Richard Ramirez, and David Berkowitz.

At one point during the show, Rivera read from *The Satanic Bible*— "Death to the weakling"—which prompted Aquino to describe the book as a polemic that was never meant to be taken literally.

A few minutes later, one young murderer on death row said he took the book literally.

In the aftermath of *Devil Worship*, Aquino, who claimed Anton LaVey had refused an invitation to appear on the show, wrote that he and Zeena met in the studio before the taping: "She defended her father and his work courageously, but Rivera's attack would have been more effectively blunted if the author of *The Satanic Bible* had been there in person." He was also quick to point out that Zeena had been gracious to both him and his wife, the former Lilith Sinclair. They would soon develop a bond that would lead to an upending of the lives of the LaVeys.

Though LaVey didn't take part in the 8/8/88 program or the Geraldo debacle, both events would have a lasting impact on him.

V. Vale had interviewed LaVey at great length and published just a small portion of their discussions in 1989's *RE/Search #12: Modern Primitives*. "LaVey was complaining about that to me," says Jack Boulware, who as editor of *The Nose* magazine published a feature with the high priest a few years later.

"I'd spilled my guts to this guy," LaVey told him. "And they barely used any of it." In fact, the introduction to the *Modern Primitives* interview promised that *RE/Search #13* would be devoted entirely to LaVey's philosophy, work, and art.

According to Blanche Barton, LaVey sat for extensive interviews with RE/Search, something he rarely would do. He trusted them and appreciated what they'd already published. "After many months of collaborating and recording, they just fell away," she says. "Unfortunately, the project never came to fruition, and the many, many hours of unedited recordings were lost."

Another story has it that V. Vale and Andrea Juno abandoned the project after LaVey refused to sever ties with Rice. Although he had played a big role in the earlier RE/Search titles *Industrial Culture*

Handbook, Incredibly Strange Films, and *Pranks!,* Rice had become persona non grata thanks to some of his public utterances and unsavory
associations. "Boyd and Anton got along great," recalls Jim Morton,
"but Boyd was, as always, dancing around the edges of all the taboos in
society. He was doing things like visiting [Charles] Manson and hanging around with skinheads."

The situation between Anton and RE/Search exploded during an
event for the *Pranks!* book and its tie-in videotape, Morton recalls, when
one panelist referred to Rice as a Nazi and announced that RE/Search
was going to distance itself from him. "This was the first time anyone
called him a Nazi, but the label stuck," he says. "Suddenly, the party
line at RE/Search was, 'If you continue to associate with Boyd, you're
as guilty as the Germans who didn't protest Hitler, and we don't want
to have anything to do with you.' Anton liked Boyd and wasn't about to
forego their friendship any more than I was."

Stuart Swezey, with Brian King, ran Amok Books—a distributor of what
they called "the extremes of information." Before Adam Parfrey started
Feral House, Swezey's brother Kenneth partnered with him on the unre-
lated publishing imprint Amok Press. Stuart suspects that Parfrey, who
published Blanche Barton's authorized biography of her live-in companion in 1990, may have instigated LaVey's withdrawal from the RE/Search
project. "If you're being interviewed by RE/Search—I love those books,
but I'm just talking about on a financial level—they're basically saying, 'It
is our book about you,'" Swezey says. "Maybe someone else comes along
and says, 'You could take all those interviews and make a really good biography, and you can get royalties.' That might be appealing."

The RE/Search books, essentially slick, high-quality, journalistic
zines, didn't have to compensate interview subjects. At the time, an
appearance in one was payment enough. "It was almost like [Vale] felt
he was doing a public service by presenting these books," Swezey says.

"I have a feeling a part of it was Adam being a little more of a hustler than Vale was."

Still, it appears LaVey was willing to risk a relatively high-profile showcase in a hip, influential, internationally distributed publication, at least in part, to reward a friend's loyalty. *RE/Search #13*, instead of showcasing the life of one uncompromising artist and thinker, became 1991's *Angry Women*, featuring interviews with numerous uncompromising artists and thinkers, including Lydia Lunch, Karen Finley, and Diamanda Galás.

In late-'80s Los Angeles, Zeena and her son became close with Richard Lamparski, one of the boy's godfathers. "On Friday he would leave school, which was right in the middle of Hollywood, and take the bus to my house," says the writer, who lived alone. "Then he would stay with me until Sunday night, or sometimes even Monday morning. Zeena would tell her babysitter to pick up her son from me." Stanton said that it was at Lamparski's Hollywood Hills home where he spent some of his happiest weekends as a child.

Lamparski had relocated to Santa Barbara when one afternoon he received a phone call from Anton.

"Richard, I have a bone to pick with you. You're never to see Stanton again—you understand that? I don't want him in the same room with you."

"Why are you telling me what I can do and what I can't do?" Lamparski responded. "What is this about?"

"The idea that you would have sex with a boy," LaVey fumed.

Stunned that his friend would make such an accusation, Lamparski thought to himself, "I'm not going to take the bait."

LaVey persisted: "Well, do you want to say anything?"

"No, I have nothing to say to you," he answered. "This proves to me what a gullible fool you are."

And that was it. Nearly two decades of friendship—done.

"He banished me from his life," Lamparski says. "I had no indication of what was happening."

XII.

Friends of the Devil

AS a kid growing up in Sweden, Carl Abrahamsson read about this leader of a San Franciscan Satanic group in men's magazines. Abrahamsson, who was intuitively drawn to the occult, admired the high priest's style and philosophy. "It was no frills, straight-to-the-core efficiency," he says, "not preposterous or escapist, looking into someone else's belly button." And he was genuinely interested in the magic, "cutting away the bullshit and using strong symbols, because they create an emotional reverberation that you can use in ritual."

Combined with his enthusiasm for trash culture, his attachment to LaVey emboldened him creatively. As a young man, Abrahamsson had become what he calls an "occultural networker," active in Thee Temple ov Psychick Youth, the British magical order founded by experimental musician Genesis P-Orridge. Abrahamsson himself had a post-punk band called White Stains. The first song they ever recorded, 1988's "Sweet Jayne," told the story of Jayne Mansfield's relationship with LaVey and the church: "If you're going to San Francisco / There's a man you should meet . . . Esoteric insights in worlds of pleasure / 'Chastity is a sickening perversion.'" When P-Orridge, who had recently met the high priest, encouraged him to send a copy to LaVey, Abrahamsson, who knew of the man's distaste for rock music, thought, "Why not? Maybe he'll think it's funny."

He didn't expect the letter he received from San Francisco.

LaVey wrote that he was honored to have inspired Abrahamsson, and that Mansfield herself would have been thrilled by the song. He called Abrahamsson and P-Orridge pioneers of the new wave of Satanism, who were shaking up the rest of the world. The letter also included an appointment to membership in the church.

"That was a mindblower when I was like twenty-one," Abrahamsson says. "Then I realized I have to go in this direction." It took him a year before he could get the money together to fly out to California. "And that was the beginning of a beautiful friendship."

On that first trip to San Francisco in 1989, Abrahamsson, who wrote his university thesis about Aleister Crowley's influence on the films of Kenneth Anger, also got to meet the auteur himself. "I came home like a mental case," he says. "But in a good way."

On his second trip the following year, Abrahamsson brought along his girlfriend, who was also a magical traveler. After dinner the first evening, he surprised his host by asking if he would consider joining them in wedlock. LaVey agreed. And on the first day of the new year (on the Gregorian calendar), LaVey led the couple into the dusty old ritual chamber, a veritable museum of artifacts. "It was like stepping into a portal and into the church's heyday," Abrahamsson says.

For Abrahamsson, this gesture was the result of his asking for something very concretely and LaVey obliging in a sign of trust and friendship. After all, this was the man who wrote an essay titled "Satanic Weddings: Why I Don't Perform Them."

It was on a visit to the Black House when Abrahamsson got LaVey to contribute keyboards to the second White Stains album, 1991's *Dreams Shall Flesh*. He requested a Scandinavian feel, and LaVey just hammered away on something that sounded like it would accompany a hambo, a traditional Swedish folk dance, which Abrahamsson captured with his cassette recorder and titled "The Satanic Hambo." "Later on, I heard some Danish guys say, 'Wow, that's an old Danish folk song,'" Abrahamsson says. "It's like a super-silly kids' song. And [LaVey] had that in his mind when I said, 'Play something Scandinavian.' And I wondered, 'Where did he hear that, and how could he memorize that?'"

Abrahamsson's obsession with preserving LaVey did not start with that release. In 1990, he bought the Swedish rights to *The Satanic Bible* and worked on the translation for years, before publishing it in 1996. Later, he made the documentary feature *Anton LaVey: Into the Devil's Den* (and wrote a companion volume); published *California Infernal*, a gorgeous book filled with Walter Fischer's photos of LaVey and Mansfield; and designed *Debauched*, a compendium of highlights from sleazy Satanic men's magazines of the '60s and '70s. "LaVey loved his stuff. He was a bona fide materialist who derived pleasure from his things," says Abrahamsson, whose own contributions have gone a long way to sate the appetites of those who derive pleasure from LaVey.

For Zeena and Nikolas, spreading the Satanic gospel meant taping an interview—more of a debate, really—in 1989 with Bob Larson, a Christian evangelist. Larson, who has been called "the Larry King of

religious radio," amassed his following by tackling such sensational subjects as child abuse, homosexuality, incest, rock music, and demonic
possession.

At the top of the show, Larson offers, inaccurately, that Anton LaVey,
the church's high priest, is now a recluse who neither does interviews
nor makes any public pronouncements. He adds that the church's
affairs are overseen by his two guests, "the chief spokespersons for the
Church of Satan."

The couple, who married the previous year, are, naturally, dressed
all in black, while their interlocutor sports a camel-colored blazer that's
a near-perfect match with his hair helmet and beard—Zeena's hair too.

For a couple seemingly on a mission to represent Satanism, they
appear to misrepresent its beliefs. First, there's Schreck's seething
homophobia. "I personally don't believe that homosexuality is a natural
practice any more than you do," he tells Larson. Then, speaking for
the Werewolf Order—not, one presumes, as a chief spokesperson for
the Church of Satan—he adds, "We do not feel that homosexuality is a
healthy or natural or safe or hygienic practice."

Then the discussion turns to Hitler, as discussions with Schreck often
do. When asked by Larson if the man who killed six million Jews was
evil, he responds, "Hitler was a masterful black magician," adding that
he doesn't believe in the concepts of good and evil. So, Larson count-
ers, he's not willing to say that someone who killed six million Jews
can't be morally quantified and called evil? "Absolutely not," Schreck
says, "nor can any act of any human being or animal be judged good or
evil."

"I agree with that," chirps Zeena.

"History decides what is good and evil," Nikolas proclaims.

When talk turns to Charles Manson, as talks with Schreck inevitably
do, Schreck says he doesn't believe Manson is guilty of the crimes for
which he's been incarcerated.

Speaking of Manson . . . "My father is now suddenly lumped into these ranks," Zeena tells Larson. "Because all around me I hear now that my father is just like Manson, just like Hitler." Why might that be, the host inquires? "Now I'm beginning to realize that maybe there are two sides to every story," she offers, "and maybe if you examine the other side that you don't hear about, you learn something that is a little more illuminating."

As for murder, they refuse to condemn that too.

As for feeding the hungry?

"We don't look for help," Schreck says. "Why should we give help to others?"

What about the people who read her dad's words and then sacrifice animals or humans in his name?

"Just because you read a book," Zeena says, "doesn't make you that thing."

"How many people have read the Holy Bible, misinterpreted it, and acted on it?" Schreck offers, sensibly.

"Do you know what John Wayne Gacy said to all of his victims?" asks Zeena rhetorically, teeing up her beau.

"He read the Twenty-Third Psalm," Schreck swings. "Should we now say that John Wayne Gacy is a Christian murderer? It's a foolish, sweeping generalization. Anyone can read a book. Mark David Chapman, who killed John Lennon, read *Catcher in the Rye*. Should we ban *Catcher in the Rye*?"

"Christianity is occultism," Schreck says later.

"Everything is a fairy tale. Christ is a fairy tale as much as Satan. It depends on what archetype you choose."

Larson, who would later turn his attention to performing exorcisms, made the resulting ninety-minute videocassette, *The First Family of Satanism*, available through his Denver ministry. Don Frew, a friend of Anton's, attended the National Religious Broadcasters Convention, a conference for evangelical Christian media professionals, where Larson premiered the tape in 1990.

"It was quite an adventure," Frew says, "because I was the only witch there."

He had been approached by Larson to talk about the book *Satanism in America*. "I had already been involved in consulting for the police on occult crime and had a bit of a reputation in that demimonde," Frew says, adding that he and his coauthors figured Larson had targeted him as the weakest link since he was the sole occultist among them and could be used to represent the whole inquiry. "I don't remember why I agreed. I probably thought it would be fun—and it was." While there, he attended a screening of Larson's video and afterward conferred with Shawn Carlson, one of the book's primary authors.

"We went to LaVey and said, 'There's a problem here. If you are going to be recommending Zeena, and Zeena's bringing Schreck, we have to distance ourselves from you. We can't be connected with this. We're sorry.'" Frew says. "Because she was going to really hurt his image."

Around this time, having endured the Satanic Panic out of the public eye, LaVey—with help from Nick Bougas, Schreck, Zeena, and Blanche—produced his own video to explain his brand of Satanism to the masses. Provisionally titled *Hail Satan!*, it featured the high priest expounding on such topics as film noir, drug use, and artists and writers he deemed Satanic (including Edward Hopper and Ben Hecht), as well as refuting hoary tropes about "breeders" and child abductors. "Instead of him having to go on these dreary talk shows and get booed off the stage, [the church] could just send a video," says Abrahamsson.

After it was done, Schreck, who, along with Zeena, had become embittered by LaVey and the church, disavowed the program. "It was not good," he says. "He was very uncomfortable before the camera. He was awkward." The video was never released in its entirety.

Soon, Zeena and Nikolas would relocate to Vienna, Austria, where they pursued their music with young Stanton in tow. But it was not an ideal move for a wild, violent kid who'd already experienced his share of trauma. After a rough few years there, which included homelessness and psychiatric hospitals, Stanton returned to the States to live with his grandparents. He and Zeena would last speak in 1995 and remain estranged for the rest of his life.

The '90s saw the resurrection of Anton LaVey as not only a kitschy pop icon, but also as a sort of elder statesman—an *éminence grisly*—for a new breed of misanthropic hipster, one whose ironic detachment, much like LaVey's, could sometimes end up flirting with fascism.

"By that point, Anton had become old school," says the occult historian Mitch Horowitz. "And when you're old school, the new scene wants to sit at your feet and gain wisdom. Anton benefited from that process."

Blanche Barton links this revived interest in LaVey directly to the Satanic Panic—more specifically to "yo-yos" like Larson and critics whose books took aim at the church. "Because they were railing against us, and many times publishing our actual Satanic Statements, describing Dr. LaVey as an evil man because he spoke out against the oppression of conventional religion . . . young adults were going to do their own research," Barton says. "They found a philosophy that embraces freedom of expression, encourages alternative lifestyles and unconventionality. He offered romance and defiance, something far more subtle and complex than what their parents and preachers were warning them against."

One thing about LaVey that appealed to those putting together zines was his accessibility. "He was a well-known figure, and also kind of frightening," says Gregg Turkington, who published zines in the early

'90s. "I could see why for any fanzine, if they had the opportunity to get an interview, that would be exciting. It legitimizes your magazine. It's one thing to interview the Circle Jerks, but it's another to be interviewing the infamous Anton LaVey."

Musician JG Thirlwell chalks LaVey's appeal up to his iconoclasm. "A lot of people were interested in exploring the dark side of the human psyche and maybe felt like this was a doorway into that," he says. "Also, it's kind of punk rock. It's something that could be really upsetting to your parents."

Thirlwell also designed covers and other graphics for *Exit*, a provocative art magazine published from 1984 to 1991 by George Petros that for a time was edited by both Petros and his friend Adam Parfrey. It attracted such notables as Robert Williams, S. Clay Wilson, Joe Coleman, Raymond Pettibon, and Devo's Mark Mothersbaugh, who contributed primitive and often sublime comics, illustrations, and collages. Though *Exit* wasn't shy about printing (lots of) swastikas and images of sexual violence, "it wasn't hateful, scolding, finger-pointing stuff," Petros insists. "It was using the currents of dissent and problems in society as materials to create works of art. Of course [it was] for shock value, because we were beyond aesthetics."

The in-your-face content may have been the main draw but, he adds, "We tried to put beauty in there. We didn't hate anybody. We left that to others and respected other people's hate."

Petros didn't run an interview with LaVey in *Exit*, but instead solicited a contribution from him for a special section on Charles Manson that was supposed to run in the sixth issue, in 1992. That magazine, which went unfinished and unpublished, was eventually collected in an *Exit* anthology and can be found online. With friend and collaborator John Aes-Nihil, Petros transcribed every Manson interview he could find, gathering aphorisms that he then commissioned artists and others to illustrate. The artists included Genesis P-Orridge and H.R. Giger;

the others, Martin Luther King Jr. assassin James Earl Ray and serial killers Richard Ramirez, Ottis Toole, and Henry Lee Lucas. Though a talented illustrator and painter himself, LaVey instead contributed a sarcastic and needling short paragraph that Petros placed in a frame. The first line reads, "The American people owe Charles Manson a debt of gratitude." The penultimate: "He is omnipresent and has been very generous with his time in helping others to cope with the pain of their own insignificance."

After *Exit* dissolved, Petros became editor of *Seconds*, a more mainstream music and culture magazine, which ran a Q&A with LaVey in 1994. That interview, conducted by Michael Moynihan, a musical collaborator of Boyd Rice's, perhaps unsurprisingly touched on two popular Mansons: Charles ("I do feel [the media have] made him out to be something that he's not—he's not the little guy with scissors who cuts little kids' fingers off") and Marilyn ("he's performing in a manner like a pied piper, through outrage").

Petros attributes LaVey's second wind, his new generation of admirers in the '90s, to the *Seconds* piece. "We got that issue into the hands of a lot of people who became influential," he says, "who went on to become the metal and punk icons." And whether they learned of LaVey through *Seconds*, those ranks would come to include Glenn Danzig, Hank Williams III, King Diamond, and countless death metal bands with spiderwebby logos.

The editor has his own theory about why LaVey was so attractive to zine creators and other alternative culture demi-celebs of the day. "It was in service of their own personality cults that they were promoting," he says. "They weren't doing it for any aesthetic or larger sociopolitical motivation. It was, 'I couldn't get your attention through doing something beautiful, so I got it through doing something horrible. How controversial of a name could I drop here, just to get people to pay attention to me?'"

Artist and publisher Shane Bugbee, a key player in this jaundiced "Art That Kills" movement, recalls his first encounter with a LaVey was seeing Zeena, not her father, on TV. "For a lot of people of my generation," he says, "that's who caught our eye—*what was that?* Because she was speaking of our generation, where Anton was of a different generation. He was an old man, so you sort of discount the old men, as I'm being discounted now by young people."

Bugbee saw his own work as a reaction to flower-powered pipe dreams. "I would tell these hippies, 'Peace and love didn't work, bro. I'm working here cleaning dishes too much and not paying any bills. You failed. I don't care how many statues you blew up—you failed us. Fuck you. You want peace and love. We're going to go with hate and violence.' And so, our artwork was all angry.

"The photocopy machine empowered us."

Even *Rolling Stone* took notice of Anton LaVey's resurgence in the new counterculture. For a profile in the September 5, 1991, issue featuring cover stars Guns N' Roses, journalist Lawrence Wright spent two weeks with Anton and Blanche and others in San Francisco. Unlike other reporters, who usually credulously parroted the high priest's claims without so much as an arched eyebrow, Wright took the initiative to investigate some of LaVey's oft-regurgitated biographical details and uncovered a few myth-busting disparities.

One: the San Francisco Police Department had no record of anyone with his name(s) having ever worked there.

Another: San Francisco never had an official city organist, so LaVey could not have been one.

And another: the San Francisco Ballet Orchestra, an ensemble LaVey said he joined as a fifteen-year-old oboist, didn't exist, and the local symphony hired to accompany the ballet had no listing for an oboist with his name.

Yet another: Paul Valentine, who ran the Mayan Theatre, told Wright that Marilyn Monroe never danced there, nor did LaVey ever work there.

But despite the clarifications and rebuttals that pepper his piece, Wright did continue to perpetuate a few falsehoods: that LaVey and Diane were married, that LaVey inspired the title character in *The Abominable Dr. Phibes*, that LaVey played the Devil in *Rosemary's Baby*.

He interviewed Michael Aquino, who accused his former mentor of losing faith and being insecure about leading an organization "that had grown beyond him." Wright also tracked down LaVey's eighty-seven-year-old father.

After Wright raised some of the discrepancies with his subject, LaVey, angered that the journalist had contacted his dad, responded, "I don't want the legend to disappear. There is a danger you will disenchant a lot of young people who use me as a role model. I'd rather have my background shrouded in mystery. Eventually you want to be recognized for what you are now."

More than thirty years later, Wright says he initially approached LaVey not as a media celebrity, but as a religious figure. "I was interested in religion and all its manifestations," he says, "especially in America where you can believe in anything you want, and if you don't see something that appeals to you, you can create your own religion. So the fact that somebody could identify with Satan and mold a brand around it really intrigued me."

And LaVey was thrilled that *Rolling Stone*, founded as a countercultural newspaper in San Francisco a year after the church, would be writing about him. "He was very welcoming," Wright recalls. "But I took that to mean he was interested in courting the readership of *Rolling Stone*, a natural target for him."

Like others who found themselves in LaVey's orbit, including Don Frew, Wright was surprised when the high priest took an interest—either genuine or feigned—in his father. "I think he had read this memoir I had written," Wright says. "I mean, he studied up, and he seemed to identify with my father. My father was a conservative banker in Dallas. He even taught Sunday school." But Wright couldn't figure out what it was about his dad that appealed to LaVey. "I began to wonder if he saw me in some way as a kind of protégé or stand-in son."

He never heard from his subject after publishing the piece, which he collected in his 1993 book *Saints and Sinners*—featuring other controversial religious and irreligious figures, like disgraced televangelist Jimmy Swaggart and atheist Madalyn Murray O'Hair—though LaVey and his followers would never forget it.

Wright returned to again explore the S-word with 1994's *Remembering Satan*, a true-crime book that investigated the story of two sisters who accused their father of heinous abuse that he, a well-liked sheriff's deputy, came to believe he committed.

As a result of that book, Wright had fallen into deep disfavor with the psychiatric community, which he had accused of creating a panic. One psychotherapist in Austin, Texas, who was behind much of the recovered memory hysteria there, was persistent in her efforts to convince him of its factual basis.

Wright had asked Richard Ofshe, the sociologist who punctured the fantasies of the father in the *Remembering Satan* case, to come talk to the district attorney about an Austin day-care case that descended into chaos. "It was horrible," Wright says. "These people went to prison for fifteen years before they were pardoned." While Ofshe was in town, he was invited to see a young man who claimed he grew up in Anton LaVey's house. Naturally, Ofshe asked Wright to join him. Wright's antagonist, the recovered memory therapist, was there. "[The kid] was talking to a group of therapists and psychologists in this small hotel conference room," Wright recalls. "And the interlocutor would say, 'You brought some artifacts from LaVey's house for the rituals. Here is this chalice and here is a *Satanic Bible* and here's a knife that they used for ritual murder. Any questions?'"

"So you grew up in Anton LaVey's house—do you remember what color the house was?" Wright asked.

The kid blanked out. "White?"

"It's probably the most famous black house in San Francisco, if not the whole country," Wright told him. "So, I guess his children were your playmates? Do you remember their names?"

"You got me," the kid said with a shrug.

"And here's the thing," Wright continues. "The therapist kept passing around the artifacts—the ritual dagger and all this stuff—as if nothing happened. I just got up and left."

Wright would go on to win a Pulitzer Prize for his book *The Looming Tower: Al-Qaeda and the Road to 9/11*, which he followed up with *Going Clear: Scientology, Hollywood, and the Prison of Belief*, a magnificent history of L. Ron Hubbard's pseudoscientific religious cult. He says he sees a kinship between Hubbard and LaVey "in their religious imagination, their inventiveness, and their capacity to build a saleable brand. In that sense, they were both very American figures. Not that I approve of their product, except that I recognize that they were talented in that direction. And their movements have outlived both of them."

Though he believes Hubbard took his self-generated faith as gospel, Wright says he's not convinced LaVey ever "crossed the line into believing his own bullshit."

Toward the end of the *Rolling Stone* profile, almost as an aside, Wright dropped a nugget of information that would cause reverberations throughout the church like the banging of a thousand gongs. He learned one evening during his time with Anton that, in a letter to

Michael Aquino, Zeena "had chosen this special day to renounce her father."

In the missive, issued from the Radio Werewolf Ministry of Propaganda & Public Enlightenment, dated December 30, 1990, Zeena informed the Temple of Set leader that the previous April she ritualistically terminated her affiliation with the Church of Satan and her relationship with her "unfather," whom she described as "ungrateful" and "unworthy." She branded Anton a "coward" who sat in his easy chair while she and others publicly defended their beliefs before frequently hostile crowds. "I believe he is, through his ostrich-in-the-sand stance, a detriment to any attempt at halting the scapegoat fever that has entered all of 'our' private lives," she wrote.

She also took issue with Blanche Barton's LaVey biography, *The Secret Life of a Satanist,* calling the book an "absurd catalogue of lies," and claiming it malignantly exploited her son, Stanton, by including a photo of him and her, without their permission, while portraying Anton "as a loving family man."

And she belittled LaVey by declaring her own pedigree: "I was born a Satanist; my unfather was raised in the mundane world of humankind where he remains."

"I have never seen any evidence that he honestly believes in the force whom he has for so long exploited as a 'good gimmick,'" she wrote, while crediting her mother, Diane, as being "the driving force of the most positive aspects of the Church of Satan."

Zeena sent the letter to Aquino in hopes of mending some fences, according to Nikolas Schreck. "She also knew what he was like, and that he would print it, and that it would bother her father tremendously." The fact that her repudiation was announced to the world in a mainstream venue like *Rolling Stone* embarrassed LaVey, says Schreck. "He didn't want people to know. He hoped we would just drift away and disappear."

At the time, LaVey dismissed Zeena's antipathy as her way of bolstering her reputation. "She feels she has a legacy to gain," he said. "I think she's got a father fixation."

Barton offered her version of the split after an article in the *Village Voice* newspaper in 2002 questioned LaVey's credentials. "Zeena Schreck got mad at Daddy because he wouldn't give her the Church of Satan," she wrote, adding, "She stomped her feet, picked up her toys and fabricated reasons to hate him. She's still doing it. Like so many celebrity kids, she's built an identity for herself by painting her father as a lying, abusive, talentless, selfish S.O.B."

During the height of the Satanic Panic, Barton says, "Schreck saw an opportunity to try to persuade Anton he was too old for this fight, and that Zeena and he were ready to take on the glamour of running the Church of Satan. He saw merchandising possibilities, no doubt, and a springboard for his musical endeavors."

Schreck says he had absolutely no interest in taking over the church, and despite appearances to the contrary, was never even a member. He blames his and Zeena's dissension on multiple factors. When he first got to know her, Zeena told him she wanted to be an actress, a musician, an artist. "She did not at any point ever want to take control of this meaningless thing that was an old man in his house," he says. And she couldn't stomach having to constantly regurgitate lies about *Rosemary's Baby* and Jayne Mansfield. "It was creating cognitive dissonance in her because she is an ethical person, unlike her father.

"She was not what people would expect a Satanist to be," Schreck adds. As a well-spoken, telegenic young woman successfully defanging accusations against the church, she made her father jealous, he says, leading Anton to try to sabotage her other public appearances and employment opportunities. His animosity reached its nadir, Schreck says, when LaVey directed a stalker of hers to a Los Angeles event she was coordinating. "That's how bad it got. That was the turning point."

Having corresponded with Michael Aquino while they lived in Vienna, after returning to America, Zeena and Nikolas—true believers, after all—joined his Temple of Set. "It was a horrific experience," Schreck says. "A lot of our tension with Aquino was that, despite his dislike of Anton, he also had this almost homophilic love of him that we found unbearable. He was such a fanboy." Chief among their disagreements was Aquino's introduction of atheistic Satanic elements into this supposedly Egyptian religion. "It didn't make sense."

Working in a zine store at the dawn of the 1990s, Reuben Radding had a front-row seat to the DIY-publishing revolution. From his station behind the register in the cramped See Hear, on East Seventh Street in Manhattan's East Village, he read them all. And for someone who used to carry around *The Satanic Bible* as a teenager in Arlington, Virginia, discovering Eugene Robinson's piece in *The Birth of Tragedy* was a revelation. "Oh, how interesting," Radding remembers thinking of LaVey's reemergence. "This thing that I felt a connection to—here's this guy and he actually has really interesting things to say."

In the early days of internet message boards, when cranks with screeching modems began to log on and make their unsolicited opinions known to complete strangers ten thousand miles away, Radding would occasionally come across comments disparaging the Church of Satan. He'd engage in flame wars with these shit-talkers—always, he says, emerging victorious. This earned him the admiration of high-ranking New York church members and an invitation to meet LaVey. So, he booked a trip to San Francisco and took a week off.

He figured he'd enjoy one memorable evening at the Black House, where Kenneth Anger also had been living at the time. But the first night led to another, then another, then another, then another. "I got to hang out in his kitchen and watch him play for three or four straight hours," says Radding, who was soon to become a bassist of some renown on New York's downtown music scene. "All I can say is this: even if it was 100 percent rehearsed shtick, it was amazing."

Maybe LaVey exaggerated stories about himself, but to Radding he wasn't just some guy puffing himself up. "He had all the skills of somebody who had done the things he claimed to have done. I watched that guy for hours play eight different keyboards like a madman—that was a guy who had played theater organs for a living. It didn't matter if he didn't do it, he could have done it. You could name some song that he barely remembered from the fucking '40s, and not only would he manage to pick it out, he'd make up this whole crazy full orchestral arrangement. It was just awe-inspiring."

One night, LaVey played a song that he asked Radding to transcribe for him. He supplied the younger musician with a recording of it, from which Radding created the sheet music, marketed it, and gave LaVey a big cut of the sales. The notation for "Hymn of the Satanic Empire, or Battle Hymn of the Apocalypse" would later be printed in LaVey's essay collection *The Devil's Notebook*.

"He was a character, and he treated people with great respect," Radding says. "It was like he was Frank Sinatra or something—you know, not a killer, but the guy who hangs with the killers."

Like many people with particular obsessions, material or otherwise, LaVey was cursed with a fear of missing out. Jim Morton saw this firsthand when he met Leon Theremin in September 1991 at a Stanford University tribute to the inventor of the strange electronic musical instrument that bears his name. "To me it was like meeting [Nikola] Tesla," Morton says. "But when I told Anton about it later, he was so pissed off." LaVey, who claimed that he used the instrument during his days as a ghostbuster to detect otherworldly intrusions, had said that at one point he was the only registered theremin player in San Francisco's musicians' union (though the union's records indicate otherwise). He loved the alien sounds it conjured.

"But nobody bothered to tell Anton because they all assumed he knew about it," Morton says.

"Because he was Anton."

During the Los Angeles riots in 1992, as the city exploded after a jury acquitted four police officers in the brutal beating of Rodney King, whom they suspected of driving while intoxicated, Larry Wessel, an indie filmmaker, was out on the streets videotaping for a documentary he was going to call *Ultramegalopolis*. As he wrapped up filming one morning, he visited his friend Adam Parfrey, who was living in LA at the time. Parfrey told him that he, too, was working on a documentary, shooting material about Anton LaVey for a film Nick Bougas was directing. Parfrey knew about Wessel's affection for *The Satanic Bible* and asked him to talk about it on camera.

"I want to shoot it right away," Parfrey told him.

"I'll go home and dress up in a black suit," Wessel said, "so I can look appropriate."

"No, no. I just want to shoot it right now, off the cuff, in my front yard."

In his red tank top and shorts, with his pageboy haircut and goggle-like specs, Wessel didn't think he was the picture of the modern Satanist, but he agreed to the ad hoc conditions and spoke about how *The Satanic Bible* made a big impact on him as a teen, presenting him with a healthy way to channel his hatred and destroy effigies of those who "irk" him. Bougas ended up using the entire interview, uncut, in *Speak of the Devil*, released the following year.

When he was invited to visit LaVey in San Francisco, Wessel didn't want to come empty-handed, so he schlepped with him a mosaic he had constructed of Anton's face that was based on the *Look* magazine cover and placed it in a big baroque frame. He wanted to present it to the high priest's first son, Satan Xerxes Carnacki LaVey, who had just arrived. And for Anton? He found a novelty shop in the city, where he asked the proprietor, "What do I get for an older guy who has every practical joke imaginable?"

"I have just the thing," the man told him as he reached under the counter, opened a drawer, and pulled out an electronic, remote-controlled whoopee cushion. Wessel also found a nice clean copy of a 78-rpm record from 1945 that was a favorite of his father's: "The Dark Town Poker Club" by Phil Harris.

As fog rolled in on this typical San Francisco evening, Wessel arrived early but pressed the buzzer exactly when he was told to. Suddenly he heard a van pull up. He turned around and saw LaVey exiting the vehicle. Blanche was driving, Xerxes—as they called the kid—was in the back. Tony, their driver, was there too.

At the time Wessel was finishing up a documentary on bullfighting, which triggered a conversation about the brutal contest between man and beast. "That's how I found out that his inspiration for playing the keyboards was when his parents took him to see a bullfight in Tijuana, at the same old bullring that I haunted, way back when he was a child," Wessell says. "Hearing those pasodobles really affected him. He committed all of the classic pasodobles to memory."

"Larry, I want to thank you for sticking your neck out for Satanism," LaVey told him that night. "I liked your section in that documentary better than anybody's. You summed up Satanism better than anyone."

Wessel admits he was a little frightened to hear that. Till then he had found LaVey to be jovial, funny, and warm. "Thanking me for sticking my neck out? I thought, 'Oh my God, what have I done? Am I in some kind of danger?'" Wessel says. "He was always getting death threats, on the telephone, in the mail, in person."

On one of Wessel's visits, LaVey showed him the "kook file." "He pulled out a photograph and a letter from one of these fans," Wessel recalls. "The fan had a bald head and a goatee, and a scowl, obviously trying to portray himself as someone who looked like Anton LaVey. But he wasn't handsome like LaVey. He was an ugly dude." LaVey just shook his head and told Wessel, "I wrote back to this asshole. I almost never write back to any of these kooks, but this particular one, I couldn't help myself." He showed Wessel a copy of the letter he'd sent.

"He wrote that he took one look at this guy's photograph," Wessel says, "and immediately wanted to flush it down the toilet."

"I asked out a brunette one year, and it turned out she was Karla LaVey."

Ron Quintana, who grew up in San Francisco in the '60s and '70s, remembers knowing about Anton LaVey and the Black House. But when he started to date his daughter circa 1992, he had no clue about her family. "She never told me for a while," he says. "She was busy. She was a real estate person, so she was always working." Quintana learned of her parentage after telling a roommate that Karla had invited him to meet "Pops" at his house in the Richmond District, around Twenty-Third Street. "Oh," his roommate replied. "Is that Anton LaVey's place?" Hearing that, Quintana approached the visit with a little trepidation, and admits to being mildly surprised at how engaging and funny the older man was. "He just seemed to enjoy life and always be in a good mood."

Quintana recalls spending one stormy Christmas Eve at the run-down Black House, what he called "an interesting place to sleep"—cats all over the place and Anton hanging in the kitchen, pumping out tiki tunes on his keyboards deep into the cold, dark night.

Blanche and Anton routinely had dinner with his father, Michael, who lived in the nearby Sunset District and had been working in real estate in his later years. "Michael was funny and flirty," she recalls, "always full of jokes." And though Michael died on August 21, 1992, his son wasn't informed until two weeks later. "[He] had gone to the hospital for abdominal pain, and we were told he died on the operating table," Blanche says, adding that his second wife didn't seem to like her step-son. "There was never a funeral or memorial, as far as we knew. We weren't called; we received a brief formal letter in the mail. Anton called and was given sparse details, but we never heard from the family again." LaVey, who Barton says received no family mementos or pictures, "was left saddened and frustrated by the whole affair."

One of the more notorious zines of the era shared its title with an old Nat King Cole song Anton LaVey loved to perform. *Answer Me!* was the feculent discharge of Jim Goad and his wife, Debbie, whose anti-social rants had the distinction of being spectacularly vile, but also well-written and often very funny.

Leading off the magazine's second issue in 1992—right before inter-views with neo-Nazi presidential candidate David Duke and *SCREW* magazine kvetcher in chief Al Goldstein, an essay titled "The Family Must Be Eliminated," *and* a serial killer Hot 100—is a conversation with LaVey, conducted at the house after the two couples returned from a (possibly facetious) meal of frogs' legs and chocolate mousse and the Goads had been treated to an organ recital live from the breakfast nook. Predictably, Jim and Anton got along infamously.

Reading the transcript of their conversation is like sitting courtside at the Wimbledon of misanthropy.

"I don't believe in equality," LaVey tells his interlocutor, in one of their first volleys, before adding, "The most equal of human beings, I would say, would be on the lowest level. . . . God must have loved them, 'cause he made so many of them." Equality is akin to the concept of reincarnation, he adds, another flight of fancy that "will allow the lowest to feel that they are equal to the highest."

Tapping into his deep well of arrogance, LaVey also speaks of the superiority of the entertainer. "Those who are the performers in life are certainly not equal to the audience, who occupies a much vaster space than the performers onstage," he says. "The performer, or the stimulator . . . is someone who deserves a little more . . . subsidizing than the person who needs stimulation and gains stimulation from that performer."

A human's greatest need in life, he declares, is stimulation: "That allows these spores in this great yeast mold to know that they're alive, that they're actually functioning."

After the topic turns to human sacrifice and LaVey tells Goad why he prefers the humiliation and degradation of one's enemies to homicide, he reveals the reason he's titillated by war: "Because it gives entire countries a chance to advocate, if not cutting the hearts out of human victims, certainly shooting them down in wholesale lots or blowing them up."

When the subject bounces to the New Testament, Goad asks, "Would you be saying that Jesus had maybe a sexual need to be crucified?" LaVey's answer? "Oh, of course, yeah."

Of course.

In the interview, LaVey explores the nature of truth. "Truth is very much a subjective thing," he says. "Because there are different kinds of truths, just like there are different kinds of love." There are "hard," "demonstrable" facts, but there's also the truth that propagandists peddle, which LaVey says, "can be altered or manipulated according to the dictates or the needs of what truth is supposed to be."

It's in the process of tackling a question about what pisses him off ("people that blame leaders," for one) when LaVey seems to explicitly answer a different question entirely—that is, does he bear any responsibility for disturbed individuals who commit misdeeds in his name? He doesn't care whether a leader is named Joseph Stalin, Adolf Hitler, Charles Manson, or white supremacist Tom Metzger—they'll always take the heat for "what the knuckleheads or the dunderheads or the stupes do to, perhaps, overextend what they have said. EACH LIVING CREATURE, whether it's human or otherwise, should be held responsible for ITS actions."

And when it comes to living creatures, LaVey sees more value in those that are otherwise than those that are human. "I wouldn't squash a spider, but I could kill a human being," LaVey says. "A spider is being the best spider he can be. . . . He meshes perfectly with nature's overall scheme. Nothing in nature is wasted, and I can't say the same thing about people."

If Adam Parfrey's Feral House was the main publishing engine that drove LaVey's popularity into the '90s, it was editor Jack Boulware and his colleagues at *The Nose* who helped expand LaVey's social orbit, leading to many lasting friendships and fruitful collaborations.

The Nose was a slick newsstand magazine that aspired to transpose the snarky, investigative, New York aesthetic of *SPY* to hip, weird San

Francisco. A few contributors, including Patton Oswalt and Marc Maron, went on to become bold-faced names themselves. Inside, profiles of Tin Pan Alley simulacrum Tiny Tim, perpetually angry televangelist Gene Scott, and bosom-fixated filmmaker Russ Meyer rubbed up against stories about adult diaper cults, celebrity wife beaters, and the grisly murder of *Hogan's Heroes* star Bob Crane.

"We used to joke in the *Nose* newsroom, 'If there isn't a beheading, we're not interested,'" Boulware says. "A story pitch had to have some sort of intensity to it." He chalks that up to the competition he faced from other, less-professional zines. "There was a shitload of magazines at that time. And there was cable television, but there wasn't streaming. I suppose the YouTube/TikTok world where young idiots eat ghost peppers and film themselves—things like that would've been a zine article twenty-five years ago."

For Boulware and others in the alternative press, the idea was to do something unique, that would get attention, "that told readers that this isn't just a world of *Entertainment Weekly* and *Vanity Fair* and *Harper's*."

In 1990, Boulware received an advance copy of Blanche Barton's LaVey bio in the mail. He'd seen the guy mentioned countless times in Herb Caen's *Chronicle* column and was curious. He ended up devouring the entire book in one day.

"The city used to be teeming with people like this," he says. "I thought LaVey was an interesting character, and I didn't know that he was still alive." Boulware wrote a review of *The Secret Life of a Satanist* for *SF Weekly*.

After the piece ran, the phone rang in his little shabby office on Seventh and Market. Barton was calling. "The Doctor would like to meet you."

They agreed to an early dinner at a restaurant in the Marina District. "He orders a steak bloody rare, and we just started talking about all kinds of stuff," Boulware says. "He was a really interesting, engaging person." The two discovered a shared fondness for old forgotten hill-billy music and flamboyant publisher Robert Harrison's scandalous magazines of the '50s, like *Whisper* and *Confidential*. LaVey, Boulware found, had a charismatic ability to draw you into a conversation even if, intellectually, you felt in over your head. "And yet he would encourage you to keep talking. Who doesn't love that?"

At the conclusion of the meal, LaVey turned to Blanche: "Should we go back to the house and get out the keyboards?"

"Yeah," she responded. "I think that would be a good idea."

Boulware, who picked up the check, felt as if he had passed some sort of test. Once at the house, they settled into the kitchen, where LaVey attacked his bank of keyboards, regaling his guest with circus music and stripper anthems. After he played for a while, he invited Boulware to sit in. The editor, who had studied piano and was a musician in high school but hadn't played in years, started poking out "Roly Poly" by Bob Wills and His Texas Playboys, a silly tune about a kid who can't stop eating. LaVey recognized the song right away. "Keep going, keep going," he urged his guest.

"I remember we were drinking horrible instant coffee out of these Church of Satan mugs," says Boulware, who was surreptitiously inter-viewing his host the whole time. "I wasn't writing anything down, but I didn't know where it was going to go. I was just like, 'How often do you get this moment?'"

A few things about LaVey stick with Boulware some thirty years after their initial encounters. One was his lack of teeth. Another was what was in his fridge. "I noticed there were a lot of juices," he says.

"I was like, Satan is fueled by fruit juice. That's pretty interesting."

With Feral House's 1992 release of *The Devil's Notebook*, LaVey's first collection of writing in two decades—and a book that had been in the works for just as long—*The Nose* team wanted to find a way to feature the author in the magazine. Having given interviews to *The*

Birth of Tragedy, Modern Primitives, and *Answer Me!,* LaVey wasn't a
stranger to the alternative press. At that time, says Boulware, "It was a
real button-pusher to run an interview with the head of the Church of
Satan. That's why *The Nose* never published an interview, because all
these others had." But what the others hadn't done was a fashion shoot,
so *The Nose* did one instead.

Unlike, say, *Vogue* or *GQ,* which relied heavily on fashion advertising to support their editorial efforts, *The Nose* never made any money
leveraging shoots. It likely didn't help that the magazine's previous fashion spreads took their cues from serial killers and the LA riots.

Regardless, along with fashion editor Becky Wilson, Boulware com-
missioned photographer Jay Blakesberg. After Boulware secured Adam
Parfrey's permission to run some book excerpts, Wilson reached out to
LaVey, who told her he was game.

On the day of the shoot, March 28, 1993, Blakesberg arrived with
his assistant at 6114. "We knocked on the door, and it just opened with
nobody there," he recalls. "It appeared to open magically by itself." It
was helped along by Tony Fazzini, whom the photographer remembers
as a guy who looked like he could have been an accountant in 1954:
horn-rimmed glasses, bald, wearing a suit with a pentagram pin on his
lapel.

For the photos, LaVey, who'd be posing with Blanche and a model,
would be wearing clothes from local retailers as well as his own vintage duds, including a chalk-striped gangster's suit, burgundy sharkskin
jacket, and a plaid sports jacket he said came from Michael's, a hab-
erdashery owned by mob boss Mickey Cohen. He'd also be handling
his bullwhip and a few of his other weapons. The stylist had brought
a safari outfit for him, which he agreed to wear, but he did balk at one
article of clothing. "No shorts," he said, firmly. "I'm not going to wear
the shorts."

Throughout the afternoon session, LaVey played along and enjoyed himself. Despite the Den of Iniquity's very low ceilings, which posed lighting challenges for Blakesberg, the cramped basement, replete with a vintage jukebox, stocked bar, and black-velvet Devil painting, made an ideal setting—though Boulware admittedly found the artificial denizens populating the scene unsettling: the man with a sailor's cap and a pump on his waist that when activated gave him an erection; the moll in garters and beret, flipping the bird; the bowtied, pencil-mustachioed barkeep; the blitzed floozy, dress hiked up above her knees, sitting in a puddle of pee. There was nothing overtly Satanic about all this, Boulware thought, and he wondered why someone would spend so much time putting together this debauched collection of mannequins. "A little Cub Scout with a giant hard-on?" he says, describing another figure. "I'm sure it was pretty hilarious if he had a dinner party in 1968 and brought the guests down there, when they'd all have cocktails and laugh at it."

Explaining their appeal, LaVey wrote in *The Devil's Notebook*, "I can enjoy their presence and there is no psychic drain."

For Boulware, the basement's beautiful Hammond organ was the main attraction. Especially impressive were the keys, some of which lit up green while others glowed red. "It was just this cheesy effect you might have seen in a Los Angeles steakhouse in 1952. But it fits in with his willingness to live in a world of nostalgia."

When the magazine finally appeared, LaVey loved the spread. "We were kind of concerned," Boulware remembers. "He seemed to be a very private guy, and here was this young bunch of misfit people doing a magazine."

The issue was a smash. And then came the back orders. "Satanists would call our office phone and say, 'I'm very interested in issue number eighteen, in particular. How many copies can I buy?' They were always very polite, very reserved."

Boulware visited LaVey a few more times after the shoot, one night looking at his Robert Harrison magazines for hours. "He had individual polybagged copies," he recalls, "and the collection was very well-organized. I thought, I bought one copy at a used shop and it was forty bucks. This guy must have invested heavily." It was really late and Boulware was struggling to stay awake, and there was LaVey, pointing out a particularly noteworthy seam of a nylon stocking on a newsprint page of an old scandal rag.

Once, Boulware brought his friend Tim Cridland to the house, thinking he and LaVey would hit it off. As "Zamora the Torture King," Cridland was eating lightbulbs, piercing himself with meat skewers, and sucking down swords with the Jim Rose Circus, a ragtag collection of human oddballs much beloved by the Lollapalooza generation. Cridland, a true carny, went in deeply skeptical of LaVey.

"Anton was trying to connect with him, and Tim had this real standoffish thing," Boulware says. "He had his own intellectual rigor around outré subjects." The editor watched the pair talk about the circus for a while and grow engaged upon realizing they knew people in common.

On some of Boulware's visits, LaVey would indulge the journalist's queries about the church. "I think that he may have calibrated this sort of conversation if someone were very interested in it," Boulware says. "But if they were very interested in it, he probably wouldn't have invited them over in the first place." They also discussed LaVey's rift with Michael Aquino. "[Aquino] thought he was going to inherit it, and LaVey didn't want him to, and [Aquino] got bitter," Boulware says. "At that point it's like you're arguing about the 4-H Club, and who's going to run it." Or, as occult author Mitch Horowitz puts it, "One was the more bombastic front man, and the other was the more melodic literary type. You see that in great partnerships all the time. But these great partnerships, with the exception of Mick [Jagger] and Keith [Richards], often split. I assume both figures want primacy, and they just can't live under the same roof."

When he started becoming close with Zeena, Nikolas Schreck says Diane, who by then was openly hostile toward LaVey, confided with him about the church's fakery, including her various aliases. There are no people, he remembers thinking, it's all just on paper. "LaVey was so paranoid. He didn't trust any real human beings to be part of a real organization. He could only micromanage all of this himself," Schreck says. "Then when he let Aquino actually try to be an administrator, and to actually have an organization, he hated the result. He couldn't stand having the control wrested from him."

"At the end, I think Anton painted himself into a corner with the church. That's why he was so lonely," Becky Wilson says. "He'd always say, 'Bring somebody to entertain me, bring somebody to talk to me,' because he didn't trust that many people. He trusted me to bring over somebody that he'd get along with. And I tried to do that."

JG Thirlwell, a shape-shifting, New York–based Australian composer and experimental musician who has performed as Scraping Foetus Off the Wheel and Manorexia, was one of those somebodies. He and Wilson had a mutual friend in Stephen Pizzurro, a.k.a. "the Pizz," a leading light of the lowbrow art movement of the '80s and '90s who specialized in fantastically garish images of hot rods and tiki culture. When Thirlwell was going to be in San Francisco for a bit in 1992, the Pizz asked if Wilson could arrange an audience with LaVey.

Though Thirlwell's ambitious music sometimes flirted with quasi-Satanic imagery (his "Descent into the Inferno" conjures a particularly ripe and nasty spirit), he himself was no dabbler. He'd read *The Satanic Bible* and *The Satanic Rituals* before the meeting, but only out of curiosity. His takeaway: "Do what you like, do what's true to you, and don't harm anyone else." He didn't find anything sinister in the books and says he wasn't surprised when the man he met that afternoon turned out to be "very sharp, acerbic, funny, and charming."

Thirlwell brought along a copy of the latest album from his project Steroid Maximus, a blend of spy jazz and avant-garde exotica, which would later inspire his work scoring the *Venture Bros.* cartoon series. "He asked me about it, examined the cover, and talked about it quite deeply," Thirlwell says. When the subject turned to keyboards, Thirlwell, an adept, asked LaVey if he ever thought of bringing computers or MIDI (musical instrument digital interface) into his arsenal so he could layer his sounds.

"No, don't need to," was the reply.

"Then, by way of illustration," Thirlwell recalls, "he fired up his keyboards and organ and proceeded to do an improvised concert for us, which lasted probably half an hour." He was changing themes, switching instruments, moving all over the place, leaving his guest astonished.

"It was amazing."

When Gregg Turkington was an obnoxious grammar school kid in the late '70s, he'd frequent a small strip mall Bible store near his family's apartment in Tempe, Arizona. Just for laughs, among the religious knick-knacks, he'd pick up seven-cent Jack Chick tracts. These ubiquitous miniature comic books by the Christian fundamentalist cartoonist and publisher depicted morality plays larded with overheated conspiracy theories. "I don't know if it was in one of the Jack Chicks or in one of the Chick-adjacent comic books," Turkington says, "but somewhere in there was a little description of the head of the Church of Satan. And there was a drawing of him, and he looked pretty diabolical." Even though he wasn't a believer, Turkington found the depiction frightening. "I was like, 'Oh shit, this guy in San Francisco started the Church of Satan.'" That was his introduction to Anton LaVey, a derogatory portrait as a scary bad guy in this little comic book.

At fifteen, Turkington moved to San Francisco where, he says, "it was a very good time to be a starving artist with a lot of crackpot ideas." He found a community that shared his interest in punk and post-punk music and avant-garde performance art. Working at Subterranean Records, which put out music by such local luminaries as Flipper and the Dead Kennedys, he learned how to record, press, and release vinyl. He began recording his own groups, like the Zip Code Rapists, releasing stuff in small editions on his own Amarillo Records. "At that time, there was never any idea that anyone really would be interested in these projects," he says. "It was fairly cheap and easy to do. And, as it turns out, people were buying them." Turkington started putting out records by other local weirdos he liked, conceptual acts rather than aggressive punk bands, artsier projects that used humor as a guiding principle. This mindset manifested in his own parodic field recordings from fast-food restaurants, adult bookstores, and airport restrooms, as well as in riotous prank phone calls, from which Turkington's semipopular alter ego, the anti-comedian Neil Hamburger, would emerge.

One evening in 1993, his roommate, Becky Wilson, arrived home from work with news that shocked him: "Oh my God, I was hanging out with Anton LaVey."

"I'm like, 'Whoa, whoa, whoa—what?'" says Turkington, who couldn't believe anyone he knew would be in contact with this mysterious man of his childhood.

Becky excitedly told him about her day styling a photo shoot at the house. "He's got these keyboards, and he played me all this music," she said, adding that she put a bug in LaVey's ear about Turkington's own pursuits. "You should meet my friend Gregg," she told him. "He puts out records. He would love to put out a record by you."

"That sounds great," LaVey told her. "Bring him by."

"It was usually like 11:00 p.m. or midnight when you would be invited over," Turkington says. The first time, Tony Fazzini opened the door and led the two young people down the nearly pitch-black hallway. After entering the small sitting room, already disoriented, they sat and waited and waited some more. Twenty minutes went by—nothing. Finally, the door swung open, and LaVey appeared in his black cape and introduced himself, and he and his new acquaintance got to talking. He politely grilled Turkington about his interests and his label, whose catalog at the time featured more than a dozen releases. They geeked out over their mutual affection for Tiny Tim, *Freaks*, and the Canadian comedy series *SCTV*, "a lot of oddball pop culture stuff that was maybe neglected," Turkington says.

"Let me play you some music," LaVey offered. "Come into the kitchen." He started performing and just kept going till deep into the morning. After a while, Turkington remarked that his playing reminded him of a record he owned, *Fantasy in Pipe Organ and Percussion,* which came out in the late '50s.

"Yeah, I know that record, by Georges Montalba," LaVey said. "Let me tell you something: I am Georges Montalba. I made that record. That is actually me under a pseudonym." He proceeded to tell Turkington about the night he was playing at the Lost Weekend, when some guys came in and offered a few hundred dollars to record him. A couple of years later, an album appears, credited to an organist named Georges Montalba and featuring LaVey's work. More Montalba records were released that LaVey said incorporated one or two songs they'd recorded of him at the bar.

"I was always really fascinated with that and would ask him about it," Turkington says. "And that's what he always said."

When a couple of the records were reissued in 2001, it was revealed that a deeply religious Christian musician named Robert Hunter played on them as the pseudonymous Montalba. "I don't know what to think," Turkington says. "I mean, it certainly sounds like LaVey, and it's also not a big prize to say, 'Yeah, I'm the one playing on this low-budget record that's pretty forgotten.' So, I felt the story checked out. Then when I saw evidence that he was playing in these places, why wouldn't they do something like this if they needed that kind of playing?"

Flattered that Turkington made the Montalba connection, LaVey asked him to whip up some kind of agreement and perhaps they could work together.

"I wrote a little thing saying I wanted to try doing a seven-inch single, a thousand copies only, a numbered limited edition, and split the money with him fifty-fifty," Turkington says. "If he liked the way it went, we could do more. But I wanted to prove to him that I was fair and honest and would do a good job and present it in a way that he liked."

He brought it over to the house the following week.

"Yeah, that sounds good," LaVey told him. "Let's do it."

Thus began their handshake deal. "He didn't need anything signed," Turkington says. "Either it was, 'You're not gonna fuck with the Church of Satan,' or it was just that he trusted me."

While Turkington and Wilson, who was putting up some of the money, were drawn to a couple of songs that featured his vocals, LaVey preferred instrumentals. "I don't sing that much," he said.

Turkington insisted he sing a bit, citing the personality in his voice. "This is what people are going to want to hear," the young man told him. "It really captures your essence."

For the A-side, they landed on "Answer Me," a 1953 German love song originally titled "Mütterlein," and previously sung by the likes of

Nat King Cole, Bing Crosby, and Petula Clark, though not in the Black Pope's sepulchral Sprechstimme.

The flipside, "Honolulu Baby," is a different animal entirely, a jaunty ditty that rose to prominence in the 1933 Laurel and Hardy comedy *Sons of the Desert* and the 1935 Our Gang short *Beginner's Luck*. It became, in LaVey's bedeviled hands, drunk-uncle karaoke at its cringiest—and finest.

"I got the whole thing pressed and in the shops pretty fast, sold out of them real fast, and came back with a check for him," Turkington recalls.

Thrilled with the response, LaVey wanted to do more.

Along with LaVey offering cassette tapes of songs, Turkington and Wilson would go over and record him in the kitchen themselves. Which led to the ten-inch extended-play *Strange Music*, whose lead-off track, "Thanks for the Memory," was best known as Bob Hope's signature song.

Cathy Fitzhugh, Turkington's girlfriend at the time, took the striking, red-drenched photo that graces the cover. She had been aware of LaVey since junior high school and impressed him the very first night they met, after identifying an old-timey song he was playing on his keyboards. She knew the Hoosier Hot Shots' version of "The Girl Friend of the Whirling Dervish" from her day job at the small indie shop Aquarius Records.

"And then Gregg dumped me," she says. "He fell in love with his coworker."

Fitzhugh feared that would be the end of her friendship with LaVey, but it only grew stronger. Barton would call her to say, "The Doctor would like to see you," and Fitzhugh found herself visiting the house almost once a week for quite a while.

"She was going over there and getting a lot of sympathy," Turkington says. "They were looking after her when she was hurting."

"[Anton] and Blanche really adored me," Fitzhugh says, "so I just felt very comfortable and comforted." Sometimes that comfort was provided at the Olive Garden at the Stonestown Galleria, where they shared many meals. And though he never left the house with LaVey, Turkington remembers him talking about the restaurant all the time: "He just thought it was so good. He loved it."

One night before heading out to eat, LaVey handed Fitzhugh a pair of vintage Spring-o-Lator pumps, high-heeled mules that miraculously didn't go clack-clack when the wearer walked. He told her the shoes, with rhinestone-embedded Lucite heels, had belonged to a famous starlet. "I have very tiny feet," she says, "and they somehow fit."

Fitzhugh figured LaVey and Barton must have been regulars at the middle-of-the-road Italian chain restaurant, famous for its unlimited breadsticks, since the staff seemed very used to them. "You were also really aware that you were at the Olive Garden with Anton LaVey," she says. "It was fun to watch people notice him. It was a scene, but he wasn't making a scene. It was just a scene because of who he was. I mean, maybe it was because I was wearing Spring-o-Lator pumps that belonged to Elizabeth Taylor too."

She recalls that LaVey, who once boasted of serving human flesh at one of his lectures, had a fairly unadventurous palate. "Everything that I'd ever eaten with him was bland and unassuming," she says. "We weren't going out and having caviar."

Like a number of women who spent time around LaVey, Fitzhugh would often wear clothes that she knew would appeal to him—in her case, vintage stockings. But she didn't expect they'd also appeal to his pets. "I'd be sitting on the couch where I know Jayne Mansfield had sat, with this semi-feral cat licking my stockinged feet."

One evening, LaVey came to Turkington with a proposal: *"The Satanic Mass* has been out of print for years and everyone wants it. Would you like to reissue that?"

Would he ever.

The *Satan Takes a Holiday* compact disc followed in 1995. This, LaVey's first full-length album of music, features sounds one would hear either riding on a carousel horse or ogling strippers in a burlesque house, not to mention the opening dirge from the *Satanis* documentary.

LaVey enlisted Blanche Barton and his friend Nick Bougas to provide vocals. Bougas, in particular, nails the old-school style of early crooners like Rudy Vallée and Russ Columbo. "They recorded some songs with [Bougas] when he visited them in San Francisco," Turkington says, "and those tracks were on one of the tapes that I was sorting through to assemble the albums."

If the *Satan Takes a Holiday* recordings have a slickness that belies their domestic do-it-yourself origins, it's because there are few instruments, and some of it was recorded on a four-track tape deck LaVey owned. When Turkington himself recorded LaVey on cassette, all he had to do was hold a decent microphone in the air. He'd then take the tapes to Tom Mallon, a producer with a studio nearby. Mallon, who has worked with such artists as American Music Club and Chris Isaak, would clean them up and equalize everything so it all sounded of a piece. Turkington even offered to get LaVey into Mallon's studio. "Nah," he responded, "I just want to record in my kitchen."

Boyd Rice had for a long while encouraged LaVey to do just that, so others could experience what he and Blanche and an elite few enjoyed. LaVey had always resisted going into a studio to record music. What was the point? "I've spent hours and hours programming these keyboards to sound exactly like the instruments that I'm trying to convey," he told Blanche. "A trumpet sounds like a trumpet. A saxophone sounds like a saxophone. I have all of my theater organs in here, all of my effects. I can't do it anywhere else."

Anton, Blanche, and a friend were listening to the *Satan Takes a Holiday* master tape in that very kitchen on February 22, 1995, when LaVey suddenly keeled over and lost consciousness. After an ambulance took him away, Blanche didn't know if he'd survive. Doctors, she later wrote, told her she had saved his life by applying cardiopulmonary resuscitation, with help from the emergency operator: "I credited the EMTs who shocked him several times, and LaVey's indomitable will to live." LaVey was soon back in fighting shape but would have no memory of the ordeal. (When it had been recommended years earlier that he replace valves in his heart, LaVey declined, and in 1990 had to be hospitalized twice with cardiac issues.)

Since only the first single was a limited edition, Turkington would keep reprinting the other records and keep bringing LaVey money. "I got the feeling that the income stream maybe wasn't what it used to be," he says, having observed LaVey's frugal lifestyle. "I would bring in these checks, a few thousand dollars each time. And I would have the accounting for them: 'We sold X number of copies, and here's your share.' They would take it, and they were grateful." He noticed that they often wouldn't deposit the checks for weeks at a time. "They were pretty casual about it. But I got the feeling that they were very appreciative to get this money coming in."

Around this time, the kitschy, space-age-bachelor-pad instrumentals of Esquivel and the lush tropical sounds of Arthur Lyman, Martin Denny, and Les Baxter were experiencing a revival in hipster music circles. And while he wasn't promoting the records as exotica/lounge artifacts per se, Turkington did see some interest from that crowd. "People were definitely like, 'Whoa, what is this?'" he says. "Not just because it was him, but that it was essentially easy-listening music." Running small ads in *The Cloven Hoof*, he figured he'd be able to attract those already predisposed.

Word of LaVey's music also made it to the incarcerated. Of the many letters he received from prisons, Turkington recalls one in particular: "'Dear Amarillo Records'—it was addressed to the record label, not to Anton LaVey—'I'm gonna be here in prison the rest of my life, and I really long for freedom. And I have no hope of ever being freed. But I was hoping that you would make this deal with me, which is: if you will get me out of jail using your powers, I will devote my life to Satan and whatever that entails.'

"Buddy, you've just written to the record label," Turkington responded. "I don't know that anyone's going to be able to help you with this, but certainly not the mail-order department of a record company."

Turkington found that his reissue of *The Satanic Mass* appealed especially to teens from the Southern United States. He could tell this from all the pentagrams they'd draw on the envelopes when requesting copies. "People were excited," he says of the records. "Not just Satanists, but curiosity-seekers, people who liked celebrity vocals. To me, if you like the music of Telly Savalas, then check out Anton LaVey, because there's so much personality."

Over the course of three years, in between records, there was a lot of socializing. While Turkington says he made "some effort not to look like a gas station employee" when he visited, LaVey always looked sharp, dressed in black, often with a tie—formal yet cordial. And despite his health scare, he showed no signs of extraordinary wear and tear. "He just seemed like an old guy," he says. "I do think there were a couple times where things were canceled because he wasn't well, or he would reschedule. But nobody ever talked to me about anything like that."

Turkington would drop off records his label released, and the next time he'd come over, LaVey would offer nuanced critiques. "I was always really flattered," he recalls. "It was my stupid bands or whatever, but he'd listened to them, and he'd discuss the packaging, the concept, the whole thing." Like the compellingly chaotic single, "Jesus, I Am Loving You," by one of Turkington's own groups, Totem Pole of Losers. "It was just a couple of weird songs," he says. "But he seemed to like the lyrics, and he asked me to sign the copy to him. It was a very unexpected turn of events."

Though he refrained from discussing the church, LaVey would sometimes classify things Turkington had done, such as building a record label, as "Satanic." "But it was more about an attitude and a philosophy toward art," Turkington says, "not about following the tenets of *The Satanic Bible.*"

One innovation LaVey likely saw as Satanic was Dine11.com, a business that collected local menus and would deliver meals from the restaurants that signed on—a kind of a proto–Uber Eats. Turkington suspects this gave LaVey a reason to not leave the house much. "I told him about this one day," he says, "and the next time I saw him, that's what he wanted to talk about: 'Gregg, it's just amazing!' That kind of thing would crack me up."

When they started making records together, LaVey presented him with a Church of Satan membership card, which Turkington says, "almost reminded me of the way a cat will put a mouse on your pillow. You know—this is how they express affection and gratitude. Because I certainly hadn't asked for this." But it wasn't as if he had any animus toward the church. The more the young man heard about it, the more he understood the appeal of some of the philosophy, especially when it came to creating interesting art. Around eighteen months after their first record, he received in the mail a large envelope containing an embossed certificate with his name on it, declaring him a priest in the Church of Satan, signed by Anton LaVey. The next time Turkington saw him, he told LaVey, "Thanks for sending that. It was really nice."

"You've done so much for me," the high priest replied.

LaVey sometimes expressed to Turkington regret that, because of his notoriety, he couldn't go out more and do things. "I don't know if it was just people harassing him," Turkington says, "not violence necessarily." One place he did frequent was Green Apple Books, a shop around a mile east of LaVey's house.

Alan Black, a clerk at the store, remembers being impressed by what he calls LaVey's "extraordinary look." "Always, he came in with a charming and spectacularly dressed lady late on a Saturday night," he says. "He was polite and calm. Always bought more than one book."

Turkington had been at LaVey's one evening when the Doctor began talking about demo tapes he would receive from metal bands he had no interest in: "You know, Gregg, these guys, they send me all this music, and you just can't even believe the names of some of these groups. Look at this tape I got here today." It was by a Florida band with a name inspired by two American cultural icons who would always figure into LaVeyan lore: Marilyn Manson.

"You're gonna make a big dent," the Black Pope told the God of Fuck, resting his hand paternally on the younger man's shoulder. "You're going to make an impression on the world."

For the rock star formerly known as Brian Warner, whose own philosophy encompassed the writings of LaVey, Crowley, and Nietzsche, those words meant everything. "Anton LaVey was the most righteous man I've ever known," Marilyn Manson wrote in his foreword to the man's essay collection *Satan Speaks!* "In a world so full of shit, Anton LaVey cut through it with the best of them."

In LaVey, Manson found a like-minded shit-stirrer—and whipping boy. "We had both dedicated the better part of our lives to toppling

Christianity with the weight of its own hypocrisy," he wrote, "and as a result been used as scapegoats to justify Christianity's existence."

The musician had first contacted LaVey in 1993 to ask if he'd play the theremin on his band's debut album, *Portrait of an American Family*. He never heard back. He did, however, pay tribute to LaVey in the song "Get Your Gunn," with the line "Selective judgments, goodguy badges / Don't mean a fuck to me." LaVey coined the phrase "Goodguy Badge" to mock those practicing performative virtue, who "make an exhibition of piety and charity." The song was inspired by the murder of an abortion doctor by a Christian fundamentalist, a crime that for Manson represented the ultimate hypocrisy: someone who identified as pro-life snuffing out another.

Manson's music—clattering, guitar-heavy, industrial goth metal—was far removed from the Tin Pan Alley LaVey preferred to visit, but that didn't matter one whit. In Manson, LaVey saw a bright, extravagant, articulate, blasphemous entertainer—someone whom, by virtue of his influence, he could see as "priesthood material."

For Manson, communicating the ideals of the Church of Satan was a mission he was happy to undertake. "I always try my hardest to bring a better understanding of Satanism to America because I have a pop status," he said. "If I explain Satanism to people in a way they can understand, it may open up their minds to it, more than if I was brandishing a pentagram."

The singer adhered to Crowley's credo "Do what thou wilt"—a lifestyle that would eventually land him in scalding water, as numerous women came forward to accuse him of physical and sexual abuse and mental anguish, allegations he has vigorously denied. And he appreciated LaVey's concepts of self-reliance, materialism, and anti-stupidity. "[Satanism is] about finding your strengths and learning to use them," Manson said. "It's about making money. It's about the need to survive and succeed in a world full of idiots."

Manson and his band were on tour in October 1994, opening for Nine Inch Nails in Oakland, when Blanche called his hotel on his day off, inviting him over for a late-night visit. After LaVey made his usual theatrical entrance, he told his guest he appreciated his stage name, which combined two extremes, but he couldn't bring himself to call him Marilyn—it made him uncomfortable, considering his relationship with the late blonde bombshell—and suggested Brian instead.

Still, LaVey didn't hesitate to share intimate details of that relationship with Manson—as well as recount his sexual exploits with Jayne Mansfield—and suggested that he was responsible for Monroe's career ascendance. "Taking credit for such things was part of LaVey's style," Manson later noted, "but he never did it arrogantly. It was always done naturally, as if it were a well-known fact."

Manson himself had just fallen into an as-yet platonic relationship with a bombshell of his own: Traci Lords, a former underage porn star he'd recently met after a show in Los Angeles. She was "very bossy and constantly playing mind games." As such, he wrote, she both "confused and captivated" him. He needed some of the older man's advice.

"I feel like you both belong together," LaVey told him, "and I think something very important is going to happen with your relationship." Manson was flummoxed, believing the vague input was itself a mind game, a way for LaVey to hold sway.

"The less people understand you," Manson figured, "the smarter they think you are."

Still, Manson left the house that morning grateful that LaVey helped him come to terms with the uneasiness he had been feeling both personally and at the world. A few days later he brought Lords over. Lords, who was up on the latest new age trends, walked in cynical. She left in silence.

Toward the end of the visit, LaVey presented Manson with a red Church of Satan membership card. "Little did I know that accepting this card would be one of the most controversial things I had done to that point," the rock star wrote.

There were other proclivities he had in common with LaVey. Later in his career, Manson, face covered in greasepaint and mouth smeared with blood-red lipstick, showcased Nazi-inspired imagery in his concerts while touring his 1996 album, *Antichrist Superstar.* Clad in a mock military uniform, he performed from a podium in front of a black, white, and red stage design that featured SS-style lightning bolts. And his 2003 album, *The Golden Age of Grotesque,* with its rune-like logo, further played with fascist tropes.

Sometimes when Cathy Fitzhugh was invited over, she'd be told, "We have a special guest coming." One night it was Manson. Fitzhugh recalls seeing the shock rocker on his best behavior, praising the older man he idolized. "We ended up talking about *Charlie and the Chocolate Factory,* since Willy Wonka was a big influence on Manson," she says. "It was great to just watch people be charmed by [LaVey]."

Returning from dinner one night with Boyd Rice, LaVey noticed that what little light there was exposed how badly the paint on 6114 California Street was peeling. "I really should take better care of this house," he told his friend. "It's been so good to me over the years." When Rice offered to paint it, LaVey demurred, but when he insisted, LaVey relented. Rice brought along his friend Harvey Stafford to help out.

"LaVey had told me that when he first painted the house black, he had a hard time finding black paint," Stafford recalls. "So he wound up having to use surplus US Navy submarine paint. This could be totally apocryphal. I don't know." Since the fence was so close to the house— Stafford figures it was less than twenty feet away—that made for a very difficult job. Then there was the sloping driveway to the garage. For Stafford, climbing a very long extension ladder up to paint the peak of the roof on a house with such a steep pitch was a scary proposition. "I have a funny memory of being at the very top of it, on the apex of the roof, and scraping eggs," he says. "I scraped a lot of eggs off that house before I painted it.

"Boyd was a sweetheart," he adds. "He's holding the ladder so I don't fall to my death or break my neck. And he's looking up to make sure I'm okay, but there are paint chips falling in his eyes. So, he looks away to brush them out of his eyes. And then he looks up again and I'm like, 'Hey, Boyd, just hold the ladder. Don't look up.'"

It was a pretty quick job, all told. They'd prepped for three or four days and got the paint on in a day or two. "I liked LaVey and liked doing things if I could help," says Stafford. "That house had a lot of problems. I couldn't really address them all."

When he painted the house, Stafford was already an artist in the underground rock scene, having created covers for albums by the Melvins and Victims Family, among others. Since much of his subject matter was cryptic and spooky, he and LaVey connected on an aesthetic level.

"I was interested in old wind-up phonographs and the 78s that you would play on them," Stafford says. "We'd sit in there and Blanche would come in from the kitchen with a tray of cookies and coffee in Baphomet coffee cups. It was all very '50s housewife. She was an incredibly gracious hostess, a very good entertainer. Manners meant a lot in that house."

Like many others, he did, however, have doubts about LaVey's genuineness. "I went in there the first time not really knowing: 'Is this guy for real? Does he really believe this shtick?' And I figured out pretty quickly, 'No, he does not,'" Stafford says. "It's his carny background extended into a lifetime performance."

LaVey would talk wistfully about his days playing the Wurlitzer at the Fox Theatre and what a crime it was that it got torn down, something Stafford, who has lived in the area since New Year's Day 1986, could relate to.

"For me in the '90s, San Francisco really was a magic place," Stafford says. "It wasn't like it is now—a very money-driven, tech-ruled place. I feel like a ghost haunting it when I walk the streets, because on every corner I can remember some cool thing that happened that had nothing to do with money. It had to do with people's imagination and their creative drive.

"The waterfront," he adds, "used to be a place where the Temporary Autonomous Zone"—the anarchist writer Hakim Bey's concept of creating ephemeral areas not bound by official oversight—"really existed in a lot of different manifestations. Every warehouse that was pioneered by artists had crazy shows: Survival Research Laboratories, punk rock shows, heavy metal shows, drag shows, themed parties on every holiday. There was plenty of fun to be had, and people knew each other and collaborated, and small creative cells merged and broke apart like amoebas."

In 1997, LaVey made Stafford a priest in the Church of Satan. "Which was kind of funny," Stafford says, "because the only thing I would've done to really deserve that is, I painted his house for free." But as Barton wrote in a note accompanying his certificate, it was because of his anachronistic interests and style and the magical evenings they spent together. LaVey felt that as a result of Stafford's metaphoric ability "to suspend time and shape reality," he deserved recognition as a magician.

"I really liked him as an example of how to age and be interesting," Stafford says, "because my whole life, I have not wanted to be the dull old man, the get-out-of-my-yard and complain-about-everything old man. I find certain curmudgeons to be quite charming—maybe he's one of them. But he was a great example of how to live the excitement of your youth well into old age."

One frequent visitor to the house during the early '90s, a university student and part-time stripper, appreciated LaVey's views about women. "How it's okay for women to be sexy, and it's okay for women to attract attention," says the friend, who requested anonymity for fear of harassment. "He actually told me, 'You're too smart for that. You need to stop stripping and finish getting your degree.' The funny thing is that people think he was some dastardly exploiter. But he was telling me, 'You're too good for that.'" Which, some would say, is not a view to be lauded at all.

He was, she discovered during their long talks, a good listener. She would often discuss with him things she could tell few others, like her double life—dancing suggestively at night and being told in her feminism class during the day that pornography is wrong. "He was like my priest," she says. "He was very understanding and compassionate in some ways."

Then he'd share with her his own problems. "He'd get panic attacks," she says. "He was always like, 'Give me some Valium.' And I'd say, 'No, I'm not a doctor.' And then he'd say, 'Stupid people don't get panic attacks.' He would tell me he had insomnia, and his heart would race, and that he had terrible anxiety."

One time when she asked him what the church was really about, he told her, "Ka-ching! Every time somebody signs up—a hundred bucks."

"I think there was a side of him that was very jaded, and he just didn't care, as long as he made his money," she says. "And he was not making a lot of money." That jadedness, she said, extended to some of his other friendships at the time: the Charlie Manson fans, the Third

Reich wannabes. "I'd tell LaVey about it and he seemed uncomfortable, but he also seemed indifferent, like, 'Eh.'

"It's this weird catch-22," she continues. "I liked the man, I liked my friendship, but I don't like the baggage."

In an article that appeared in 1994, LaVey told Darby Romeo and Kerin Morataya, of the witty feminist punk zine *Ben Is Dead*, that he enjoyed speaking with smaller outlets and folks on "what they call the cutting edge." He attempted to flatter the pair with the promise that "doors will open for you if this is done well." But before they could even commence the interview, it was time to eat. Onward to the Olive Garden!

Once there, the writers tried to convince LaVey that it would be in his best interest to allow them to get the conversation on tape. It was a request that he refused, telling them, "I've had bad experiences with tape recorders. I've been burned before," before adding, curiously, "I feel there is a lot of personal response or interpretation that should be left to the interviewer."

The pair discovered that LaVey was still smarting over Lawrence Wright's *Rolling Stone* shellacking from three years earlier. LaVey resented that he was made out to be a bad guy by a writer he claimed had an agenda. "This guy comes along and he tries to steal memories away from me. I mean, that's what people live for—memories."

Back at the house, and inside a bathroom, Romeo noticed near the toilet a waxed corn cob on a string (a nod to their use by American settlers as tools for ass-wiping). She also found five baby-name books on a stool. "Though there was an unconcealed love for Xerxes," she wrote, "each time the child was brought up he was referred to as a 'genetic experiment.'"

"It was very engineered," LaVey clarified, "a lot of thought went into it. We are working on new ways to raise children. For example, what would it be like to grow up without the sound of TV, with homeschooling . . . ?" After all, he himself learned much more after dropping out of high school.

"I don't want to sound like I'm building a master race," he added, "but if there are more kids like our baby, and selective breeding ensues . . . we will, once again, have women who look like women, and men who look like men."

Anton was thrilled to have spawned a son, whom he called his "little pal." "His cardiologist said Xerxes added years to his life," Blanche Barton recalls, "and Anton said the day Xerxes was born was his happiest one."

LaVey taught him to respect and love animals, curling his fingers into a half-fist and patting Xerxes's hand, saying, "Paw to paw." He also brought the toddler to gun shows. Although LaVey was never able to take his son shooting, by the age of three Xerxes had learned the basics of gun safety, Barton says: "Never touch the trigger until you're ready to shoot, never point a gun at anything you don't intend to shoot, and treat every firearm as if it's loaded."

They'd watch movies together—Laurel and Hardy, Abbott and Costello, *Frankenstein*, *Dracula*, and other Universal monsters. "Anton wasn't one for throwing a ball around in the park, but we did go to a few playgrounds where he pushed Xerxes on the swing," Barton says. "He was protective of Xerxes and liked to keep him near him. We went out for long drives to various places around the Bay Area, and Xerxes met plenty of interesting people."

Lisa Carver, Boyd Rice's pregnant girlfriend, was nothing if not an interesting person. And she was neither impressed nor amused when her beau brought her to the house to meet his good friend. "Already I can't stand Anton," she later wrote, "the way his sailor's cap is set at a jaunty angle, the way Tony, the silent manservant, hovers at his shoulder like a human epaulet." Carver—a zine-maker who as out-there musician and performance artist Lisa Suckdog released songs with titles like "Will I Ever Do Anything with My Clothes On?" and "I Want to Die"—was no shrinking violet, but in LaVey she saw "a delirious, decrepit pervert."

He regaled his new guest with the usual keyboard recital interspersed with the usual reminiscences of his (real or imagined) days as a carny, police shutterbug, and ecdysiast's accompanist. He dropped the usual names—Mansfield, Monroe, Togare—with the weight of the anchor on the *Queen Mary*. He expounded on theories about DNA, sperm, and urine. Blanche mentioned to her that their son, who kept night hours like Pops, had never met another child. He was nearly a year old.

In her memoir, *Drugs Are Nice*, Carver also brought up other LaVeys: Karla, who claimed her dad loved animals and children, and Zeena, who accused her dad of abusing his animals and her mother. "It is said that Anton loved Zeena so much," Carver wrote, "that her son Stanton, born when Zeena was fourteen, was both Anton's grandson and son." Carver went on to speculate that Zeena's behavior and motivations resembled those of a molested daughter, before concluding, "her quest is a valiant one: to destroy the one who destroyed her." She later told *SPIN* magazine, in a 2008 profile of Stanton, that Rice, who previously had been romantically involved with Zeena, had shared the story with her.

When asked about the conjecture, Stanton told *SPIN*, "That was totally slanderous, but she got hers. My girlfriend beat her up."

Carver admitted his girlfriend, Szandora, did indeed jump her before Stanton entered the fray, but added that they didn't really hurt her—and she got a fistful of Szandora's hair out of the deal. (Years later, through therapy to recover memories, Carver learned that she herself had been abused by her own father.)

Richard Lamparski had heard the gossip about his godson and would tell anyone who asked that he knew nothing of its veracity. "But if you're going to pose as the Devil's representative on Earth," he reasons, "people get to say whatever they damn well please about you."

In a 2021 Q&A with Eugene Robinson, who had interviewed Anton decades earlier, Stanton revisited the rumor. "I am just as curious as ever as to the true identity of my biological father," he said, discounting as "total lies" his family's claims about his parentage, which would come to include a neighborhood delinquent and a fisherman just passing through town.

Whether wondering out of genuine curiosity or indulging in vicious sensationalism, Stanton volunteered to Robinson: "So how likely is it that Anton is my father? . . . I'd give it 51% credible, 49% incredible."

Sharon LaVey, who married Stanton in 2018, says he resented the fact that he couldn't get a straight answer from his grandmother. "I was there for some of those arguments," she says. "It was very frustrating to see him go through that.

"He and his grandmother might have had a better relationship if she just told the truth. I have two little boys that have Stanton's DNA"—twins Richard and Kenneth, named after Stanton's godfathers, Lamparski and Anger—"and someday if we do a DNA test, we might get to know who his father is."

Barton—who says the truth is simply that Zeena got pregnant by a boyfriend and wanted to keep the baby—can only imagine what drove Stanton to make such a pronouncement. "I suppose he would have thought that being Anton's child would be more prestigious than being his grandson," she says, "even if it meant sullying Dr. LaVey's reputation in the worst possible way."

Thomas Thorn was another rock musician who was invited into LaVey's orbit. He had been a fan of *The Satanic Bible* since picking it up at age eleven at a newsstand in Evanston, Illinois. "I liked the pageantry and the power that was portrayed in it," he says. "It wasn't until later on that I really understood the philosophy." As a self-proclaimed "outsider," he felt the book spoke to him.

"There was a supernatural element, but there was also a lot of mental strategy and those sorts of things going on," he says. "*The Satanic Bible* offered me the opportunity to participate in that. Everybody was looking for a how-to manual."

And what he learned eventually found its way into his music. He was a nightclub bouncer and aspiring keyboardist when the group My Life with the Thrill Kill Kult, who were about to embark on their first major US tour, came calling. "They were the standard two-men-dressed-in-leather gay guys playing electronic disco," he says. "They're like, 'We want this bald-headed thug to be our keyboard player, because that would be totally against the whole image.' There was a lot of playing-with-devil-worship imagery in that band, particularly in the earlier music."

He left after a couple of years to form the Electric Hellfire Club, whose records, such as *Burn, Baby, Burn!* and *Satan's Little Helpers*, were rife with forked-tongue-in-cheek references to drugs, serial killers, demonic possession, and the sigil of Baphomet. The title of the song "Invocation/Age of Fire" from their first album was lifted from *The Satanic Bible* and is, Thorn says, "meant to be a rock anthem built around a New Satanic Age—this empowering ideal." He even dedicated 1995's *Kiss the Goat* to recent arrival Satan Xerxes Carnacki LaVey.

Though he was friendly with New York–based church leaders Peter Gilmore and Peggy Nadramia, he resisted signing up. "Because I'm not a joiner," he says, adding that he felt some of his lifestyle choices were incompatible with membership in the Church of Satan. "No self-respecting Satanist would ever use mind-altering drugs. And I'm like, 'Well, I guess I'm not a self-respecting Satanist.'"

In 1996, his band was on tour in San Francisco with opening act Boyd Rice doing his solo noise thing. "We had an awful night," Thorn remembers. "Everybody got really drunk, got in a huge fight. Half the people quit the band, and I woke up in the morning having had the most miserable day ever."

The day brightened—or darkened, depending on one's point of view—when Rice invited him over for a very long visit with LaVey. Upon their arrival, Blanche steered them into a room and onto a deep leather couch before leaving to fetch the Doctor.

"You must rate pretty high," Rice nudged him.

"Why is that?"

"Because you get the ritual chamber," Rice said. "Everybody else just gets to meet LaVey in the kitchen."

The man Thorn met was hardly the sickly, doddering old coot Zeena's narrative had suggested. And while it was obvious to Thorn that LaVey knew of his work, he says, "I'm not so naïve as to think that they hadn't just talked about eight different bullet points about who I was."

Still, the musician was taken aback by his host's generosity of spirit. "He said that he wanted to bring me into the priesthood, because what I had accomplished was certainly worthy of that."

When it was time to leave, Thorn recalls, "he looked me right in the eye and said, 'Thomas, I want you to always remember I'm very proud of you.' It was really powerful.

"Looking back," he adds, "he knew there was a chance he was never going to see me again. So what he was doing was imprinting upon me that my last words from Anton LaVey were that he was proud of what I had done and what I was doing, which is cool, it's heavy. I don't want to diminish it by calling it strategy, but there was a level of strategy involved—things that he was doing to make sure that the church continued on in his absence in ways that he thought were good, important, and valid."

XIII.

Legacy of Evil

LaVEY called Ragnar Redbeard's *Might Is Right*, the racist, sexist, and anti-Semitic screed that he excerpted for a chapter in *The Satanic Bible*, "probably one of the most inflammatory books ever written." When an independent publisher named Shane Bugbee approached him to contribute a foreword to a new centennial edition, LaVey thought there was no one more qualified to write an introduction, since the book has been linked so indelibly with him.

The journey of the request to LaVey began, unwittingly, with Marilyn Manson. Bugbee had released a bootleg live CD of the shock rocker that he had grabbed off a video he shot of a concert. As a joke, he put LaVey's post office box as the record label's address. "I was just fucking around like, 'Church of Satan—let's send some shit to LaVey,'" Bugbee says. He then started mailing LaVey his zines. He was surprised when he got a response that LaVey didn't want to kill him.

Bugbee was convinced he had to wrangle LaVey's participation in the Redbeard reprint after meeting a neo-Nazi who wanted to advertise in the program book he was putting together for the Milwaukee Metal Fest. "I'm not saying this word because I don't like him," Bugbee says. "He's an actual fucking Nazi Party member."

In those days, the underground was still underground. "So, you dealt with racist people," Bugbee says. "You dealt with haters. You just dealt with it." When the Nazi found out Bugbee was a Satanist, he gave him a copy of *Might Is Right*, admitting that it was his bible. Intrigued by the connection, Bugbee pitched LaVey in a letter. "I said, 'I'm going to do this with or without you, and I'm going to point this at you. I want to give you the chance to explain yourself in an interview and in the foreword to the book. Because Nazis gave me the same book and they're telling me it's their bible too.'"

For Bugbee, this revelation was just too wild to resist. "I just know that none of the goths in the world know that the Nazis love this book too," he says. "And I'm going to make money off that. I wrote LaVey that letter, and he loved it."

In the foreword to the 1996 reprint, LaVey waxes ecstatic about the book's forbidden attraction: "What I saw should not have been in print. It was more than inflammatory. It was sheer blasphemy. As I turned the pages, more blasphemy met my eyes. Crazy as it was, I found myself charged at the words. People just didn't write that way."

The day before appearing at the first annual Bay Area Anarchist Book Fair in March 1996, Bugbee hand-delivered the book to LaVey at home. He proudly boasts he was the last person LaVey made a priest in the Church of Satan.

"Blessed are the powerful . . . Cursed are the feeble, for they shall be blotted out!" LaVey proclaimed in one of *The Satanic Bible*'s more outrageous passages (cribbed from *Might Is Right*). It was a sentiment he'd harbor for a lifetime.

"He was enamored of the aesthetic of power," says Mitch Horowitz, "and he wrote very plainly about being enamored of the Nazi aesthetic." As did Michael Aquino.

Indeed, in a 1972 issue of *The Cloven Hoof*, Aquino's lead editorial expanded upon that very appeal: "The skull-and-crossbones may seem a rather juvenile insignia for a paramilitary organization, but, as the trademark of the S.S., it produced the same intimidation of opponents that the 'Jolly Roger' did during the days of sea piracy. In time the Nazis' already-dynamic swastika was rendered even more striking by turning it askance."

In an essay titled "The Jewish Question? Or Things My Mother Never Taught Me," LaVey discussed the first time he read the notorious anti-Semitic document *The Protocols of the Elders of Zion*, which purported to be the Jewish blueprint for world domination. "My instinctive reaction was, 'So what's wrong with THAT? Isn't that the way any master plan should work?" Later in the piece he asked, "What is 'tyranny'? Despotism? Is it all so bad, if so attractively packaged that it's demanded?"

In another essay, "A Plan," LaVey proposed that Satanists' attraction to certain aspects of both Judaism and Nazism were not necessarily contradictory, since Jews have been despised throughout history for their lack of Christian values, and the Nazi aesthetic "is grounded in black," as is that of young people drawn to Satanism. "To be a Satanist is, by association, already to be aligned with the universal devil Jew," he wrote.

"It will become easier and more convincing for any Satanist to combine a Jewish lineage with a Nazi aesthetic," LaVey concluded, "and with pride rather than with guilt and misgiving."

His fascination with Nazism notwithstanding, he was still born of Jewish parents, an adolescent when Hitler carried out his atrocities. How could he thread this poison-tipped needle? "Well, because he wasn't a humanist," says Eugene Robinson. LaVey felt—correctly, Robinson thinks—that people are largely shit. But, as LaVey told him, "I don't play pedigrees."

Still, LaVey's friend Richard Lamparski recalls the high priest being very touchy about any mention of his Jewish roots. "I brought it up once, in the underground playroom," Lamparski says. "He stopped in the middle of the ladder, turned around, looked at me, and said, 'We don't talk about that.'"

Back in the church's early days, LaVey encountered members of the American Nazi Party and the anti-communist Minutemen, whom he considered insecure products of arrested development. They almost always needed to overcompensate for some physical disability, chronic illness, or sexual or social deficiency, he believed, by inflating their egos by affiliating with extremist groups. They also couldn't function without a leader. If someone like George Lincoln Rockwell, founder of the American Nazi Party, deserved any respect at all, LaVey thought, it was because he appeared to the public as an evildoer with far more power, followers, and money than he actually had. (Which could also have been said of LaVey himself.) LaVey imagined that it must have been particularly humiliating for Rockwell's acolytes to see their man gunned down while leaving, of all places, a laundromat.

In the *Birth of Tragedy* interview, LaVey railed against psychic vampirism, "where the strong constantly pull the weak up at the cost of their own strength." He said that ever since he was a teen, he believed in the idea of social stratification, based on someone's ability to "pass the sensitivity test of being . . . one of the new class of super people."

"If this sounds of course fascistic, so be it," LaVey added. "I've been accused of being everything from extreme left to extreme right."

LaVey, who believed Hitler's greatest mistake was employing racist concepts, targeting specific ethnicities, went on to describe the Nazi strongman as someone who also "didn't compromise himself." He imagined that the Führer's associates were not forced to join him at gunpoint, a description that could apply to LaVey and his church—and one that was not lost on him: "So [Hitler] said, in a sense, as I would say or anyone else in a semblance of power would say, 'Welcome to my world! If you like it or you feel comfortable, if it's your bag, your thing too, then we'll enjoy ourselves.' Otherwise, the door swings both ways . . ."

Though he might not have been interested in the politics of racism or homophobia, LaVey was attracted to fascist imagery as the embodiment of power. "Everybody says, 'Yeah, the Nazis—Hugo Boss designed their uniforms,'" his friend Carl Abrahamsson says. "You could say that that's despicable whitewashing, in a way. On the other hand, it's also true they look good. And they would look good even on the most liberal and nice person."

The imagery has been absorbed into the culture in other significant ways. "I'm thinking of the artist Tom of Finland, and all those S&M pictures of gay men," Horowitz says. "What else is that but the Nazi aesthetic to some degree?"

That's the look of the leathermen in Kenneth Anger's 1963 celebrated short film *Scorpio Rising*, which is drenched in representations of the occult, queerness, Nazism, and biker chic. And that's no coincidence. "The leatherman image, if you go down to its roots, is really kind of fascistic-looking," says LaVey interviewer Jack Fritscher, who, as founding editor in chief of *Drummer* magazine, was a pioneer of that scene. "It is taken out of war clothing worn by American soldiers, because war surplus provided the first biker and leatherman clothing. We'd shop at army surplus stores."

"Look at our culture [now]," says Horowitz. "Darth Vader, Loki—who are these guys supposed to be? And people love them—they're on every lunchbox—including people who profess to hate Satanism. They love [*Star Wars*'s] stormtroopers. They love Maleficent. Our culture is in love with [fascist villains], for better or worse."

Don Frew says his friend LaVey had "a fascination rather than a flirtation with fascism, because he was always fascinated with anything in psychology or society that granted one person or group control over another." That's why he was trying to attract politicians, celebrities, and businesspeople to the church. "Because in our society, those are really the three groups of power." As time went on, it became harder for LaVey to bring into the fold the people he wanted, and he was attracting more of the ones he didn't.

Still, LaVey's authoritarian leanings bothered many, including his friends. "Anton turns the appetite for power into the delusion of individual control," wrote Jacques Vallée, "a repulsive illusion, darkly reminiscent of the early Nazi."

In explaining LaVey's appeal, Vallée cited Hitler's membership in the occultist and ethnonationalist group the Thule Society, and his "exceptional gift of eloquence." "Could a similar vision arise now?" Vallée wrote. "At the Altamont feast of hippiedom, three hundred thousand lovers of rock music stoned on grass, acid and testosterone were mesmerized and controlled by a handful of disciplined Hells Angels. One kid was murdered in full view of the apathetic crowd. Mick Jagger was on stage singing 'Sympathy for the Devil.' . . . [Anton] treads on dangerous ground when he rides on such imagery to shock his middle-class audience."

When Vallée confronted LaVey with criticisms that the church played to a neo-Nazi sentiment, the high priest brushed them off. "He claims as evidence his friendly relationship with Sammy Davis Jr. and people of all races and creeds," Vallée wrote. "Anton mocks would-be 'satanists' who feel obligated to display hatred for everyone. 'These people are not occultists,' he says, 'they're just sick.'"

San Francisco socialite Willy Werby said she and her husband, Don, had attended LaVey's Halloween parties "until a group of guys showed up in Nazi uniforms, which made us uncomfortable—and we ended the practice."

LaVey's extremist leanings also turned off Burton H. Wolfe, author of his first biography, who wrote at the end of that very book that although he had experimented with Satanism, he dropped out "when LaVey began developing his Church into a harsh, vindictive, crypto-fascist style organization." (LaVey characterized this as Wolfe's way of saving face for having participated. The two men remained friendly for many years after the book's release.)

Even Xerxes would later admit he was confounded by his father's appreciation of *Might Is Right*, as well as Satanists' overall fascination with fascistic imagery. "I suppose the goal is to be as shocking as possible," he said, "but it is quite bizarre given my family's heritage."

Gregg Turkington had dear friends who expressed disappointment that he had become close with LaVey, considering these preoccupations. "Because that shit is not for me," he says. "It wasn't stuff that came up. All I could do was say, 'In my experience, this guy is not like that.' He's talking about a lot of Jewish entertainers that he likes. And, of course, we know his own heritage was Jewish. He just didn't seem to have that in his DNA—in my experience." Nevertheless, Turkington couldn't understand why LaVey was aligning himself with some on the extreme right, other than for effect. "My experience was just hanging out with a funny old Jewish man."

From the perspective of a bohemian artist, Harvey Stafford wanted to see an interesting life for everyone, a bigger banquet table with more things on it, so he was able to look past some unpleasantness. "I can't say I was that interested in tweaking people by playing off of the history of fascism," he says. "But that said, Boyd and Anton were complicated people, and it's part of what made them exciting and interesting to be around. They were certainly not bland."

Stafford says that during the rise of QAnon—a sort of mass psychosis that, not unlike the Satanic Panic, afflicted a small but vocal contingent of the easily manipulated—all he could think was, "God, fuck these guys! They totally ruined it all!" Time was, you could sit at a bar with friends and try to determine who knew more about that tennis-shoe-wearing UFO suicide cult. Conspiracy theories used to be fun things to discuss.

"But," Stafford says, "it's all been shit on by these weird, paranoid rednecks who watch right-wing television."

Or as LaVey once opined about astrology, "If enough people are motivated by a hoax, then the hoax becomes as reality."

Margie Bauer became aware of LaVey as a teen in the late 1980s. Thanks to a boyfriend who studied metaphysics, she had access to an extensive occult library, which included LaVey's books as well as *The Devil's Avenger*, which was the one she read first. After writing LaVey a letter telling him how much of an impact his philosophy had made on her, in 1994 Blanche called to say she and the Doctor would like to have her over. And over again.

Bauer worked as a server, usually the dinner shift, at a tiki-style supper club called the Caribbean Zone. It was a warehouse that had been converted into a total environment out of LaVey's dreams—complete with foliage, a waterfall, and a crashed aircraft, actually the remains of an old tour plane used by the rock band the Doobie Brothers, which was suspended above the bar.

Since Bauer was already visiting the house two or three times a week, LaVey and Blanche asked her if she'd be interested in helping out with administrative work, processing memberships, answering letters, writing promotional materials (such as "The Satanic Youth Communiqué," an FAQ for budding acolytes), contributing pieces to *The Cloven Hoof*, and scouting rare books for use in articles. With the current media attention, various projects in progress, and a child on the premises, they could certainly use the help.

Her workday at the Black House typically began around midnight, when they all would gather in the kitchen over coffee and snacks, "Blanche and I typing away at our respective work," Bauer says, "often with a cat on one knee and baby Xerxes on the other." LaVey would be at his keyboards supplying the soundtrack. After a few hours, they would relax in the purple room and watch a movie or three. On a few occasions Bauer introduced films to LaVey that he would end up loving, including *Cobb*, starring Tommy Lee Jones as Ty Cobb, the so-called meanest man in baseball, and *Shining Through*, a World War II drama with Michael Douglas and Melanie Griffith that won the Razzie Award for Worst Picture of 1992.

She was also a student of LaVey's, learning applications of lesser magic, the manipulation techniques he served up in *The Compleat Witch*, a book, she says, that spoke to her.

Usually, she'd find herself heading home at eight or nine in the morning. And though she wasn't paid a wage, she'd often receive unexpected, generous envelopes on birthdays and holidays.

"He is probably the most genuine person I have ever known," she says. "If he liked you, he allowed you to just be yourself and leveled no criticism—in a way that I've rarely experienced with anyone else. I mean, you can tell the Devil anything, right? He really did love all the little personality quirks and foibles that we all have."

Bauer was at the house one mild fall evening, doing her administrative duties while ensconced in a small room off of the Den of Iniquity. She had not seen LaVey on her last few visits; she figured he just wasn't up for company. But she also knew that something felt different that night.

She'd been there for a few hours when, suddenly, Xerxes came rushing down wrapped in his coat. He was followed by his mother, who told Bauer, "I have to let you out; we've had some things come up."

"She was an amazing actress," Bauer has said, "like nothing was wrong." Bauer's husband was already waiting outside in their car to pick her up, and as the couple sat puzzled about what was transpiring, an ambulance stopped in front of 6114 California Street. They watched as the attendants carried a body from the house and loaded it into the vehicle.

Anton Szandor LaVey was taken to St. Mary's Hospital, two and a half miles away, where he died shortly before 9:00 a.m. on Wednesday, October 29, 1997, of pulmonary edema, an abnormal buildup of fluid in the lungs often resulting from a bad ticker. He was sixty-seven when he met his maker in San Francisco's first Catholic hospital.

As if to bookend a life filled with question marks followed by exclamation points, his death certificate initially listed his expiration date as October 31.

Halloween.

"I will never die," LaVey calmly told interviewer Joe Pyne in 1967, not long after founding the church.

"You won't?"

"No, of course not, I've made arrangements."

We all want to live forever, LaVey explained—who among us wants to die? "We're like little children that are put to bed before we really want to go to bed. . . . You don't know how many people are going to come to your funeral. You don't know what your wives—your husbands—are going to be doing afterwards."

Not to mention your daughters.

Evil Wilhelm picked up the ringing telephone. A familiar female voice was on the line.

"Ding-dong, the witch is dead!" it gleefully announced.

"I was the first call Zeena made when he died," he says.

Zeena also phoned into Bob Larson's nationally syndicated religious radio show the day after Anton passed with a bizarre claim: she had put a curse on him, and it worked. She was taking responsibility for her unfather's death.

For her part, Blanche sent out a more (or less) traditional, if typically fanciful, death notice. In it she attributed his rheumatic heart disease to a "Fever of Unknown Origin" he caught when he visited Europe at the end of WWII, and managed to squeeze in mentions of Jayne Mansfield, Sammy Davis Jr., the two Marilyns, and *Rosemary's Baby*.

On Tuesday, November 4, three days after Xerxes's fourth birthday, the family held an intimate funeral ritual at Woodlawn Memorial Park in Colma. In a large chamber that usually accommodated some fifty mourners, the small group began the ceremony by ringing a bell and invoking the four Crown Princes of Hell: Satan, Lucifer, Belial, and Leviathan. Then came the "Invocation to Satan," from *The Satanic Bible*, commanding the forces of eternal darkness to bestow their power. The service included a recitation of "The Men That Walk with Satan"—a poem by Robert E. Howard—as well as some passages from "The City of Dreadful Night," by Scottish poet James Thomson. To herald the dead, Blanche recited in both English and Enochian the Eleventh Enochian Key (with the memorable closing line "Be friendly unto me, for I am your God, the true worshipper of the flesh that liveth forever!").

"We spoke from our hearts, spending some time memorializing Anton," Blanche says. "His corporeal form was present with us, and we said our painful goodbyes." They rang the bell to conclude the ceremony and closed with the final phrase from *The Satanic Rituals*'s "Homage to Tchort": "Forget ye not what was and is to be! Flesh without sin, world without end! So it is done." With that, LaVey's body was wheeled down a narrow, black-draped corridor leading to the crematory oven. "We all retreated to the glare of the outdoors," Blanche recalls. "Karla and I hugged outside, watching the smoke rise as Anton's body was consumed by the flames."

Karla drafted the veteran local publicist Lee Houskeeper to make the official announcement after her father had been dead for a week. Thursday, November 6—the day she wanted to open the house for a press conference—was also the day Houskeeper was accompanying His All Holiness Bartholomew I, ecumenical patriarch of the Eastern Orthodox Church, on the spiritual leader's visit to bless the new Annunciation Cathedral in San Francisco's Mission District. "I was being shadowed by Secret Service officers when Karla and I met to make the plan," Houskeeper says. "I told her that I didn't want my representation of Bartholomew to become the story, and since her father was already dead, one more day wouldn't make any difference."

The dozen or so reporters and camera people who crammed into the airless parlor that Friday saw a skull atop an organ, daggers on the wall, and at the center of the room, a life-size replica of Anton LaVey on loan from the San Francisco Wax Museum at Fisherman's Wharf. The purpose of the press conference was for Karla and Blanche to present a united front: they both would be carrying on LaVey's work.

"We will continue in his footsteps to do as he directed to keep the Church of Satan going and keep it strong," Karla said.

The women spoke about his philosophy and what he signified. "He did believe in the Devil," Blanche said at one point. "He believed in magic. He practiced it religiously."

Karla cut her off with a clarification. "He didn't believe in a devil with horns and tails."

A few days later, Blanche sent out a solicitation on church letterhead requesting essays and tributes for a commemorative issue of *The Cloven Hoof* dedicated to the man she described as "angry, selfish, driven."

The Karla-Blanche alliance would prove to be short-lived. With her real-estate job, Karla had little time for the quotidian tasks required of the organization and, unlike Blanche, had no interest in maintaining the Black House as a potential historical site. And in January 1998, LaVey's eldest child filed a petition in probate court seeking to be appointed executor of her father's estate, which owing to settlements and bankruptcy amounted to just $60,000 (mostly from book royalties). In dispute was a handwritten, one-paragraph, unnotarized will dated March 9, 1995, in which LaVey apparently appointed Blanche executor and left "all writings, artwork, property and holdings" to her and ongoing book royalties to be held in trust for their son. Karla labeled the document a fraud, saying that her father "was not of sound and disposing mind and was under the influence of medication" when it was composed as he recuperated from a hospital stay. She also claimed that as his sole caregiver, Barton "threatened to leave him if he did not do what she wanted."

Blanche denied the allegations and accused Karla of falsely calling herself a high priestess in the church, despite having not participated in its operation for some time. She also said that since Zeena had been estranged from her father, LaVey's younger daughter deserved nothing from his estate.

Nearly thirty years later, Blanche says she knew full well LaVey's hurriedly conceived document wouldn't hold up to legal scrutiny, but she submitted it out of a sense of personal obligation. "If I hadn't presented it," she says, "I would have felt guilty."

She, Zeena, and Karla ended up reaching a settlement in January 1999, agreeing to share in future royalties and divide the personal property. Blanche would also continue to administer the Church of Satan, which she soon entrusted to High Priest Peter Gilmore and High Priestess Peggy Nadramia, a married couple long active in the church from their home base of New York.

Zeena's campaign to destroy Anton's legacy continued apace. In February 1998, just a few months after Anton's death, she and Nikolas Schreck—with whom she briefly ran a Satanic tchotchke shop called Hellhouse of Hollywood (located, somewhat improbably, at 6666 Hollywood Boulevard)—published online what they called a "brief checklist" purportedly debunking many of her father's more notorious biographical claims, regarding, among other things, the creation of the church, Anton's nonexistent role in *Rosemary's Baby*, his "affair" with Jayne Mansfield, church membership numbers, and his supposed wealth. She also alleged that he abused his pets and her mother and pimped out female disciples.

In 2012 Zeena publicly reaffirmed her enmity toward her unfather, calling him a lazy con man who never planned ahead or took care of his family, because "that is the nature of LaVeyan Satanism: Get what you can, live only in the here and now, care only about yourself, and get other people to care for you.

"It's like you're one big infant."

Zeena and Schreck later moved to Berlin, took up Tantric Buddhism, and then amicably divorced. Her resemblance to the pop star Taylor Swift turned her into a viral social media meme in the 2020s.

Conversely, Zeena's own estranged son, Anton doppelgänger Stanton, continued to beat his grandfather's truculent drum, leading his own

sect, the Ordo Satanas (sign-up fee: $66.60), and becoming a ubiqui-
tous presence on the Hollywood goth-industrial music scene. He briefly
ran a Sunset Boulevard shop with John Aes-Nihil called Odium, selling
racist skinhead music and books on fascism, Black power, Satanism,
and serial killers—what he called "intellectual smut"—before hawking
Devil-themed merchandise on his own website. In December 2022,
Stanton died from an accidental drug overdose while treating pain
from back surgery. At the time, he had been helping to curate an Anton
LaVey exhibition for the Graveface Museum in Savannah, Georgia.

Karla, having relinquished the Church of Satan to Blanche, started
up an organization called the First Satanic Church and promoted a
long-running music/burlesque/variety show in San Francisco called
Black X Mass. Anton's son, Satan Xerxes (now known as Ethan Clarke),
grew up to become a visual anthropologist specializing in pop culture
and war.

Not long after LaVey died, Gregg Turkington, who was then living in
Melbourne, Australia, got a call from Adam Parfrey. The publisher told
him that before he passed, LaVey had been working on a book. Both
Parfrey and Blanche thought Turkington would be the right person to
make sense out of the hundreds of pages of essays he'd left unfinished.
Flattered, Turkington agreed to take on the daunting project. "Adam
gave me a page count," he recalls, "and what I finally put together was
maybe a third of what I was given."

Turkington admits that he minimized the pieces that read more
didactically Satanic in favor of funnier bits that best captured the personality of the man he knew. "Some of the stuff I was given was like red
meat for the crowd that was looking for doctrine and ritual from the
head of the religion."

He brought up his concerns with Parfrey. "If you're asking me to do this," Turkington said, "that was never my real area of interest." He had hoped to inject the same sense of playfulness into this collection that he and Becky Wilson helped bring to LaVey's records. "That's probably why that book came out the way it did," he says. "You could have that same pile of essays and have a very different book that was sterner and more frightening."

Turkington admits to being initially surprised by the preponderance of essays fetishizing women who pissed themselves, but figured, "This is his thing—let's get it in there." When he found two pieces covering the same theme, he would thread them together. Though not the most emblematic of LaVey's writings, this collection, titled *Satan Speaks!*— published in 1998 and featuring a cover illustration by the rock poster artist and church member Coop—is certainly the most entertaining. The brief treatises are by turns flippant and provocative, inscrutable and revelatory, mundane and really out-there.

In "Stereo: Scam of the Century," LaVey shakes his Luddite fist at advancements in audio technology, lamenting, "A flute becomes as stentorian as a trumpet; a triangle as distracting as a timpani roll."

In "Why Walk?" he claims to have met a man in a wheelchair who told him he could actually stroll just fine but decided, "Why bother?" Ultimately, LaVey applauds this act of public dishonesty ("getting special advantages without expending money or effort"), as it revealed someone ahead of his time.

In "The Sneeze," he waxes rhapsodic about a young lady he knew who would involuntarily pee when she *achoo-ed*. "It may have distressed *her*," LaVey admits, "but it excited *me*."

In "The Nose Bubble," he describes the appeal of dangling fake plastic snot from one's nostrils in order to give others a false sense of superiority.

In "Why I Can't Make Money," he confesses, "I've never learned the value of money because my goals have always been attainable without money. . . . If I lack financial wealth, I have the next best thing: an appearance of it."

In "Don't Bathe," he calls the titular activity "against my religious principles," "like suicide," "very unhealthy," and "unkind to other animals, in that it renders a human unpredictable and often unjustly untrustworthy."

"To be fair," Turkington says, "the book probably does reflect my own taste more than if he had been left to his own devices and had finished it." Ultimately, Parfrey was pleased with Turkington's editorial choices and that the book immortalized LaVey's humorous side. And Turkington enjoyed his first and last experience as an editor.

As for the music he released by LaVey, after his death Turkington waved the white flag, deciding he didn't want to deal with the chaotic estate. He initially licensed some of it to another label. "Eventually I just washed my hands of the whole thing, because there just seemed to be too much confusion and too many parties involved," he says. "I liked working with him. I didn't have any need to try to squeeze money out of recordings of someone who is now gone. In fact, I have a lot of tapes of more songs. I could probably put together a couple more albums."

In a memo dated "15 June XXIII A.S." (a.k.a. 1998), Blanche wrote to church members on official letterhead. She was pleading for donations to help save her home. To help satisfy his palimony settlement, LaVey had been forced to sell it in 1993 for $240,000 to his old friend and patron Donald Werby, who allowed him to keep living there. (Werby himself was no stranger to scandal. In July 1990, he pleaded guilty to two misdemeanor counts of statutory rape of teen prostitutes and two misdemeanor counts of contributing to the delinquency of a minor. He had been indicted the previous August on twenty-one felony counts alleging he bought sex from minors with cocaine and money, and was later hit with a felony bribery charge. He received a one-year suspended sentence and a $300,000 fine, and was placed on three years' probation.) Blanche's current landlord, Cass-Bagley Corporation, partly owned by Werby, wanted to tear the Black House down to build apartments. A rumor that Marilyn Manson was going to buy it never mutated into a reality.

"I don't like to beg for money: that's one reason why I became a Satanist, in defiance of all the rip-off, 'gimmee-gimmee' churches," Blanche wrote. "But these are special circumstances." She proposed that if she were able to retain the house, she might offer tours and perhaps return to conducting rituals and seminars there. "If every person who has ever been influenced by Anton LaVey's writings sent in just one dollar to fund this special preservation project, we'd have more than enough money to buy the property and restore it."

Her appeal failed to scare up the requisite funds, and on July 22 she was served with an eviction notice. She and her four-year-old son would need to flee the Dilapidated House that Satan Built.

A month later, Harvey Stafford received a call from Grux, the leader of the experimental music group Caroliner and a friend of Karla and Anton's, to see if he could help clear out some stuff from 6114 and move it into a storage facility. Stafford, who had an Econoline van, dropped everything to drive over. What he saw shocked him. "There were several people there squabbling over every last scrap of anything," he says.

He witnessed a pithy exchange over a rusty old vacuum cleaner as well as what he describes as "a not very nice exchange over a piece-of-shit mimeograph machine" that supposedly was especially valuable because *The Cloven Hoof* had been printed on it. "I'm like, 'It's a piece of junk, nobody really cares. And you can't prove it. You've got no provenance.' But whatever."

On the morning of August 22, Blanche had been scheduled to walk through the house with Zeena, Karla, and their attorneys to appraise the value of specific items they were considering moving to a mutually agreed-upon safe place. Even though she had been ordered to leave the house, they were still going through probate—establishing the division of the estate—and had been told by that court not to remove anything. "My attorney was not present," Barton says, "but had told me that all parties had agreed that perhaps five to ten of our most precious items could be removed that morning, and that anything that was taken out should be inventoried and documented." She had friends bring Xerxes to Fisherman's Wharf for a few hours, not wanting to subject him to the activities and uncertain of the mood that would accompany this mix of adversarial personalities.

Nikolas Schreck, who was there with Zeena, recalls walking into a "very dramatic" scene. "After all of the hatred and enmity," he says, "Blanche had to let us in." Once inside, he removed the large Baphomet adornment that hung over the mantel in the ritual chamber. "I took it down and broke it, snapped it, and ritually tried to destroy everything that had to do with the energy of [LaVey] and the Church of Satan," he says.

"There were no attorneys present, and certainly no inventory or documentation," Barton says. "I was in the back of the house, trying to list the important items in the kitchen—Dr. LaVey's keyboards, some original movie posters, and other memorabilia—while Zeena and Karla were already lining their trucks up in front with a dozen friends, carting things from the front chamber, down the brick steps, without any care, packing, or organization."

Since she was facing eviction, Barton figured that if Karla and Zeena wanted to foot the bill for transport and storage until the probate court divided the estate, "this was the painful but prudent path." She made certain Boaz, their snake, and Zambezi, their cat, were safe in the kitchen, told her father—who had moved in downstairs earlier that year—that she needed to be with Xerxes, and then split.

Schreck recalls the house's interior resembling a tomb—no organization, just piles and piles of stuff. "Nothing had ever been moved," he says. "If it was put there in 1978, it was still there. It was completely stagnant and dusty. Everyone who went there got sick. It was like there was some kind of rot in the air, and it stank."

Stafford remembers the place looking "really fucked up." He was, however, finally able to see parts of the house that had previously been off-limits. "I had no idea from going to visit—because you only went to these particular rooms—but that was the time I started looking at the foundation. I was like, 'Shit, this thing is eaten up with termites, and the sill plate on the foundation is gone, and the concrete foundation is crumbling.' It was a mess."

But it all felt so very apt. "It was a haunted house. It fit right into his shtick."

In a small room at the back, where a broken pane of glass had exposed the interior to the elements, Stafford saw boxes upon boxes of old issues of *The Cloven Hoof* and what turned out to be correspondence to the church. "Every letter written to the church was in those boxes. And they were dated on the ends, just like boxes of tax records. Nobody there seemed to give a shit about those."

That same day, Stafford also got to walk into the ritual chamber. "There was someone associated with the church that got the Leslie speakers, which was quite a score," he says, of the uncommon audio gear typically used with Hammond organs. "Anton LaVey's Leslies? Jesus! It's like Tony Iommi's amp head. It's pretty fantastic."

Barton returned in the evening to find that walls had been knocked down, the bedrooms had been trashed, and the premises could no longer be secured. After sorting through the debris, she grabbed some clothes and toys. "We spent that night in a hotel in San Bruno, near the airport," she says, "and never slept in the Black House again."

She has called what transpired that day "an obscene rape of the Black House." Vintage 78-rpm records lay in pieces on the ground. Valuable books from a carefully curated library were strewn on the sidewalk. "The girls later accused me of stealing because things they remembered had disappeared," she says. "A few weeks later, they claimed an entire storage unit they'd arranged had been breached and cleaned out."

LaVey's friend Don Frew had been working for years at Shambhala Booksellers, a metaphysical shop next to Berkeley's storied Moe's Books, when he heard that someone from Moe's who lived on California Street was helping to clear stuff out of the house. After the Moe's employee inquired about a stack of legal boxes, Blanche allowed him to take it. When Frew expressed interest in the boxes, the neighbor let them go for around $200.

The boxes offered an evanescent history of the Church of Satan, a time capsule into an at-times thriving cottage industry of like-minded egoists and misanthropes. Among other things, they contained completed order forms for church merchandise, such as books, wall hangings, records, and jewelry; subscription renewals for *The Cloven Hoof*; information requests from teachers, homemakers, college students, retailers, kids, and prisoners (at least one of them signed in blood); mailings; invoices; membership applications; warlock exams; requests for the high priest's counsel; updates from grotto leaders; prisoner mail addressed specifically to Karla; and letters exchanged between Anton and Marcello Truzzi, Burton H. Wolfe, Kenneth Anger, and others. Frew added the material to the collection of the Adocentyn Research Library, where just outside Berkeley, he and his wife, Anna Korn, maintain a trove of thousands of books on paganism, Satanism, UFOs, and other arcane subjects.

The Black House was demolished in 2001 and replaced in 2008 with a nondescript beige-and-olive three-unit condominium. Even the house number—6114—disappeared, no longer recognized by the city of San Francisco as a legitimate address.

There went the neighborhood.

Mitch Horowitz admits he came late to LaVey. "I felt—probably like [other] people on the occult scene do—that Anton and the Church of Satan served to detract from the groundedness or the seriousness of what we were attempting to do," the historian and author says, "and that terms like 'Satanism' or 'Satanist' were epithets that we didn't want to apply to ourselves."

Around the fall of 2017, Horowitz felt his own metaphysical search undergoing changes. He was deeply dissatisfied with the manner in which much of the alternative spiritual culture—and himself with it— was framing the journey within the terms of the Abrahamic religions: Judaism, Christianity, and Islam. "Here's God up here, or Heaven up here, and something called Hell or Satan down here," he says. "I began to question those reference points because they're conceptual, like all religious reference points are. Every religion is made by human hands, and yet by dint of overwhelming familiarity and cultural repetition for centuries, we come to feel that these are the coordinates of reality. And there's no evidence for that whatsoever. These are decisions that were made by human beings who were in struggles, fought wars. There were movements that rose to ascendance, there were movements that descended. And like every culture, ours got made by those perceptions."

He became very interested in what, in his estimation, was a greater neutrality toward what might be called "the demonic" in Old Testament scripture. Horowitz—who grew up in a traditional Jewish household and had an Orthodox bar mitzvah—was intrigued by how the name of the demon Azazel was intoned in synagogue during Yom Kippur, the Jewish Day of Atonement. In this context, Azazel represents a desolate location where a scapegoat bearing the sins of the Jews was cast out. Horowitz came to realize that even a term like "demon" in its original Greek was a neutral term, similar to how "spirit" is used today. "There wasn't a negative value behind it," he says. "It was only in late biblical antiquity, and then post-biblical antiquity, that this Greek term was remade as something maleficent."

Horowitz recalls receiving a copy of *Occulture*, a book of essays by the high priest's friend Carl Abrahamsson, and reading a chapter titled "Anton LaVey, Magical Innovator." "I remember feeling a charge go through me," he says, "as one sometimes does when you encounter a book or a movie or a song or a piece of art, and you feel, 'There's something uniquely important for me in this.'

"I immediately grokked to the kind of protean self-creation that Anton was talking about," he adds, "his idea of the Total Environment, creating that total aesthetic around yourself." Horowitz felt liberated by the ability to talk about the pursuit of personal power in a way that wasn't negative, that predisposition to view it as inherently corrupt. "And I saw that Anton articulated some of this with a seriousness that I hadn't understood."

Anton LaVey—he's just Ayn Rand with pentagrams! That's a description Horowitz has heard a lot. "To a degree, that's true," he says. "But unlike Ayn Rand, Anton was not so burdened by an economic ideology that had suffocated out all other considerations."

In LaVey's view, you can create, maintain, and live inside your own bespoke domain and pursue personal power—yet his philosophy is hardly circumscribed. It's flexible. If you're an adult responsible for others, and if happiness to you means making them happy, then it's impossible to be totally selfish. You have to be able to let others in.

"It doesn't preclude a sense of belonging," Horowitz says. "So it's not a philosophy that expects you're going to become a libertine." Even when LaVey was conducting the Satanic baptism of his daughter Zeena, Horowitz adds, "I don't mean this to sound glib, but he's still spending time with his family. You know—there's Anton with his kid."

The church emerged in 1966 as a mix of performance art, satire, ritual, and self-help, and then developed into something more substantial—an unusual trajectory for this kind of cabalistic group. "Frequently the spiritual superstar will enter the scene as if bearing the tablets from Sinai," Horowitz says. "For Carlos Castaneda, it's Native American wisdom. For the Maharishi Mahesh Yogi, it's transcendental meditation. For somebody else, it's a marriage of physics and spirituality.

"For Anton," he continues, "it was a wish to lampoon the hypocrisies of mainstream spirituality, along with what he saw as the sugar sweetness that was not yet to play out in the media image of the Summer of Love, but which he witnessed firsthand in San Francisco. He decided to take a sledgehammer to them, while at the same time making himself famous."

With LaVey, Horowitz observes, there was always a tension between responsibility and revulsion. He was all in, until he wasn't. "Obviously he was deeply attached to the occult aesthetic and occult ceremonies," Horowitz says. "He came up with plenty of rituals himself, or adapted them from other works. But he was also so anti-orthodoxy and anti-belief, he grew disdainful of people taking these things so seriously. Suddenly they started to think of this really being a church, which actually the organization has perpetuated, and to some extent Anton perpetuated, by awarding all these different degrees and this tone of orthodoxy about what does and doesn't constitute a Satanist. What could be less Satanic than that? 'Here's how you have to be a rebel, and there's no other way to be a rebel.' There was always that tension within

Anton, but he always left enough ambiguity so that the individual could find their way within his work."

Marcello Truzzi once said of his friend, while paraphrasing George Orwell, "If you wear a mask long enough it sticks to your face. Then it becomes your face." In other words, if you commit to the bit with such extreme devotion, it's bound to change you. "I respect that," says Horowitz, "because every actor is told, 'Never break character.' No matter what happens during the show—if the ceiling falls in, if somebody utters the wrong line—you can recover from every mishap. But you can't recover from breaking character.

"And Anton"—publicly at least—"never broke character."

Though not completely aligned with LaVey's belief system, the high-profile Wiccan Don Frew has a similar appreciation for what he created. "Reading LaVey today you go, 'Oh, of course! Like, what's the big deal?'" he says. "It's hard to put it in context and realize how revolutionary it was at the time, because if you take 'Satanic' off it, it just doesn't seem that weird or crazy. It was a legitimate religio-philosophical movement that LaVey wanted to explore, and he could explore it more easily with other people.

"Satanism was just the window dressing on it. It was a window dressing that worked at the time and didn't work later. But that was built into LaVey's Satanism from the beginning. He dug his hole; he was stuck in it. As he got older, he was aware of it."

Any group that's concerned with the inflation of the ego, Frew believes, is going to tear itself apart over time because the individuals won't be able to work with one another unless there's a strong control at the heart. "And without LaVey at the center," he says, "the Church of Satan is not doing a hell of a lot."

As evidenced by his splits with Michael Aquino and Zeena, LaVey didn't want anybody challenging him, but that also meant when he died there would be no charismatic leader to take over. "I think he could see that, that this was all coming to nothing," Frew says. "And that was really affecting him."

While the church, under the auspices of Peter Gilmore and Peggy Nadramia, remains an active concern, as of 2024, that activity largely has been relegated to cyberspace, where they maintain a comprehensive website—replete with essays, interviews, historical articles, and podcasts—as well as a presence on social media, including a highly rational and witheringly droll X (formerly Twitter) account.

The church also has inspired a number of contemporary offshoots, chief among them the Satanic Temple—based in the witch haven of Salem, Massachusetts—which shares some of the superficial trappings of LaVeyan Satanism: the macabre iconography, the performative rituals, the sex-positiveness, the metaphoric recognition of the Devil as an adversarial figure. The Satanic Temple, however, has inverted LaVey's philosophy, rejecting his Social Darwinist views and glorification of authoritarianism. Instead, it is a tax-exempt, nontheistic religion, a social justice organization rallying—and, perhaps more effectively, suing—on behalf of marriage equality and reproductive rights and against Christian privilege and corporal punishment, among other causes. For its best-known protest, in 2018 the Satanic Temple briefly installed a nearly nine-foot-tall winged-goat Baphomet statue in front of the Arkansas State Capitol building where a Ten Commandments monument also stood.

Lucien Greaves, who founded the Satanic Temple with a similarly pseudonymous Harvard University buddy, Malcolm Jarry, in 2013, has admitted using LaVey's church as "a starting point"—and even contributed illustrations to a limited-edition reprinting of *Might Is Right* published by Shane Bugbee—but has since distanced his group from the Church of Satan, explaining on the temple's website: "The Church of Satan expresses vehement opposition to the campaigns and activities of The Satanic Temple, asserting themselves as the only 'true' arbiters of Satanism, while The Satanic Temple dismisses the Church of Satan as irrelevant and inactive."

And like the Church of Satan, it has also weathered episodes of internal discord, which led Joseph Laycock, author of *Speak of the Devil*, a history of the Satanic Temple, to pose this rhetorical conundrum: "How can you have an *organization* of people dedicated to total individual freedom and empowerment?"

On Halloween 2017, Lethal Amounts, a Los Angeles gallery dedicated to outlaw art, hosted an event called "Disobey," a memorial of sorts, nearly twenty years to the day after Anton LaVey ceased to walk among the living. At the magic-themed Black Rabbit Rose nightclub right off Hollywood Boulevard, goths, punks, occultists, and the Lucifer-curious descended into the velvety, ornate space to mingle with the likes of Karla LaVey, Kenneth Anger, Boyd Rice, Misfits front man Glenn Danzig, and the night's DJ, Matt Skiba of the rock band Alkaline Trio. There, they took in an astonishing collection of LaVeyan artifacts, including original artwork by the man himself, photos by Walter Fischer from the book *California Infernal*, and the organ from the ritual chamber, on loan from former Radio Werewolf drummer Evil Wilhelm, upon whom it was bestowed by Zeena.

"Karla's funny," says Evil Wilhelm, recalling the event. "She's like, 'Let's take a picture with the organ. Oh, wait, I need my horns!' And this guy runs and grabs her purse and takes out her little stick-on horns. These LaVeys are great at always having a slave around to get their horns."

For Evil Wilhelm, the highlight of the evening came when the ninety-year-old Anger ripped open his shirt to reveal the infamous LUCIFER tattoo spelled out across his chest. For others, it may have been the performance by a Satanic doo-wop group. For others, it may have been the ritual in which a blood-drenched woman was proffered to the goddess Lilith. For others still, it may have been the long, digressive, and illuminating onstage conversation between Boyd and Karla, two longtime acquaintances reminiscing about the bad old days.

After they decided to take questions from the audience, someone asked Karla if her father had, in all honesty, sported a tail until his teens.

"Yes, that's absolutely true," Anton's eldest kid quickly responded. And with a flourish that surely would have made Pops beam with atta-girl pride, she doubled down.

"Both of my parents had tails."

Though she didn't elaborate on her mother's dorsal stub, her father's, she clarified, was technically a pilonidal cyst—a common condition that sometimes manifests as a golf ball–sized bump—which she cited as one of the reasons the military wouldn't have him. That's nothing like a caudal appendage, which, according to LaVey's authorized biography, "seems to occur about one in every 100,000 births." Both claims run counter to what Burton H. Wolfe wrote in *The Devil's Avenger*: "He had no claws, tail, horn stumps, or yellow eyes—although his eyes were rather narrow and glinting."

"He was born with a tail," Karla reiterated. "Both my parents had to have their tails removed.

"That's absolutely true."

Hails

FIRST, big thanks to everyone who agreed to be interviewed for this book—or, at the very least, answered an email or sent a message—and that includes Carl Abrahamsson, Bobby Neel Adams, John Aes-Nihil, Blanche Barton, Margie Bauer, Carol Sturm Smith Beaumont, Alan Black, Jay Blakesberg, Jack Boulware, Shane Bugbee, Martyn Burke, Michael Butler, Wayne Chonicki, Mary deYoung, Raechel Donahue, Gabe Essoe, Evil Wilhelm, Cathy Fitzhugh, Don Frew, Jack Fritscher, Michael S. Glick, Damon J. Goldstein, Walt Harrington, Mitch Horowitz, Lee Houskeeper, Hawk Koch, Richard Lamparski, Sharon LaVey, Steve Leialoha, Thomas Lipscomb, Stuart MacKenzie, Peter Mintun, Jim Morton, George Petros, Lisa Petrucci, Jose Pineda, Ana Maria Quintana, Ron Quintana, Reuben Radding, Eugene S. Robinson, Nikolas Schreck, Dr. David Smith, Harvey Stafford, David Steinberg, Edward Millington Stout III, Stuart Swezey, Jay Thelin, JG Thirlwell, Thomas Thorn, Gregg Turkington, Jacques Vallée, Spencer Waldron, Larry Wessel, Becky Wilson, Lawrence Wright, and Gary Zellerbach.

This book wouldn't exist were it not for the divine guidance and encouragement of my editor, Ben Schafer, and agent, Roger Freet.

As usual, Steve Korn and his X-ray vision saved me from myself.

Peggy Nadramia, who herself has written a number of illuminating articles about Anton LaVey and the church, supplied copious research materials, for which I am eternally grateful. Thanks also to William J. Butler for the access.

Fist bumps go to Marci Ballard, Matt Birkbeck, Jamey Duvall, James Evenson, Sean Howe, Justin Humphreys, Virginia MacDonald, Dennis McNally, Josh Modell, Tom Prince, Joel Selvin, Mark Suppanz, Christina Ward, and John Yohalem for providing either crucial contacts or vital assistance. And two enthusiastically raised devil horns to the Supersuckers for inspiring the book's title.

I'd also like to extend my deepest appreciation to Don Frew (again) and Anna Korn at the Adocentyn Research Library of Albany, California.

As always, eternal love to Helen Brod, the late Mike Brod, and the Boyle and Silverman families.

And, finally, I am truly blessed to have the unwavering trust and support of Rachel and Sasha, my beautiful angels, without whom . . .

Sources and Notes

INTERVIEWS for this book were conducted in person or via telephone, Zoom, Messenger, or email between December 2022 and March 2024. To distinguish these interviews from previously published material, I have attributed the quotes to their speakers in the present tense. Additionally, I consulted many secondary sources, including newspapers, magazines, books, videos, podcasts, social media posts, essays, legal papers, and ephemera, which are listed here if they're not cited within the text itself. I accessed many of the newspaper articles on Newpapers.com and checked out some rare books and video from the Internet Archive digital library. All personal correspondences between Anton LaVey, his family, and others—as well as Church of Satan administrative documents and copies of *The Cloven Hoof*—are from the collection of the Adocentyn Research Library of Albany, California.

INVOCATION

1 **"Please dim the lights":** Will Stevens, "Satanic Rites at Marriage," *San Francisco Examiner*, February 1, 1967.

1 **He stands before:** These and other details from the wedding have been sourced from the Reuters news footage titled "USA: Satanic 'Wedding' Performed in California," January 31, 1967, https://reuters.screenocean.com/record/438957, as well as "Anton LaVey Performs Satanic Wedding Rite for John Raymond and Judith Case," KPIX-TV, February 1, 1967, Bay Area Television Archive, https://diva.sfsu.edu/collections/sfbatv/bundles/238408.

2 **Raymond places:** Judith Case, as told to Ruth Perlberg, "We Were Married by the Devil!" *True Confessions*, June 1967.

3 **"Well, that's it":** Stevens, "Satanic Rites at Marriage."

3 **Among them:** Ibid.

4 **"Reporters clustered"**: Don Donahue, "Satiating Satan," *Berkeley Barb*, February 3, 1967.

4 **a wailing fire truck**: "Nude Dresses Up Wedding Held in a Den of Satan," *Detroit Free Press*, February 2, 1967.

4 **"It was awfully"**: Stevens, "Satanic Rites at Marriage."

4 **"She is the altar"**: Jonathan Root, "When the Devil's Own Fall in Love . . .," *San Francisco Chronicle*, February 1, 1967.

4 **"cold, unyielding slab"**: "It Was a Helluva Wedding," *New York Daily News*, February 2, 1967.

4 **"conceived not in heaven"**: Root, "When the Devil's Own Fall in Love . . ."

4 **"I am an ordained"**: Ibid.

4 **"I did it just as"**: Stevens, "Satanic Rites at Marriage."

4 **"They were both Christian"**: "It Was a Helluva Wedding."

5 **"Do you mean"**: Donahue, "Satiating Satan."

5 **"This marriage is as valid"**: Root, "When the Devil's Own Fall in Love . . ."

5 **"As you step off"**: Donahue, "Satiating Satan."

5 **mandrake root**: Ibid.

5 **eucalyptus oil**: "'Satanic' Wedding Alarms from Beginning to End," *Bismarck Tribune*, February 1, 1967.

5 **Gavin Arthur**: "A Satanic Bride in Black," *San Francisco Examiner*, January 31, 1967.

5 **An indignant Arthur**: Gavin Chester Arthur, "Editor's Mail Box: No Gift," *San Francisco Examiner*, February 8, 1967.

5 **One journalist noted**: Donahue, "Satiating Satan."

6 **"I consider it"**: Rob Haeseler, "Satanic Bid for Legality," *San Francisco Chronicle*, August 17, 1967.

6 **"We're not saying"**: Ibid.

6 **Bedecked in a black**: "Anton LaVey on *The Joe Pyne Show*," YouTube video, uploaded by Rev. Draconis Blackthorne, www.youtube.com/watch?v=Kqb54 soKU8M.

7 **John Raymond decided**: John Raymond, "The Satanic Verses: How One Man Helped Get the Church of Satan Off the Ground," *SF Weekly*, July 1, 1998, https://archives.sfweekly.com/sanfrancisco/the-satanic-verses /Content?oid=2135424.

8 **"As soon as we attended"**: Case, "We Were Married by the Devil!"

8 **Case's father, Edward**: "A Satanic Bride in Black."

8 **"After the last guest"**: Raymond, "The Satanic Verses."

8 **"We really pulled it off"**: Ibid.

CHAPTER I

9 **A caudal appendage**: Abraham Alarcon, Edgar Armijo, Daniela Cisneros, Jose Facio, Jorge Gutierrez, Susana Hernandez, Gerardo Muñoz, and Josue Rueda, "Human Tail in a Newborn," *Journal of Pediatric Surgery Case Reports* 76,

January 2022, ScienceDirect, www.sciencedirect.com/science/article/pii/S22 13576621003195.

9 **But that's exactly:** Blanche Barton, *The Secret Life of a Satanist: The Authorized Biography of Anton Szandor LaVey,* revised edition (Port Townsend: Feral House, 2014), 25.

9 **Chicago's Franklin Boulevard:** Burton H. Wolfe, *The Black Pope: The Authentic Biography of Anton Szandor LaVey* (self-published e-book, 2008), 17.

9 **"It really was":** Lawrence Wright, "Sympathy for the Devil," *Rolling Stone,* September 5, 1991.

9 **When he was:** Barton, *The Secret Life of a Satanist,* 25.

9 **Once while camping:** Wright, "Sympathy for the Devil."

9 **The intense pain:** Barton, *The Secret Life of a Satanist,* 25.

10 **when he was a teenager:** US Census Bureau, "1950 Census of Population and Housing," www.ancestry.com/imageviewer/collections/62308/images /43290879-California-142209-0024?treeid=&personid=&queryId=b274 802b-a24f-43cf-b80f-3e364f1505b9&usePUB=true&_phsrc=iuI286&_phstart= successSource&pId=265347410.

10 **before it was amended:** Wolfe, *The Black Pope,* 17.

10 **Gertrude, twenty-seven:** US Census Bureau, "Fifteenth Census of the United States: 1930—Population Schedule," www.ancestry.com/discoveryui -content/view/83754470:6224?tid=&pid=&queryId=5eadd05c-6192-404c-bf57 -2722eb6f1485&_phsrc=iuI292&_phstart=successSource.

10 **Michael, a Chicago native:** US Census Bureau, "Thirteenth Census of the United States: 1910—Population," www.ancestry.com/discoveryui-content /view/112668219:7884?tid=&pid=&queryId=cec4a9a2-7531-4815-8169-7e00fa 51407a&_phsrc=iuI303&_phstart=successSource.

10 **Born in Cleveland:** Wolfe, *The Black Pope,* 18.

10 **Baris worked:** US Census Bureau, "Twelfth Census of the United States: Schedule No. 1—Population (1900)," www.ancestry.com/discoveryui-content/view /38917402:7602?tid=&pid=&queryId=488dcfc4-c466-4f86-91f9-4b547470 8740&_phsrc=iuI305&_phstart=successSource.

10 **moved his family:** US Census Bureau, "Fifteenth Census of the United States: 1930—Population Schedule."

10 **his parents journeyed:** "Modesto California City Directory, 1933," www .ancestry.com/discoveryui-content/view/249879054:2469?tid=&pid=&query Id=b54981c4-8281-4cf3-9527-950fb291d0b2&_phsrc=iuI311&_phstart=succes sSource.

10 **Within three years:** Voter registrations, precinct No. 201, Marin County, CA, 1936–1940, www.ancestry.com/discoveryui-content/view/60469994:61066 ?tid=&pid=&queryId=6b637845-ac91-44c2-9ad2-279d9b9686eb&_phsrc =iuI333&_phstart=successSource.

10 **By 1940:** Michael Joseph Levey draft registration card, serial No. 1054, www .ancestry.com/discoveryui-content/view/18959591:2238.

11 **As an adolescent, he:** Barton, *The Secret Life of a Satanist*, 20.

11 **"I never was":** Ibid.

11 **As a member:** "Larkspur Cubs Hold Fine Parents Night," *San Anselmo Herald*, April 17, 1941.

12 **registered Democrats:** Voter registrations, precinct No. 201, Marin County, CA, 1936–1940.

12 **"From a young age":** Barton, *The Secret Life of a Satanist*, 21.

12 **He liked brass:** Ibid., 22.

12 **At Tamalpais:** Pat Goulder, "Elaborate Christmas Program for Public This Friday Evening at 8:15 in Assembly Hall at Tamalpais Hi," *San Anselmo Herald*, December 13, 1945.

12 **he managed to sneak:** Barton, *The Secret Life of a Satanist*, 23.

12 **Another exhibition:** Ibid., 23–24.

12 **Incubator Babies:** Walter Burroughs, managing ed., *Official Guide Book: Golden Gate International Exposition* (San Francisco: Crocker Company, 1939), 95.

12 **at around five:** Barton, *The Secret Life of a Satanist*, 30.

13 **A defender:** Ibid., 21.

13 **"It had all":** *Speak of the Devil: The Canon of Anton LaVey*, directed by Nick Bougas, 1993, YouTube video, uploaded by Eviliv3, www.youtube.com /watch?v=EKA9qtoT9To.

13 **For school:** Barton, *The Secret Life of a Satanist*, 24.

13 **He claimed:** Ibid., 25.

13 **in spring 1945:** Ibid., 26.

13 **LaVey, instead:** Ibid., 21.

14 **learned secrets:** Ibid., 28–29.

14 **A salesman named:** Record of prisoner, William LaVey (alias William Levey), United States Penitentiary, McNeil Island, Washington, www.ancestry.com /discoveryui-content/view/15091:1253?tid=&pid=&queryId=cc9f93ae-0720 -44b8-8c83-631993802e5c&_phsrc=iuI328&_phstart=successSource.

14 **in spring 1947:** Barton, *The Secret Life of a Satanist*, 32.

14 **during feeding time:** Ibid., 33.

14 **began playing:** Ibid., 34.

14 **Not only would:** Ibid., 35.

14 **LaVey's name is:** Bill Antes and Justus Edwards, eds., *Clyde Beatty Circus 1947 Season Route Book & Souvenir Program*, https://digital.library.illinoisstate.edu /digital/collection/p15990coll5/id/14491/rec/17.

15 **spent some time:** Barton, *The Secret Life of a Satanist*, 38–39.

15 **Around this time:** Ibid., 39–40.

15 **"I knew that":** Wright, "Sympathy for the Devil."

15 **Later, he told:** Fred Harden, "Anton LaVey: Disciple of the Devil," *Hustler*, December 1979.

15 **onetime roommate:** Gerald Nachman, "Stage and Screen," *Oakland Tribune*, August 11, 1967.

16 **The pair:** Wright, "Sympathy for the Devil." Barton, *The Secret Life of a Satanist*, 47.

16 **He'd tell another:** Harden, "Anton LaVey: Disciple of the Devil."

16 **"She approached sex":** Ibid.

16 **By 1949:** US Census Bureau, "1950 Census of Population and Housing."

16 **picked up the odd gig:** Barton, *The Secret Life of a Satanist*, 53–54.

16 **he said he bluffed:** Ibid., 53.

16 **the college had no:** Wright, "Sympathy for the Devil."

16 **"I would be hired":** Barton, *The Secret Life of a Satanist*, 54.

17 **One night at:** Ibid., 55.

17 **"I'd be in the crib":** "Boyd Rice and Karla LaVey interview 10/31/2017," video, Internet Archive, https://archive.org/details/BoydKarla.

17 **"There is no God":** Wright, "Sympathy for the Devil."

17 **After the SFPD later:** Ibid.

17 **he was picking up work:** Barton, *The Secret Life of a Satanist*, 58.

17 **Clients began:** Burton H. Wolfe, *The Devil's Avenger* (New York: Pyramid, 1974), 58.

18 **On the first:** Email to the author from Lori Ponton Rodriguez, assistant treasurer and membership, Musicians Union Local 6/AFM6, San Francisco, June 13, 2023.

18 **In 1956, his parents:** Wolfe, *The Black Pope*, 53.

18 **He later said:** Barton, *The Secret Life of a Satanist*, 63.

18 **Mary Ellen Pleasant:** "Mother of California Civil Rights Movement," *Gold Chains: The Hidden History of Slavery in California*, American Civil Liberties Union of Northern California, www.aclunc.org/sites/goldchains/explore /mary-ellen-pleasant.html.

CHAPTER II

Author interviews with Steve Leialoha, Edward Millington Stout III, John Aes-Nihil, and Blanche Barton.

20 **"Anton was playing":** Stanton LaVey, "1959: The Year Diane Met the Devil," BaphometX (blog), October 11, 2021, www.baphometx.com/post/1959-the -year-diane-met-the-devil.

20 **In December:** Allen Brown, "The Question Man: How to Get Along with People," *San Francisco Chronicle*, December 16, 1959.

20 **On May 10:** "Circus Daze for Organ Society," *San Mateo Times*, May 9, 1960.

20 **at a performance:** "Organ Concert at Capuchino," *San Mateo Times*, October 13, 1960.

21 **And it wasn't:** "'Wedding Fraud': Divorcee Sues Kin of Kennedy Aide," *San Francisco Chronicle*, November 18, 1961.

23 **who at twenty-six:** "8 Women Join Police Force," *San Francisco Examiner*, June 7, 1949.

23 **a former marine:** "San Francisco Policewomen Arrest Crime—Instead of Criminals," *San Francisco Chronicle*, November 13, 1949.

23 **One late:** "Woman Cop Shoots S.F. Man," *San Francisco Chronicle*, August 25, 1963.

24 **When he was:** "The Lady Cop Who Shot Fast," *San Francisco Examiner*, February 27, 1964.

24 **LaVey testified:** "Jury Hears Two Versions of a Shooting," *San Francisco Chronicle*, February 27, 1964.

24 **Dee was acquitted:** "That Lady Cop in New Trouble," *San Francisco Chronicle*, April 30, 1964.

24 **charged with:** "Woman Cop Suspended," *San Francisco Examiner*, April 30, 1964.

24 **suspended ninety days:** "Woman Cop Suspended 90 Days," *San Francisco Examiner*, June 2, 1964.

24 **Still, she:** "Police Promotions by the Score," *San Francisco Chronicle*, January 1, 1972.

24 **Twelve years:** "Yesterday's Second Big Deal: A Trike Accident," *San Francisco Examiner*, June 22, 1984.

24 **In Carole's:** Wright, "Sympathy for the Devil."

24 **It was at:** Barton, *The Secret Life of a Satanist*, 74.

25 **Over time:** Michael Aquino, *The Church of Satan, Volume I*, eighth edition (self-published paperback, 2013), 26–27.

25 **multitudinous volumes:** *Satanis: The Devil's Mass*, DVD, directed by Ray Laurent, 1970 (Seattle: Something Weird, 2003).

26 **a chamber where:** Aquino, *The Church of Satan, Volume I*, 27.

CHAPTER III

Author interviews with Raechel Donahue and Dr. David Smith.

29 **In 1965:** "Anton LaVey and Family on Children's TV Show," YouTube video, uploaded by Danny Shipman, www.youtube.com/watch?v=QxvWE3OHRQs.

30 **Togare was nine:** Wolfe, *The Devil's Avenger*, 73.

30 **The big cat was named:** Europe, Registration of Foreigners and German Persecutees, 1939–1947 for Georg Kulovits, www.ancestry.ca/discoveryui-content/view/12830469:61758?tid=&pid=&queryId=87a8d3b2-274f-4125-91c7-3d76a51a2f98&_phsrc=qCC35&_phstart=successSource.

30 **mingling with:** Herb Caen, "It's Your Dime, Start Reading," *San Francisco Chronicle*, April 20, 1965.

30 **teaching kindergarteners:** Peter Hartlaub, "Our San Francisco: Satanic Priest Raised Lion in S.F. and Then Things Got Really Wild," *San Francisco Chronicle*, October 30, 2023.

30 **the Golden West:** Eloise Keeler, "Deadline Is Near for Cat Show," *San Francisco Examiner*, September 19, 1965.

31 **"We just don't":** Jonathan Root, "S.F.'s Own: A Quarter Ton of Loving Lion," *San Francisco Chronicle*, April 22, 1966.

31 **Diane, who admitted:** Mildred Schroeder, "She's Married to Magic," *San Francisco Examiner*, June 21, 1966.

31 **three days later:** "Keene vs. Togare: S.F. Politician on a Lion Hunt," *San Francisco Chronicle*, April 25, 1966.

31 **"You know":** Charles Denton, "Sorcery Practiced Here," *San Francisco Examiner*, September 8, 1966.

31 **Kenneth Anger:** Wolfe, *The Devil's Avenger*, 71.

31 **Novelist Stephen:** Wolfe, *The Black Pope*, 61.

31 **Dr. Cecil Nixon:** "Now, Getting Back to Isis and Her Zither . . . ," *San Francisco Chronicle*, September 3, 1945.

31 **another called Galatea:** "Want to Be Mystified? Just Call on Dr. Nixon," *San Francisco Examiner*, June 9, 1931.

31 **LaVey claimed another:** Wolfe, *The Devil's Avenger*, 71.

32 **"the medieval":** Barton, *The Secret Life of a Satanist*, 76.

33 **"Calling it":** Dave Smith, "'Head Satan' Speaks—to Set Record Straight," *Los Angeles Times*, July 17, 1970.

33 **"Satan as a red devil":** Randall H. Alfred, "The Church of Satan," in Charles Y. Glock and Robert N. Bellah, eds., *The New Religious Consciousness* (Berkeley: University of California Press, 1976), 189.

33 **forbade the use:** Ibid., 186.

33 **the Berkeley campus:** Ibid., 193.

33 **Alcohol, however:** Ibid., 186.

33 **a spiked punch:** Ibid.

34 **"desire successes":** Edward J. Moody, "Magical Therapy: An Anthropological Investigation of Contemporary Satanism," in Irving I. Zaretsky and Mark P. Leone, eds., *Religious Movements in Contemporary America* (Princeton: Princeton University Press, 1974), 358.

34 **Many suffered:** Ibid, 360.

34 **"assorted psychological":** Ibid., 359.

34 **"The new member":** Ibid., 366.

34 **the shibboleth ritual:** Ibid., 378–379.

34 **Alfred also observed:** Alfred, "The Church of Satan," 189.

35 **Diane would soon:** Anton LaVey letter to Marcello Truzzi, October 14, 1969.

35 **"At the present time":** Church of Satan handout, undated.

36 **the *Chronicle*:** John L. Wasserman, "Mostel Film at Festival," *San Francisco Chronicle*, October 13, 1966.

36 **Matt Cimber:** "Mickey, Jayne May Remarry," *San Francisco Examiner*, July 21, 1966.

36 **Less than:** "Jayne Mansfield Wins Custody," *San Francisco Chronicle*, October 16, 1966.

37 **"That candle":** Barton, *The Secret Life of a Satanist*, 91.

37 **Or maybe:** May Mann, *Jayne Mansfield* (New York: Pocket, 1974), 198.

37 **According to LaVey:** Barton, *The Secret Life of a Satanist*, 90.

37 **the SFIFF:** "Fun and Games," *San Francisco Examiner*, October 30, 1966.

38 **conducting a Halloween:** Charles Denton, "Bewitching Thoughts," *San Francisco Examiner*, November 6, 1966.

38 **donning a pith helmet:** Gerald Adams, "A Debutante's Big Splash," *California Living,* the magazine of the *San Francisco Examiner* and *Chronicle,* November 6, 1966.

39 **The big cat:** Florabel Muir, "Jayne's Son in 2d Surgery," *New York Daily News,* November 29, 1966.

39 **According to May Mann:** Mann, *Jayne Mansfield,* 225.

39 **LaVey claimed:** Barton, *The Secret Life of a Satanist,* 92.

39 **Zoltan developed:** "Jayne Mansfield's Son, 6, Recovering," *San Francisco Examiner,* December 8, 1966.

39 **LaVey said:** Barton, *The Secret Life of a Satanist,* 92.

39 **She would sneak:** Ibid., 97.

39 **She would ring:** Ibid., 100.

39 **she phoned:** Herb Caen, "San Franciscaena," *San Francisco Chronicle,* December 15, 1966.

39 **LaVey claimed that:** Barton, *The Secret Life of a Satanist,* 101.

39 **Brody would:** Ibid.

40 **"Togare has become":** Ivan Sharpe, "Jungle Cats Are Making Dandy Household Pets," *San Francisco Chronicle,* December 27, 1966.

40 **Vigne, another:** Noir Gallery brochure, San Francisco, undated.

40 **Loralee, a mystic:** Fellowship of Isis website, www.isisofutah.org/loreon-vigne.

40 **And by January:** Will Stevens, "Rise of S.F. Satanist Church Cult," *San Francisco Examiner,* January 29, 1967.

40 **LaVey received:** Peggy Nadramia, "From the Church of Satan Archives," Church of Satan website, www.churchofsatan.com/from-the-cos-archives/.

41 **"We're in the":** Aquino, *The Church of Satan, Volume I,* 39.

41 **Weber had gone:** "'Satan' Must Pay His Due," *San Francisco Examiner,* February 24, 1967.

41 **Weber told the judge:** "Court Tells Sorcerer to Fork Up," *San Francisco Chronicle,* February 25, 1967.

41 **"I'll make":** Jack Rosenbaum, "She's No Lady," *San Francisco Chronicle,* March 9, 1967.

41 **She was dancing:** Susan Atkins with Bob Slosser, *Child of Satan, Child of God* (San Juan Capistrano: Menelorelin Dorenay's Publishing, 1977/2005), 65.

41 **She was already:** Ibid., 70.

41 **But come:** Ibid., 71.

42 **"We can live":** Ibid., 72–73.

42 **"a smash hit":** Ibid., 73.

42 **"having failed":** Herb Caen, "Tripe a la Mode de Caen," *San Francisco Chronicle,* March 29, 1967.

42 **The show, the drugs:** Atkins, *Child of Satan, Child of God,* 73.

42 **On the front door:** Ibid., 143.

43 **"She stated that":** Vincent Bugliosi with Curt Gentry, *Helter Skelter: The True Story of the Manson Murders* (New York: Bantam, 1975/1995), 639.

43 **"She was a junkie":** Eugene S. Robinson, "Anton LaVey/The Church of Satan," *The Birth of Tragedy* 4, November 1986–January 1987.

43 **LaVey surmised:** Ibid.

43 **"In the end":** Barton, *The Secret Life of a Satanist*, 82.

44 **LaVey regarded as "kooks":** Arthur Lyons, *Satan Wants You: The Cult of Devil Worship in America*, paperback edition (New York: Mysterious Press, 1989), 90.

44 **By March:** Ernest Lenn, "Beware Mr. Lion, the D.A. Is Out on a Richmond Safari," *San Francisco Examiner*, March 8, 1967.

44 **The grievance:** Ernest Lenn, "Bill Blake Bill Bars Beasts," *San Francisco Examiner*, March 13, 1967.

45 **Assistant DA:** William Chapin, "A Sorely Tried Sorcerer," *San Francisco Chronicle*, March 15, 1967.

45 **In his mug shots:** Wolfe, *The Black Pope*, 142.

45 **He said he'd:** Russ Cone, "Blake's 'No Animals' Law Blocked," *San Francisco Examiner*, March 29, 1967.

45 **At municipal court:** "Rival Hunters Closing in on S.F. Sorcerer's Lion," *San Francisco Examiner*, March 16, 1967.

45 **LaVey was granted:** Cone, "Blake's 'No Animals' Law Blocked."

45 **Four days later:** Baron Muller, "Zoo Experts, Cops Called to Cage Lion and Jaguar," *San Francisco Examiner*, April 1, 1967.

46 **"Togare was quite":** Ibid.

46 **Togare had pawed:** Scott Thurber, "Togare Spirited Away," *San Francisco Chronicle*, April 4, 1967.

46 **"It's as if":** "Togare to the Zoo!" *San Francisco Examiner*, April 3, 1967.

46 **"The neighbors":** Ibid.

47 **LaVey was found:** "Sorceror Fined for Lion's Roar," *San Francisco Chronicle*, May 13, 1967.

47 **"I think it":** "Anton LaVey and Terry Hallinan Outside Courtroom," May 12, 1967, Bay Area Television Archive video, https://diva.sfsu.edu/collections/sfbatv/bundles/238407.

47 **Togare lived:** "A Squad of Quads," *San Francisco Examiner*, January 19, 1969.

47 **"for whatever reason":** Tippi Hedren with Theodore Taylor, *The Cats of Shambala*, paperback edition (New York: McGraw-Hill, 1986), 73.

47 **himself mauled:** "Miscued Lion Mauls Director," *Fresno Bee*, July 9, 1978.

47 **Hedren brought:** Hedren, *The Cats of Shambala*, 83.

48 **Before a crowd:** David Lamb, "'Sorcerer' Baptizes Child in Bizarre Anti-Religious Rite," *Red Bluff Daily News*, May 24, 1967.

48 **"In the name":** Anton Szandor LaVey, *The Satanic Mass* CD, Murgenstrumm Records, 1968/2019.

49 **"I always felt":** Lamb, "'Sorcerer' Baptizes Child in Bizarre Anti-Religious Rite."

49 **"It took me":** Zeena LaVey, introduction to Anton Szandor LaVey, *The Satanic Witch*, reprint of *The Compleat Witch* (Los Angeles: Feral House, 1989), unpaginated.

49 **For the journalists:** Lamb, "'Sorcerer' Baptizes Child in Bizarre Anti-Religious Rite."

50 **"The last time":** Al Ricketts, "A 'Happening' Took Place at Tokyo's New Latin Quarter," *Stars and Stripes*, February 1, 1967, https://75.stripes.com/archives /happening-took-place-tokyos-new-latin-quarter.

50 **The image:** "Jayne's Mansfield's Daughter Held," *Terre Haute Tribune*, June 19, 1967.

51 **he had been injured:** "Jayne's Daughter Held as Runaway, Custody Debated," *Philadelphia Daily News*, June 22, 1967.

51 **In the early:** John Wirt, "Lost Highways: Jayne Mansfield's Last Days in Louisiana," *64 Parishes*, winter 2017, https://64parishes.org/lost-highway-jayne -mansfields-last-days-in-louisiana.

51 **LaVey later shared:** Barton, *The Secret Life of a Satanist*, 88.

52 **Kenneth Anger:** *Mansfield 66/67*, film, directed by P. David Ebersole and Todd Hughes, the Ebersole Hughes Company, 2017.

52 **"Curses shmurses":** Ibid.

52 **On October 23:** Jack Rosenbaum, "Locks and Keys," *San Francisco Examiner*, October 24, 1966.

52 **the astrologer:** Herb Caen, "Pocketful of Notes," *San Francisco Chronicle*, April 7, 1965.

52 **"This cat":** Raymond Strait, *The Tragic Secret Life of Jayne Mansfield* (Crossroad Press: 1976/2016 digital edition), location 2897.

52 **"I'm a Catholic":** Ivan Sharpe, "Jayne Finds a Mod Man," *San Francisco Chronicle*, January 19, 1967.

53 **LaVey planted:** Marilyn Beck, "Give in to Lust, Anger, Greed: Jane [sic] Joined the Devil," *Dayton Journal Herald*, February 28, 1967.

53 **"Anton is a good":** Marilyn Beck, "Celebrity Closeup," *Macon News*, March 6, 1967.

53 **"This book":** Mann, *Jayne Mansfield*, 5.

53 **"Anton LaVey":** Ibid., 230.

53 **LaVey later:** Anton LaVey letter to Marcello Truzzi, June 12, 1974.

54 **The day after:** Steve Pelletiere, "A Memory of Jayne: Actress and S.F. Sorcerer," *San Francisco Chronicle*, July 1, 1967.

54 **"a lewd, lascivious":** Wolfe, *The Devil's Avenger*, 174.

54 **"Jayne was not":** Harden, "Anton LaVey: Disciple of the Devil."

CHAPTER IV

Author interview with Hawk Koch.

55 **"When the sorcerer":** Shana Alexander, "The Feminine Eye: The Ping Is the Thing," *Life*, February 17, 1967.

55 **He let his:** Email to the author from Lori Ponton Rodriguez, Musicians Union Local 6/AFM6, June 13, 2023.

56 **These appearances:** Alfred, "The Church of Satan," 193.

56 **mostly white, middle-class:** Ibid., 194.

56 quarterly costume parties: Ibid., 188.

56 while he witnessed: Carl Abrahamsson, *Anton LaVey and the Church of Satan: Infernal Wisdom from the Devil's Den* (Rochester: Inner Traditions, 2022), 333.

56 In July 1967: Marcello Truzzi letter to Anton LaVey, July 16, 1967.

57 mock other occult: Anton LaVey letter to Marcello Truzzi, November 11, 1969.

57 For his part: Raymond Buckland, *Witchcraft—Ancient and Modern* (Queen Victoria Press, 1970/2017), 159.

57 "Although Crowley": Ibid., 161.

57 In September: Marcello Truzzi letter to Hugh Hefner, copied to Anton LaVey, September 8, 1967.

57 In its annual: "Seventh Annual Dubious Achievement Awards for 1967," *Esquire*, January 1968.

57 On Sunday: Sexual Freedom League, classified advertisement, *Berkeley Barb*, December 1–7, 1967.

58 One of the attendees: Wolfe, *The Devil's Avenger*, 216.

58 In the mortuary: Lynn Ludlow, "S.F. Sailor Gets Satanic Services," *San Francisco Examiner*, December 12, 1967.

58 "He chose": "Sailor's Soul Consigned to Devil in Rites at SF Satanic Church," *Salinas Californian*, December 12, 1967.

59 Cosseboom, introduced to: Peri Cosseboom, interviewed by Adam Roberts, others, *The Devil You Know Podcast*, episode 130, September 6, 2019, podcast audio, www.youtube.com/watch?v=hu2xKxkOxsM&list=PLwzUgKv9z RGW2UAcDuQ0kYfrdDeCODE2.

59 Cosseboom's young son: Ibid.

59 "Who cares?": Ibid.

59 "By all the powers": Ludlow, "S.F. Sailor Gets Satanic Services."

59 Olsen's parents: Dexter Waugh, "Sailor's Satanic Funeral," *San Francisco Examiner*, December 11, 1967.

60 After the burial: Ludlow, "S.F. Sailor Gets Satanic Services."

60 The archbishop: "Navy Role in Burial Protested," *San Francisco Examiner*, December 13, 1967.

60 After leading: Wolfe, *The Devil's Avenger*, 16.

60 "A preparation": Ibid., 17.

61 Then, members: Ibid.

61 "With that": Ibid., 17–18.

61 "When LaVey": Ibid., 18.

61 "To conclude": Ibid., 20–21.

61 By early 1968: Marcello Truzzi letter to Anton LaVey, January 24, 1968.

62 petition for: Marcello Truzzi letter to Anton LaVey, May 23, 1968.

62 As for the former: Church of Satan handout, undated.

62 Truzzi, who rejected: Marcello Truzzi letter to Anton LaVey, January 24, 1968.

62 As Truzzi: Anton LaVey letter to Marcello Truzzi, May 13, 1968.

62 **University of San Francisco:** Anton LaVey letter to Marcello Truzzi, September 13, 1968.

62 **As a presenter:** Pat Montandon, *The Intruders*, paperback edition (Greenwich: Fawcett Crest, 1976), 15–19.

64 **Invited to:** Anton LaVey letter to Marcello Truzzi, June 7, 1968.

64 **LaVey was already:** Jack Rosenbaum, "Our Man on the Town," *San Francisco Examiner*, July 16, 1968.

64 **In a letter:** Anton LaVey letter to Marcello Truzzi, July 1968.

64 **"It didn't chop":** Jack Fritscher, *Anton LaVey Speaks: The Canonical Interview* (Sebastopol: Palm Drive Publishing, 2021), 26.

65 **On Wednesdays:** Church of Satan handout, undated.

65 **"the most disturbing shape":** Anton Szandor LaVey, *The Devil's Notebook* (Los Angeles: Feral House, 1992), 112.

66 **until they were deemed:** Barton, *The Secret Life of a Satanist*, 145.

66 **One sympathetic:** Jeff Berner, "Astronauts of Inner Space," *San Francisco Sunday Examiner & Chronicle*, June 23, 1968.

66 **He had returned:** Aquino, *The Church of Satan, Volume I*, 48–49.

67 **"an affirmation":** Ibid., 51.

67 **"I have made":** Ibid.

67 **Aquino, who had been:** Ibid., 56.

CHAPTER V

Author interviews with Gary Zellerbach, Carol Sturm Smith Beaumont, and Mitch Horowitz.

69 **169 paperbacks:** Marcello Truzzi, "The Occult Revival as Popular Culture: Some Random Observations on the Old and the Nouveau Witch," *The Sociological Quarterly*, winter 1972, 16–17.

70 **these pearls of wisdom:** Merla Zellerbach, "A Charm Course for Witches," *San Francisco Chronicle*, July 19, 1967.

70 **The invitation read:** Merla Zellerbach, "Costume Parties Making Life Difficult," *San Francisco Chronicle*, July 24, 1967.

70 **In line with:** Joan White, "Pat Stages a Dream Party," *San Francisco Examiner*, July 31, 1967.

70 **"Fred said":** Anton Szandor LaVey, *Satan Speaks!* (Port Townsend: Feral House, 1998), 5.

70 **Goerner brought:** Peggy Nadramia, "So It Was Written: The History of *The Satanic Bible* by Anton Szandor LaVey," Church of Satan website, www.churchofsatan.com/the-history-of-the-satanic-bible/.

71 **Soon, LaVey:** Ibid.

71 **It would contain:** Anton LaVey letter to Marcello Truzzi, June 7, 1968.

71 **Marcello Truzzi had been:** Marcello Truzzi letter to Anton LaVey, April 28, 1968.

71 **LaVey expressed:** Anton LaVey letter to Marcello Truzzi, May 13, 1968.

71 **As talks:** Nadramia, "So It Was Written."

71 **When Hamilburg:** Ibid.

72 **When more months:** Ibid.

72 **He had signed:** Peggy Nadramia, "The Satanic Mass—A Shot Heard Round the World," Church of Satan website, www.churchofsatan.com/the-satanic-mass/.

72 **The cover:** Anton LaVey letter to Marcello Truzzi, August 2, 1968.

72 **He had hoped:** Nadramia, "The Satanic Mass."

72 **In late August:** Mike Resnick, . . . *Always a Fan: True Stories from a Life in Science Fiction* (Cabin John: Wildside Press, 2009), 297.

73 **"It was dull":** Ibid., 297.

73 **Resnick suggested:** Ibid., 298.

73 **No doubt:** Anton LaVey letter to Marcello Truzzi, September 13, 1968.

73 **In a letter:** Ibid.

74 **"Anthony Levy":** Resnick, . . . *Always a Fan*, 298.

74 **a voodoo doll:** Anton LaVey, "Letters from the Devil," *National Insider*, October 12, 1969, reprinted in *Letters from the Devil*, designed by Kevin I. Slaughter (Baltimore: Underworld Amusements, 2010).

74 **in explicit, step-by-step:** Anton LaVey, "Letters from the Devil," *National Insider*, September 28, 1969.

74 **In a phone call:** Resnick, . . . *Always a Fan*, 298.

74 **"Did he take":** Ibid., 299.

74 **In one letter:** Anton LaVey, "Letters from the Devil," *National News Exploiter*, October 29, 1972.

75 **He delivered:** Anton LaVey letter to Marcello Truzzi, October 15, 1968.

75 **"Just say it":** LaVey, *Satan Speaks!*, 5.

77 **But the letter:** Anton LaVey letter to Marcello Truzzi, May 13, 1968.

78 **Though he called:** Nadramia, "So It Was Written."

78 **It had been decided:** Anton LaVey letter to Marcello Truzzi, March 17, 1969.

78 **Randall Alfred:** Alfred, "The Church of Satan," 183–184.

79 **"were all components":** Ibid., 185.

79 **Marcello Truzzi's wife:** Anton LaVey letter to Marcello Truzzi, October 14, 1969.

79 **More than twelve thousand:** Julie Morris, "Acts Billed, Didn't Appear," *Detroit Free-Press*, November 7, 1969.

79 **According to author:** Arthur Lyons, *The Second Coming: Satanism in America* (New York: Dodd, Mead & Co., 1970), 125.

80 **Relieved that:** Anton LaVey letter to Marcello Truzzi, November 11, 1969.

80 **There, on November 19:** Nadramia, "The Satanic Mass."

80 **At least that:** "Rock Rolling into the Occult as Disks, Niteries Yen That Ol' Black Magic," *Variety*, November 5, 1969.

80 **Such a disappointment:** Nadramia, "The Satanic Mass."

80 **When *Variety*:** "Steppenwolf, Bobby Goldsboro, Ruth Brown, Chas. Ives, Rouvann, 'Super-Black Blues' Top New LPs," *Variety*, December 31, 1969.

81 **Murgenstrumm's principals:** Nadramia, "The Satanic Mass."

81   **But when he received:** Nadramia, "So It Was Written."

82   **In fact, LaVey lifted:** Anton Szandor LaVey, *The Satanic Bible*, eightieth printing (New York: Avon, 1969/2005), 33.

83   **In the opening:** LaVey, *The Satanic Bible*, 25.

83   **"Satan," LaVey later writes:** Ibid., 55.

83   **"If God":** Ibid., 61.

83   **"The Satanist":** Ibid., 41.

83   **"Is it not":** Ibid., 44.

83   **"With all":** Ibid., 43.

83   **"Wise to the ways":** Ibid., 113.

84   **"Satanism *does not*":** Ibid., 70.

84   **"It is an established":** Ibid., 67.

84   **"she should":** Ibid., 71.

84   **"Satanism represents":** Ibid., 51.

84   **"a poseur":** Ibid., 103.

84   **"Hitler was no fool":** Ibid., 82.

85   **whose first printing:** Truzzi, "The Occult Revival," 27.

85   **He appeared locally:** Peggy Nadramia, "Addendum to 'So It Was Written: The History of *The Satanic Bible*,'" Church of Satan website, www.churchofsatan .com/addendum-to-the-history-of-the-satanic-bible/.

86   **whose host would:** Steve Allen, *Curses! Or . . . How Never to Be Foiled Again* (Los Angeles: J.P. Tarcher, 1973), 17–20.

86   **"I suspect that":** Deirdre LaRouche, "Satan, the Modern Liberator," *St. Louis Post-Dispatch*, December 27, 1970.

86   **it was reported:** Bob Williams, "'Satan's Bible' Found on Pair," *Billings Gazette*, July 26, 1970.

86   **LaVey called Baker:** Maitland Zane, "The Cannibalism Case—A Psychiatrist's Opinion," *San Francisco Chronicle*, July 17, 1970.

87   **more than one million:** Email to the author from Andrew Yackira, development editor, HarperCollins Publishers, March 27, 2024.

CHAPTER VI

Author interview with Lisa Petrucci.

89   **The movie was:** George Anderson, "Stage & Screen," *Pittsburgh Post-Gazette*, January 15, 1970.

89   **In an interview:** Jeanne Miller, "The Anything-Goes Church," *San Francisco Examiner*, March 3, 1970.

90   **It opens with:** *Satanis: The Devil's Mass*, DVD.

92   **As an actress:** "To Act with Miss Anglin," *New York Times*, April 26, 1927.

92   **appeared on the radio:** "Baroness on Waves," *Belvidere Daily Republican*, April 8, 1927.

92   **in the '40s:** Herb Caen, "It's News to Me: Pocketful of Notes," *San Francisco Chronicle*, June 17, 1948.

92   **and '50s:** "Teazle's Tidbits . . . ," *San Francisco Chronicle*, September 6, 1952.

92 **He made the front page:** "Cupid Wins Over Iron Bars in Unique Romance," *San Francisco Chronicle*, October 8, 1926.

92 **Later, his wife:** "New Trouble Stalks Baron de Plessen," *San Francisco Examiner*, January 2, 1930.

97 **Anger, who'd been:** Kenneth Anger letter to Anton LaVey, September 10, 1969.

97 **When LaVey finally:** Anton LaVey letter to Kenneth Anger, October 13, 1969.

97 **In a profile:** Gerald Nachman, "Stage and Screen: Black Power," *Oakland Tribune*, March 17, 1970.

97 **Bonewits later wrote:** Isaac Bonewits, "My Satanic Adventure, or I Was a Teen-aged Satanist! (Version 2.3)," 2005, www.neopagan.net/SatanicAdventure.html.

97 **Opening night:** "'Satanis' Opens in SF," *Centra Costa Times*, March 1, 1970.

97 **Lenore Cosseboom:** Peri Cosseboom, *The Devil You Know* podcast.

98 **critic Stanley:** Stanley Eichelbaum, "Exploitation for Satan," *San Francisco Examiner*, March 5, 1970.

98 **In his *San Francisco*:** John L. Wasserman, "The Devil and His Works," *San Francisco Chronicle*, March 5, 1970.

98 **"LaVey gives plenty":** "Satanis, The Devil's Mass," *Variety*, March 11, 1970.

98 **"skillfully made":** Richard Ogar, "Deviled Ham? Oi Vey LaVey!" *Berkeley Barb*, March 6–12, 1970.

98 **In a piece:** Nick Kazan, "Life and Leisure: The Cult of the Occult," *Newsweek*, April 13, 1970.

100 **Although Ray Laurent:** "Ray Laurent," Internet Movie Database, www.imdb.com/name/nm0491272/?ref_=fn_al_nm_1.

CHAPTER VII

Author interviews with Thomas Lipscomb, Spencer Waldron, Martyn Burke, Wayne Chonicki, Jack Fritscher, and Richard Lamparski.

102 **He even had a title:** Peggy Nadramia, "The Compleat Story of *The Compleat Witch*, or, What to Do When Publishers Fail," Church of Satan website, January 14, 2022, www.churchofsatan.com/the-compleat-story-of-the-compleat-witch/.

103 **He quoted his desired advance:** Ibid.

103 **After seeing:** Ibid.

103 **It wasn't long:** Ibid.

104 **He was tasked:** Alden Whitman, "Lipscomb New Chief Editor of Dodd, Mead Unit," *New York Times*, December 12, 1970.

104 **LaVey's own book:** Nadramia, "The Compleat Story of *The Compleat Witch*."

105 **besides, the book was late:** Ibid.

105 **On May 20, 1970:** *The Jean Shepherd Show*, May 20, 1970 episode, www.radioechoes.com.

106 **The book, he wrote:** Jean Shepherd, introduction, *1929 Johnson Smith & Co. Catalogue*, reprint (New York: Chelsea House, 1970), v.

106 **Earlier in his radio career:** Esther Inglis-Arkell, "The Bizarre True-Life Tale of the Hoax Behind the Book *I, Libertine*," *Gizmodo*, February 18, 2015, https://gizmodo.com/the-bizarre-true-life-tale-of-the-hoax-behind-i-libert-1686572112.

106 **By July 1970:** Smith, "'Head Satan' Speaks—to Set Record Straight."

106 **"I wanted to create":** Barton, *The Secret Life of a Satanist*, 115.

107 **Some grottos:** *The Cloven Hoof*, September/October 1973.

108 **Armed with the addresses:** Aquino, *The Church of Satan, Volume I*, 131.

109 **Adrian-Claude Frazier:** Adrian-Claude Frazier letter to Anton LaVey, November 20, 1970.

109 **He assured LaVey:** Adrian-Claude Frazier letter to Anton LaVey, December 25, 1970.

110 **Which explains why:** Aquino, *The Church of Satan, Volume I*, 113–115.

110 **Frazier responded:** Ibid., 116.

110 **In Michael Aquino's eyes:** Ibid., 120.

110 **Still, Aquino stayed on:** Ibid., 151.

110 **That number has:** Alfred, "The Church of Satan," 194.

110 **On December 9:** Adrian-Claude Frazier letter to Anton LaVey, December 9, 1971.

111 **Patricia Hall:** "Not Our Witch, Says Satanist," *San Francisco Chronicle*, May 9, 1970.

111 **By the following month:** Jacquin Sanders, "Tenets of Satanism: Sex and the Black Mass," *Honolulu Advertiser*, June 2, 1970.

111 **That summer:** Smith, *Los Angeles Times*, July 17, 1970.

111 **"If someone waltzes up":** Ibid.

111 **"Manson is just":** Ibid.

112 **"civility, good manners":** Ibid.

112 **"Because yours":** Church of Satan notice, undated.

112 **Arthur Lyons was visiting:** Jacques Vallée, *Forbidden Science 2: California Hermetica, The Journals of Jacques Vallée* (San Antonio: Anomalist, 2017), Kindle, location 803.

112 **"he sincerely believed":** Ibid., location 810.

113 **"What do these people":** Ibid., location 820.

113 **a curious advertisement:** *Miami Herald*, December 2, 1970.

114 **Anton, who had heard:** Anton LaVey letter to Kenneth Anger, October 13, 1969.

115 **"looks mean everything":** Anton Szandor LaVey, *The Satanic Witch*, reprint and retitling of *The Compleat Witch* (Port Townsend: Feral House, 2003), 18.

115 **"is an animal first":** Ibid., 13.

115 **Jayne Mansfield:** Ibid., 131.

115 **"natural odors":** Ibid., 95–96.

116 **The sharp aroma:** Ibid., 106.

116 **In a letter dated:** Nadramia, "The Compleat Story of *The Compleat Witch*."

116 **Though LaVey boasted:** Barton, *The Secret Life of a Satanist*, 156.

117 **He assured friends:** Anton LaVey letter to Marcello Truzzi, November 22, 1970.

117 **"Dr. LaVey resides":** John M. Kincaid, undated Church of Satan form letter.

121 **in LaVey's case:** "TV and Radio Highlights Today," *Minneapolis Tribune*, April 12, 1971.

121 included marriage: Carole Clifford, "Hell Hath No Fury . . . ," *Montreal Star*, March 20, 1971.

121 "merely a distaff-oriented": Harlan Ellison, *The Other Glass Teat* (New York: Ace, 1975), 378.

121 "The concept": Ibid., 379.

121 "genuinely fascinating": Ibid., 381.

121 flying to Los Angeles: Nadramia, "The Compleat Story of *The Compleat Witch*."

122 "frank and oft-times": Martie Kazura, "LaVey Writes 'Bewitchery Bible,'" *Cincinnati Post & Times-Star*, March 13, 1971.

122 "It's fun to read": Bobby Mather, "Bobby Mather on Books," *Detroit Free Press*, February 28, 1971.

122 "The demonic lore": Isabel Edwards, "How to Be a Sensuous Witch," *Minneapolis Tribune*, March 7, 1971.

122 "While some": Robyn Rickard, "Learning the Witch Craft . . ." *Honolulu Advertiser*, March 19, 1971.

122 "More delicate": Larry Harmon, "Books," *El Paso Times*, March 7, 1971.

123 In 1972: Barton, *The Secret Life of a Satanist*, 115.

127 He believed ritual: Anton LaVey letter to Marcello Truzzi, August 2, 1968.

130 "I don't feel": Fritscher, *Anton LaVey Speaks*, 7.

130 "What is far worse": Ibid., 11.

130 "Why the hell": Ibid., 12.

132 "We had barely": Vallée, *Forbidden Science* 2, location 1379.

133 the Department: "Fencing Around with Satan's Aide," *San Francisco Examiner*, September 21, 1971.

133 "You'd think": Herb Caen, "Eat More 3-Dot Journalism," *San Francisco Chronicle*, September 20, 1971.

133 Its dedication page: Anton Szandor LaVey, *The Satanic Rituals* (New York: Avon, 1972), unpaginated.

133 That last personality: Anton LaVey letter to Marcello Truzzi, July 1968.

133 "a kinky gift": John Richmond, "Last Minute Bargains," *Montreal Star*, December 23, 1972.

134 "When he sits": Vallée, *Forbidden Science* 2, location 1998.

134 Like Vallée: Ibid., location 2091.

134 who he claimed: Anton LaVey letter to Marcello Truzzi, June 23, 1971.

134 "Either he has no": Vallée, *Forbidden Science* 2, location 2161.

135 "There we spoke": Ibid., location 2689.

135 "People need": Ibid., location 2688.

135 "I supply": Ibid., location 2693.

CHAPTER VIII

Author interviews with David Steinberg and Jack Boulware.

137 "I wanted": Sammy Davis Jr. and Jane and Burt Boyar, *Why Me? The Sammy Davis, Jr. Story* (New York: Farrar, Straus and Giroux, 1989), 209.

138 "I was curious": Ibid., 208.

138 "I'd read enough": Ibid.

138 As Davis enjoyed: Ibid., 208–209.

138 "Everyone there": Ibid., 230–231.

138 In an interview: Maxine Sanders, interviewed by Kate Hutchinson, *The Last Bohemians* podcast, https://podcasts.apple.com/gb/podcast/maxine-sanders-the-witch-queen-on-casting-spells/id1453507847?i=1000471299162.

138 Christopher Jones: Lina Das, "The Final Affair of Roman Polanski's Murdered Wife, Sharon Tate," www.dailymail.co.uk/femail/article-478867/The-final-affair-Roman-Polanskis-murdered-wife-Sharon-Tate.html.

139 "Don't get involved": Davis, *Why Me?*, 209.

139 TV comedy pilot: *Poor Devil*, directed by Robert Scheerer, 1973, YouTube video, uploaded by the Official Sammy Davis Jr., www.youtube.com/watch?v–lAcj9CfLkcg.

139 Arne Sultan: "Sammy Davis Jr. Set to Star in Comedy Series Next Season," *Kokomo Tribune*, February 4, 1973.

139 Davis said: Steve Hoffman, "Sammy Singing His Best but He Wants a Comedy Series," *Cincinnati Enquirer*, December 21, 1972.

140 Word had it: Buck Biggers and Chet Stover, "NBC Gets Sammy Davis, but Not as 'Poor Devil,'" *San Bernardino County Sun*, April 20, 1973.

140 "beautifully done": Aquino, *The Church of Satan, Volume I*, 259.

140 LaVey also sent: "Christopher Lee 1975," YouTube video, uploaded by Colin Grimshaw, www.youtube.com/watch?v=SgK54Vc-GZ0.

141 In mid-March: Aquino, *The Church of Satan, Volume I*, 259.

141 "The original": Ibid., 261.

141 While at the theater: Ibid., 262.

142 The following month: Ibid., 261–262.

142 But then in June: Ibid., 263.

142 In LaVeyan jargon: Barton, *The Secret Life of a Satanist*, 233.

142 By August: Aquino, *The Church of Satan, Volume I*, 265.

143 LaVey wrote: Ibid., 266.

143 "Lee said Sammy": Zeena Schreck. "Interview with Zeena: Remembering Christopher Lee at Halloween Time," *Zeena Art* (blog), October 27, 2020, www.zeenaschreck.com/blog/category/christopher-lee-at-halloween-time.

143 Aquino would: Aquino, *The Church of Satan, Volume I*, 267.

144 "Anton and Sammy": Ibid.

144 "a true star": Ibid., 269.

144 "It was a turn-on": Davis, *Why Me?*, 209.

144 "However bizarre": Sammy Davis Jr., "Hollywood in a Suitcase, Part 4: A Touch of Satanism and Lessons in Love," *New York Daily News*, September 11, 1980.

144 "a 'coven'": Davis, *Why Me?*, 209.

144 "Sammy told me": *Comedians in Cars Getting Coffee*, season 11, episode 1, "Eddie Murphy: I Just Wanted to Kill," created by Jerry Seinfeld, 2019, Netflix.

144 "Mr. Davis is now": *The Cloven Hoof*, September/October 1973.

CHAPTER IX

Author interviews with Gabe Essoe, Michael S. Glick, Ana Maria Quintana, and Michael Butler.

147 **He was once again:** Adrian-Claude Frazier letter to Michael Aquino, March 2, 1973.

148 **Diane wrote:** Diane LaVey letter to Adrian-Claude Frazier, March 6, 1973.

148 **In February 1974:** Adrian-Claude Frazier letter to Anton LaVey, February 23, 1974.

148 **Another grotto:** Anton LaVey letter to Marcello Truzzi, February 28, 1973.

148 **The Stygian:** Anton LaVey letter to Marcello Truzzi, July 22, 1972.

148 **"I'd step off":** Barton, *The Secret Life of a Satanist*, 113.

149 **LaVey predicted:** Anton LaVey letter to Adrian-Claude Frazier, June 3, 1973.

149 **"This film allows":** Marty Gunther, "Satanist Calls Film a Boon for Christians and Devil-Worshippers," *National Tattler Special: Exorcism*, spring 1974.

149 **The author:** Wolfe, *The Black Pope*, 4.

149 **An article:** Mary Every, "Black Pope Simmers Down," *Santa Barbara News-Press*, November 14, 1974.

149 **he also told:** Anton LaVey letter to Marcello Truzzi, April 23, 1974.

149 **He said he had grown:** Anton LaVey letter to Marcello Truzzi, July 12, 1974.

150 **"Since that film":** Fritscher, *Anton LaVey Speaks*, 26.

151 **he came in contact:** Paul Talbot, "The Devil in Hollywood: The Films of Anton LaVey," *Screem* 19, 2009.

151 **In a letter:** Anton LaVey letter to Kenneth Anger, October 13, 1969.

151 **The appearance:** *The Cloven Hoof*, month unknown, 1969.

151 **Still, LaVey worked:** Talbot, "The Devil in Hollywood."

151 **In 1970:** John Austin, "Occult Film Rise Seen," *Los Angeles Evening Citizen News*, May 22, 1970.

152 **"That film still":** Fritscher, *Anton LaVey Speaks*, 27.

152 **Alda, who claimed:** Joyce Haber, "Nonmovie Star Quality Contributes to Alda's Ability to Turn 'Em On," *Los Angeles Times*, September 6, 1970.

152 **"a bomb":** Michael Aquino, *The Cloven Hoof*, November 1971.

152 **LaVey claimed:** Anton LaVey letter to Marcello Truzzi letter, June 23, 1971.

152 **Michael Aquino:** Michael Aquino, *The Cloven Hoof*, February 1972.

153 **"The producers":** Talbot, "The Devil in Hollywood."

153 **announcing in November:** "Sandy Howard Announces 10 Projected Films," *Los Angeles Times*, November 8, 1974.

154 **Bryanston offered:** "'The Devil's Rain' to Start Shooting Jan. 27," *Los Angeles Times*, January 1, 1975.

154 **The company:** Ellen Farley and William K. Knoedelseder Jr., "Butchie, the Mogul," *Los Angeles Times*, June 27, 1982.

154 **Fuest, however:** Anthony Petkovich, "Robert Fuest: He Was Making Mad Films!" *Psychotronic Video* 41, 2004.

154 "I never": Justin Humphreys, *The Dr. Phibes Companion* (Albany: BearManor Media, 2018), 14.

155 after Mercedes McCambridge: Anton LaVey letter to Marcello Truzzi, October 18, 1974.

155 LaVey had just: Ibid.

155 "It seems reasonable": Aquino, *The Church of Satan, Volume I*, 393.

155 LaVey himself admitted: "Devil on Loose at Film Site," *Victoria Advocate* (Victoria, Texas), March 12, 1975.

156 "a terribly difficult": Robert Fuest audio commentary track, *The Devil's Rain*, Blu-ray, directed by Robert Fuest, 1975 (Los Angeles: Severin Films, 2017).

156 "There was a cloud": Ibid.

156 "The Mafia": Tom Burman interview, *The Devil's Rain*, Blu-ray.

157 "Terribly nice": Petkovich, "Robert Fuest."

157 "was rather like": Aquino, *The Church of Satan, Volume I*, 391.

159 "I was dreading": "Movie on Satan Bedeviling Cast."

159 "very charming": Ibid.

159 "I wondered": Jeanne Miller, "Could My Image Take Playing the Devil?" *San Francisco Examiner*, July 8, 1975.

159 "But once the film": Ken Williams, "Ernest Borgnine: Veteran Actor Has a 'Devilish' Time with New Film," *Journal-News* (Hamilton, Ohio), July 21, 1975.

159 "I believe": Miller, "Could My Image Take Playing the Devil?"

159 "Of course": "Movie on Satan Bedeviling Cast."

160 "This current": Ibid.

160 "What the hell": Tom Burman interview, *The Devil's Rain*, Blu-ray.

160 Albert, soon: Anton LaVey letter to Marcello Truzzi, April 8, 1975.

160 "I suppose": William Shatner with David Fisher, *Up Till Now: The Autobiography* (New York: Thomas Dunne, 2008), 166.

160 "Things went": Dick Russell, "Anton LaVey: The Satanist Who Wants to Rule the World," *Argosy*, June 1975.

160 A photographer: Shatner, *Up Till Now*, 167.

161 "I was grappling": Ibid.

161 "like a sort": Petkovich, "Robert Fuest."

161 "I have no idea": Tom Skerritt interview, *The Devil's Rain*, Blu-ray.

161 "He glommed": Lawrence Wright, *Going Clear: Scientology, Hollywood, & the Prison of Belief* (New York: Alfred A. Knopf, 2013), 150.

161 "She gave me": Church of Scientology, *What Is Scientology?* (Los Angeles: Bridge Publications, 1998), 233.

162 claimed to have: Peggy Nadramia and Peter Gilmore interview, *The Devil's Rain*, Blu-ray.

162 "My career": Church of Scientology, *What Is Scientology?*, 233.

162 "You may simply": Russell, "Anton LaVey."

162 "wasn't a talented": Talbot, "The Devil in Hollywood."

162 "I resent it": Russell, "Anton LaVey."

163   **Another disaster:** Robin Adams Sloan, "The Gossip Column," *New York Daily News*, March 30, 1975.

163   **just as the Vatican:** "Vatican Calls Satan Real, Not a Fantasy, but Issues Cautions," *New York Times*, June 27, 1975.

163   **"Indeed Satan":** Michael Aquino, "Quo Vadis?" *The Cloven Hoof*, July/August 1974.

164   **Roger Ebert:** Roger Ebert, "Reviews: The Devil's Rain," *Chicago Sun-Times*, August 15, 1975, RogerEbert.com, www.rogerebert.com/reviews/the-devils-rain-1975.

164   **Richard Eder:** Richard Eder, "Film: 'The Devil's Rain,'" *New York Times*, August 8, 1975.

164   ***Variety* labeled:** Robe., "Film Reviews: The Devil's Rain," *Variety*, June 24, 1975.

164   **According to Rex:** Rex Reed, "Summer Hits: Kern Musical, the Krals; Movies Miss," *New York Daily News*, August 8, 1975.

164   **"the most striking":** Aquino, *The Church of Satan, Volume I*, 392.

164   **"Robert Fuest":** Gabe Essoe, *The Book of Movie Lists* (Westport: Arlington House, 1981), 159.

164   **Having eventually:** Farley and Knoedelseder, "Family Business, Episode 3: 'The Fall,'" *Los Angeles Times*, June 27, 1982.

165   **"the ultimate":** Michael Adams, *Showgirls, Teen Wolves, and Astro-Zombies: A Film Critic's Year-Long Quest to Find the Worst Movie Ever Made* (New York: It Books, 2010), 107.

165   **"Since the":** Michael Aquino, *The Church of Satan, Volume II: Appendices*, eighth edition (self-published paperback, 2013), 362.

165   **Aquino told LaVey:** Aquino, *The Church of Satan, Volume I*, 411.

165   **He did not:** Aquino, *The Church of Satan, Volume II*, 360.

166   **LaVey responded:** Ibid., 374.

166   **"If you want":** Ibid., 375.

166   **Not long after:** "Sky Riders," *Variety*, December 31, 1975, https://variety.com/1975/film/reviews/sky-riders-1200423657/.

166   **"I did feel":** Farley and Knoedelseder, "Family Business, Episode 3: 'The Fall.'"

167   **Peraino received:** "8 in 'Deep Throat' Case Receive Prison Sentences," *New York Times*, May 1, 1977.

167   **went on to gross:** "All Time Domestic Box Office," The Numbers, https://the-numbers.com/box-office-records/domestic/all-movies/cumulative/all-time/4901

CHAPTER X

Author interviews with Jacques Vallée, Don Frew, Blanche Barton, Stuart MacKenzie, Mary deYoung, and Nikolas Schreck.

169   **In April 1976:** Vallée, *Forbidden Science* 2, location 5207.

169   **It also warned:** James A. Finefrock, "The Great Mutilation Mystery," *San Francisco Examiner*, April 19, 1976.

169   **"I'd have known":** Vallée, *Forbidden Science* 2, location 5213.

170 **"It may"**: Finefrock, "The Great Mutilation Mystery."

171 **"Among the fakeness"**: Ibid., location 1300.

171 **"To the chagrin"**: Ibid., location 1311.

171 **"Anton fails"**: Ibid., location 1319.

171 **Vallée rejected**: Vallée, *Forbidden Science* 2, location 1897.

171 **In 1978 he was offered**: Burton H. Wolfe letter to Anton LaVey, July 7, 1978.

172 **One of her father's**: Burton H. Wolfe letter to Zeena LaVey, September 13, 1975.

172 **For Anton's part**: Anton LaVey letter to Marcello Truzzi, May 22, 1979.

173 **She told**: Bethaney Lee, "Zeena LaVey Advocates Free Education," *The Guardsman*, October 19, 2016, http://theguardsman.com/zeena-schreck -advocates-free-education/.

173 **Stanton, however**: Stanton LaVey, Facebook post, July 30, 2022, www .facebook.com/szlavey/posts/pfbid028wpVglSxMAAfFMsRzV95sFXs ZrGdyJ2Y8ZNiqdHX8Bf2PDvI'Pp9XN3vX3rbAcEWBl.

174 **in the late '50s**: Jack Stevenson, *Land of a Thousand Balconies: Discoveries and Confessions of a B-Movie Archaeologist* (Manchester: Critical Visions/Headpress, 2003), 48.

176 **LaVey himself**: LaVey, *The Satanic Bible*, 96.

179 **On October 31**: Federal Bureau of Investigation, Anton LaVey file, https:// vault.fbi.gov/anton-lavey-part-01-of-01/anton-lavey-part-01-of-01. The story of LaVey's run-in with the FBI is expanded upon in David Gambacorta, "Satan, the FBI, the Mob, and the Forgotten Plot to Kill Ted Kennedy," *Politico*, January 12, 2020, www.politico.com/news/magazine/2020/01/12 /fbi-satan-mobplot-kill-ted-kennedy-097180.

182 **"*Michelle Remembers* is"**: Leonore Fleischer, "Highest Game in Town," *Washington Post*, November 25, 1979.

182 **"The only group"**: Michelle Smith and Lawrence Pazder, MD, *Michelle Remembers* (New York: Congdon & Lattès, 1980), 117.

183 **A footnote**: Smith and Pazder, *Michelle Remembers*, 259.

183 **Adjoining a reference**: Ibid., 299.

183 **"I find it"**: Peggy Nadramia, "From the Church of Satan Archives."

184 **The court ruled**: *LaVey v. Smith*, March 4, 1982, C-81-3643 MHP, Northern District of California.

184 **In LaVey's defense**: Ibid.

184 **Nevertheless, on March 4**: Ibid.

185 **In 1983**: Robert Rheinhold, "Collapse of a Child-Abuse Case: So Much Agony for So Little," *New York Times*, January 24, 1990.

185 **Charges were soon dropped**: Ibid.

185 **Prosecutors, armed**: Debbie Nathan, "I'm Sorry," *Los Angeles Times Magazine*, October 30, 2005.

185 **At a cost**: Rheinhold, "Collapse of a Child-Abuse Case."

187 **He refused to defend**: Barton, *The Secret Life of a Satanist*, 249.

187 **LaVey told one**: Walt Harrington, "The Devil in Anton LaVey," *Washington Post Magazine*, February 23, 1986.

187 **"I contacted him"**: Annette Lamothe-Ramos, "Beelzebub's Daughter," *Vice*, September 25, 2012, www.vice.com/en/article/yv53ex/beelzebubs-daughter -0000175-v19n4.

188 **"I knew these"**: *Satan Lives*, film, directed by Sam Dunn, Scot McFadyen, and Manfred Becker, 2015 (Toronto: Banger Films).

188 **"[Anton] lived in a dream"**: Lamothe-Ramos, "Beelzebub's Daughter."

190 **She claimed**: Stephen G. Bloom, "Devil of a Palimony Dispute," *Sacramento Bee*, September 22, 1988.

191 **"I have no idea"**: Stanton LaVey, July 30, 2022, Facebook post.

191 **In the lawsuit**: Hegarty/LaVey Property Agreement, April 25/26, 1985, as published in Aquino, *The Church of Satan, Volume II*, 419–420.

193 **By 1991, it appeared**: Wright, "Sympathy for the Devil."

193 **In 1988**: Linda Goldston, "Devil Duo Was a Match Made in . . . ," *New York Daily News*, September 11, 1988.

194 **Her suit, he said**: Bloom, "Devil of a Palimony Dispute."

194 **Diane amended**: Diane Hegarty First Amended Complaint, Case #891863, Superior Court of the State of San Francisco, December 7, 1988, as published in Aquino, *The Church of Satan, Volume II*, 426–434.

194 **The following June**: Anton LaVey Answer to First Amended Complaint, Case #891863, Superior Court of the State of San Francisco, June 1, 1989, as published in Aquino, *The Church of Satan, Volume II*, 435–437.

194 **The court**: Paul Avery, "Church of Satan Founder Hoping for New Hearing," *San Francisco Examiner*, September 19, 1991.

194 **On September 27**: Superior Court Order, Case #891863, Superior Court of the State of San Francisco, September 27, 1991, as published in Aquino, *The Church of Satan, Volume II*, 438.

194 **his average net income**: Anton LaVey declaration, Chapter 11 Case #91-34251, United States Bankruptcy Court, Northern District of California, April 22, 1992, as published in Aquino, *The Church of Satan, Volume I*, 429.

195 **The case was eventually converted**: United States Bankruptcy Court, Northern District of California, Chapter 7 Case #91-34251TC, March 10, 1993, as published in Aquino, *The Church of Satan, Volume II*, 449.

195 **"On the platform"**: William Lindsay Gresham, *Nightmare Alley* (New York: New York Review Books, 1946/2021), 68.

195 **Movies that ranked**: Blanche Barton, *We Are Satanists: The History and Future of the Church of Satan* (La Quinto: Aperient Press, 2021), 658–659.

CHAPTER XI

Author interviews with Walt Harrington, Eugene S. Robinson, Jim Morton, Bobby Neel Adams, Evil Wilhelm, Nikolas Schreck, Harvey Stafford, Jack Boulware, Blanche Barton, Stuart Swezey, and Richard Lamparski.

202 **"That interview"**: Boyd Rice, *The Last Testament of Anton LaVey* (Denver: Hierarchy, 2019), 9.

204   **It was before:** Ibid., 110–113.

208   **The program was to commence:** Ibid., 6.

208   **Schreck and Rice previewed:** "NON (US) Interview KPFA 1988," You-Tube audio, uploaded by the Uncouth Youth, www.youtube.com/watch?v =v7roW35FaRU.

209   **Schreck called:** "Radio Werewolf: 8/8/88 Rally," video, Internet Archive, https:// archive.org/details/Radio-Werewolf-8-8-88-Rally.

209   **Schreck had been in contact:** Chuck Ross, "Devilish Time for Geraldo," *San Francisco Chronicle*, September 13, 1988.

209   **"Shortly before":** Zeena Schreck, "Flashback 8-8-88: Interview Excerpts from the Forthcoming Book, *Phantoms: The Rise of Deathrock from the L.A. Punk Scene*," *Zeena Art* (blog), August 8, 2018, www.zeenaschreck.com/blog /flashback-8-8-88-interview-excerpts-from-forthcoming-book-phantoms -the-rise-of-deathrock-from-the-la-punk-scene.

209   **"He had a crush":** George Petros, *Art That Kills: A Panoramic Portrait of Aesthetic Terrorism 1984–2001* (London: Creation, 2007), 199.

210   **"We're gathered":** "Radio Werewolf: 8/8/88 Rally."

210   **Schreck managed:** Ibid.

210   **"Musically, the event":** Rice, *The Last Testament of Anton LaVey*, 7.

210   **"When the time":** Zeena Schreck, "Flashback 8-8-88."

211   **"the Church of Satan's":** Joshua Bote, "A Little-Known Satanic Rally, Held in '80s San Francisco, Foretold 2021's Obsession with Conspiracy," *SFGate*, July 30, 2021, www.sfgate.com/sfhistory/article/Church-of-Satan-8-8-88-rally-San -Francisco-Lavey-16333009.php.

211   **Parfrey said years:** Petros, *Art That Kills*, 199.

211   **"I could have":** Genesis P-Orridge and Anton LaVey in conversation in Carl Abrahamsson, *Anton LaVey and the Church of Satan*, 339.

212   **A photo of Heick:** James Ridgeway, *Blood in the Face: The Ku Klux Klan, Aryan Nations, Nazi Skinheads, and the Rise of a New White Culture* (New York: Thunder's Mouth Press, 1995), 186.

212   **"I was not at all":** Zeena Schreck, "Flashback 8-8-88."

213   **"Anton was saying":** "Radio Werewolf: 8/8/88 Rally."

213   **"It's important":** Ibid.

214   **"normal life":** Ibid.

215   **"When the lines":** Bote, "A Little-Known Satanic Rally."

217   **Even though sponsors:** Edwin Diamond, "Winners and Sinners: Media," *New York Magazine*, December 19–26, 1988.

217   **seen in nearly:** Jay Sharbutt, "Cauldron Boils Over Geraldo's 'Devil Worship,'" *Los Angeles Times*, October 27, 1988.

219   **"She defended":** Aquino, *The Church of Satan, Volume I*, 423.

221   **Stanton said that:** Stanton LaVey, "The Man Who Sold the World: My Times with Adam Parfrey," BaphometX (blog), May 14, 2018, www.baphometx.com /post/the-man-who-sold-the-world-my-times-with-adam-parfrey.

CHAPTER XII

Author interviews with Carl Abrahamsson, Don Frew, Nikolas Schreck, Mitch Horowitz, Blanche Barton, Gregg Turkington, JG Thirlwell, George Petros, Shane Bugbee, Lawrence Wright, Reuben Radding, Jim Morton, Larry Wessel, Jack Boulware, Jay Blakesberg, Becky Wilson, Ron Quintana, Cathy Fitzhugh, Alan Black, Harvey Stafford, Richard Lamparski, Sharon LaVey, and Thomas Thorn.

225 "Satanic Weddings": LaVey, *Satan Speaks!*, 118.

225 "the Larry King": Jay Grelen, "Evangelist Bob Larson Still Stirring Things Up," *Fresno Bee*, January 25, 1986.

226 At the top: "The First Family of Satanism Bob Larson Talk Back (1989)," YouTube video, uploaded by Andreas Göransson, www.youtube.com/watch?v=XGdcCUmHbAk.

228 such topics as: Abrahamsson, *Anton LaVey and the Church of Satan*, 330–333.

232 For a profile: Wright, "Sympathy for the Devil."

236 In the missive: Aquino, *The Church of Satan, Volume II*, 404–405.

237 "She feels": Wright, "Sympathy for the Devil."

237 "Zeena Schreck": Blanche Barton, "The Georges Montalba Mystery," Church of Satan website, August 13, 2002, www.churchofsatan.com/georges-montalba-mystery/.

243 Leading off: Jim Goad, "Calling Dr. Satan," *Answer Me!* 2, 1992.

248 For the photos: "Look Like Hell," *The Nose* 18, 1993.

249 "I can enjoy": LaVey, *The Devil's Notebook*, 139.

255 it was revealed: D. Shawn Bosler, "Devil in Disguise," *Village Voice*, July 30, 2002, www.villagevoice.com/devil-in-disguise/.

258 "I've spent": Blanche Barton quoted in *Iconoclast*, film, directed by Larry Wessel, 2010.

259 Anton, Blanche: Barton, *We Are Satanists*, 233–234.

259 LaVey was soon: Ibid., 234.

259 When it had: Barton, *The Secret Life of a Satanist*, 252.

262 "You're gonna": Marilyn Manson, with Neil Strauss, *The Long Hard Road Out of Hell* (New York: ReganBooks, 1998), 171.

262 "Anton LaVey was": Marilyn Manson, foreword, *Satan Speaks!*, XI.

262 "We had both": Manson, *The Long Hard Road Out of Hell*, 164.

263 "make an exhibition": LaVey, *The Devil's Notebook*, 20.

263 "I always": Boyd Rice, "I Think the Children Have Come for Me," *Seconds* 40, 1996.

263 as numerous women: Rania Aniftos and Anna Chan, "A Timeline of Abuse Allegations Against Marilyn Manson," Billboard.com, December 14, 2023, www.billboard.com/lists/marilyn-manson-abuse-allegations-timeline/may-2021-another-ex-sues-for-rape/.

263 "[Satanism is] about": Neva Chonin, "Marilyn Manson Just Trying to Help Those Misfit Kids," *San Francisco Chronicle*, March 10, 1999.

264   **Blanche called:** Manson, *The Long Hard Road Out of Hell*, 164.

264   **After LaVey:** Ibid., 168.

264   **"Taking credit":** Ibid., 169.

264   **"very bossy":** Ibid.

264   **"The less":** Ibid.

264   **Still, Manson:** Ibid., 170.

264   **A few days:** Ibid.

264   **"Little did":** Ibid.

265   **"I really should":** Rice, *The Last Testament of Anton LaVey*, 132.

269   **smaller outlets:** Darby Romeo and Kerin Morataya, "Kerin and Darby Get Down with the Devil, Anton Szandor LaVey," *Ben Is Dead* 24, 1994.

271   **"Already I can't":** Lisa Crystal Carver, *Drugs Are Nice: A Post-Punk Memoir* (New York: Soft Skull, 2005), 165.

271   **"a delirious":** Ibid., 168.

271   **He regaled:** Ibid., 166.

271   **He expounded:** Ibid., 167.

271   **"It is said":** Ibid., 169.

271   **"her quest":** Ibid., 171.

271   **She later:** Marc Weingarten, "Speak of the Devil," *SPIN*, September 2008.

272   **Carver admitted:** Ibid.

272   **Years later:** Zoe Zolbrod, "The Sunday Rumpus Interview with Lisa Carver," *The Rumpus*, February 5, 2012, https://therumpus.net/2012/02/05/the-sunday-rumpus-interview-with-lisa-carver/.

272   **"I am just":** Eugene S. Robinson, "A Satanic Incest Inquest: 5 Easy Pieces w/Church of Satan Scion Stanton LaVey," *Look What You Made Me Do* (Substack), October 24, 2021, https://eugenesrobinson.substack.com/p/a-satanic-incest-inquest-5-easy-pieces.

272   **"So how likely":** Ibid.

CHAPTER XIII

Author interviews with Shane Bugbee, Mitch Horowitz, Eugene Robinson, Richard Lamparski, Carl Abrahamsson, Jack Fritscher, Don Frew, Gregg Turkington, Harvey Stafford, Margie Bauer, Evil Wilhelm, Blanche Barton, Lee Houskeeper, and Nikolas Schreck.

277   **"probably one of":** Amy Bugbee and Shane Bugbee, "The Doctor Is In . . . ," *MF* 3, accessed at www.churchofsatan.com/interview-mf-magazine/.

278   **"What I saw":** Anton LaVey, foreword in Ragnar Redbeard, *Might Is Right* (centennial edition, 1996), excerpted in David A. Johnson, "Instructive Bad Reading, Part I: Dissecting Fascism with the Help of 'Might Is Right,'" *The Cascadia Advocate* (blog), August 21, 2020, www.nwprogressive.org/weblog/2020/08/instructive-bad-reading-part-one-dissecting-fascism-with-the-help-of-might-is-right.html.

279   **"Blessed are":** Ragnar Redbeard, *Might Is Right* (Chicago: Dil Pickle Press, 1927), 32.

279   "The skull-and-crossbones": "That Other Black Order," *The Cloven Hoof*, April 1972.

279   "My instinctive": LaVey, *Satan Speaks!*, 71.

279   "is grounded": Ibid., 20–21.

279   "It will become": Ibid., 22.

280   LaVey encountered: Anton LaVey letter to Marcello Truzzi, June 26, 1969.

280   "where the strong": Robinson, "Anton LaVey."

282   "Anton turns": Vallée, *Forbidden Science* 2, location 1332.

282   "exceptional gift": Ibid., location 1362.

282   "He claims": Ibid., location 1384.

283   "until a group": Willy Werby, letter to the editor, *SF Weekly*, July 1–7, 1998.

283   "when LaVey began": Wolfe, *The Devil's Avenger*, 216.

283   LaVey characterized this: Michael Moynihan, "Anton LaVey: A Fireside Chat with the Black Pope," *Seconds* 27, 1994.

283   Even Xerxes would: Abrahamsson, *Anton LaVey and the Church of Satan*, 231.

284   "If enough people": Church of Satan tract as quoted in Alfred, "The Church of Satan," 186.

286   "I have to": Abrahamsson, *Anton LaVey and the Church of Satan*, 156.

286   "She was an": Ibid.

286   Anton Szandor LaVey: Larry D. Hatfield, "Celebrity Satanist, True '60s Hell-raiser, Off to Join His Master," *San Francisco Examiner*, November 7, 1997.

286   "I will never die": "Anton LaVey on *The Joe Pyne Show*," YouTube video.

287   she had put: Bob Larson, *Larson's Book of Spiritual Warfare* (Nashville: Thomas Nelson, 1999), 145.

288   "We will continue": Karen Hunt, "Church of Satan Founder LaVey dies," *Santa Cruz Sentinel*, November 8, 1997.

288   "He did believe": Susan Sward, "Satanist's Daughter to Keep the 'Faith,'" *San Francisco Chronicle*, November 8, 1997.

289   And in January: Boulware, "A Devil of a Time."

289   In dispute: Don Lattin, "Satan's Den in Great Disrepair," *San Francisco Chronicle*, January 25, 1999.

289   Blanche denied: Ibid.

290   She, Zeena: Ibid.

290   In February 1998: Zeena LaVey and Nikolas Schreck, "Anton LaVey: Legend and Reality," www.coursehero.com/file/130464949/Anton-LaVey-Legend-andRealitypdf/.

290   reaffirmed her enmity: Lamothe-Ramos, "Beelzebub's Daughter."

291   Sunset Boulevard shop: Ron Athey, "Apocalypse Culture Now," *LA Weekly*, May 29, 2002, www.laweekly.com/apocalypse-culture-now/.

291   Karla, having relinquished: Tony DuShane, "Nightlife: Black X Mass," *San Francisco Chronicle*, December 21, 2006.

291   Anton's son: "RU35: Visual Anthropologist Ethan X Clarke on Politics, Culture, Film, Art—Rendering Unconscious," YouTube video, uploaded by Trapart Film, April 26, 2021, www.youtube.com/watch?v=evXVB2ZSwoI.

292   **"A flute"**: LaVey, *Satan Speaks!*, 57.

292   **"getting special"**: Ibid., 77.

292   **"It may have"**: Ibid., 105.

292   **he describes**: Ibid., 131.

292   **"I've never learned"**: Ibid., 132.

293   **"against my"**: Ibid., 134.

293   **To help satisfy**: Boulware, "A Devil of a Time."

293   **Werby himself**: Malcolm Glover, "Hotelier Changes Plea to Guilty in Sex Case," *San Francisco Examiner*, July 6, 1990.

294   **on July 22**: Barton, *The Secret Life of a Satanist*, 269–270.

297   **"an obscene rape"**: Ibid., 270.

298   **demolished in 2001**: "F.A.Q.: The Black House," the Church of Satan website, www.churchofsatan.com/faq-the-black-house/.

301   **Marcello Truzzi**: Harrington, "The Devil in Anton LaVey."

302   **For its best-known**: Jamie Ducharme, "The Satanic Temple Protested a Ten Commandments Monument in Arkansas with Its Baphomet Statue," *Time*, August 18, 2018, https://time.com/5370989/satanic-temple-arkansas/.

302   **"a starting point"**: Lucien Greaves, "Correcting the Church of Satan 'Fact Sheet,'" *The Lucien Greaves Archive*, https://luciengreaves.com/correcting -the-church-of-satan-fact-sheet.

302   **"The Church of Satan"**: "Church of Satan vs. Satanic Temple," the Satanic Temple website, https://thesatanictemple.com/pages/church-of-satan-vs-satanic -temple.

303   **"How can you"**: Helen Lewis, "A Satanic Rebellion," *The Atlantic*, October 1, 2023, www.theatlantic.com/ideas/archive/2023/10/social-justice-rebellion -satanic-temple/675481/.

303   **the performance by**: August Brown, "Ritual Shift," *Los Angeles Times*, January 5, 2018.

304   **the long, digressive**: Rice and LaVey interview, Internet Archive.

304   **"seems to occur"**: Barton, *The Secret Life of a Satanist*, 25.

304   **"He had no claws"**: Wolfe, *The Devil's Avenger*, 24.

Index